THE SOUL
of
ADOPTION

THE SOUL
of
ADOPTION

CATHERINE E. POELMAN

Eagle Gate
Salt Lake City, Utah

*For those who perpetuate
the miracle of adoption*

Library of Congress Cataloging-in-Publication Data

Poelman, Catherine E., 1943-
   The soul of adoption / Catherine E. Poelman.
      p.   cm.
   Includes bibliographical references.
   ISBN 1-57345-655-1 (pbk.)
   1. Adoption.   I. Title.
   HV875.P63   2000
   362.73'4—dc21   00-024520

Printed in the United States of America   18961-6645
10 9 8 7 6 5 4 3 2 1

CONTENTS

PREFACE

Adoption is an exquisite grafting of humankind. For both the birth and adoptive parents it is a defining transition, a deliberate lunge beyond childbearing. For the child it is permanent relocation accompanied by the hope of increased opportunity. Over a lifetime it may induce wondrous adaptation, proportionate to the complexities of attachment. Successful participants learn to comprehend the needs of everyone involved and afford those individuals freedom to choose and grow in ways consistent with their unique personalities and talents. Boundless and unwavering love can develop.

Thirty years ago my husband and I adopted a child. Nine years ago we fostered another. We worked to raise them with faith and love—just as we did our other children—to be obedient to the commandments of our Heavenly Father. But we weren't the only ones who felt connected to them. Their biological parents also wanted (and felt they needed) to have contact with the children. And these other parents did not share our beliefs and practices. This experience gave me some comprehension of the need for tolerance and flexibility in adoption.

When I returned to the university to study current trends in psychology after most of our children were grown, I thought I had already developed some understanding of the uniform qualities in human nature. But I discovered that genetic and environmental factors produce amazing diversity. Scientific study of personal characteristics and behaviors still fails to account for the most powerful ingredient in all of us—the quality and worth of each soul. I became suspicious of the generalities that circulate regarding adoption. So I started my own collection of accounts given by children who had been adopted—including those who had become adults—and by their birth and adoptive parents. Though many participants shared the same religious convictions I do, others joined in the adoption circle from a variety of cultural origins. Every narrative I have recorded and shared here holds surprises; the uniqueness of individual souls transcends averages. The marvel of adoption begins to distill a pattern: The human spirit is divinely resilient, and abiding love secures eternal relationships.

I believe the soul of adoption is manifest in the souls of the participants and in the Lord who watches over them. He sanctions the worthy use of this legal and spiritual covenant. For me, the real-life experiences in this book are more engaging and valid than many of the psychological studies I have summarized. Specific examples can be practicably understood, and they are the most powerful tools for comprehending and applying significant insights to the multiplicity of human souls.

Although the names and places in the individual accounts have been changed to protect privacy, I have been meticulously true to the words and tenor of their tellers. Their candor is unedited in order to fully inform. When examples of children who are especially challenging seem to predominate, it is not because they are usually in the majority. All of us—including our biological children—are sometimes challenging; and it is life's challenges that not only teach but also motivate us.

The far-reaching consequences of adoption make early careful and straightforward evaluation of whether to participate especially critical. It is not that the endeavor doesn't require faith—it requires tremendous inspiration and courageous faith—but adoption may also utilize all the cumulative wisdom and thorough preparation available at each stage in the life-encompassing process. Both the stories and the studies shared in this book confirm the virtue and ardor of adoption.

Now faith is the substance of things hoped for.
Hebrews 11:1

1
DON'T WORRY
THE IMPACT OF DECISION

All mortals are born innocent, but into surprisingly diverse circumstances. Adoption is a timeless equalizer—spreading opportunities and challenges around. This book values the unique contribution of each individual who participates in the adoption process. The qualities of a human soul ultimately prevail over every other aspect of adoption. The birthparents, the child, and the adoptive parents all bring their own gifts and dreams to the adoption experience, and the demands of life will assuredly test them.

Hope is the instrument by which inert dreams become active realities. "Hope cometh of faith," assured Ether, and "maketh an anchor to the souls of men, which would make them sure and steadfast" (Ether 12:4). Hope is power that exists in every individual; nurtured, hope is motivation for a lifetime. Children who were adopted may be blessed by the hope they see in the adult world. Birthparents retain the hope that their child will receive all the opportunities life offers. Adoptive parents sustain the hope that their child will achieve success and find happiness. Regardless of the circumstances necessitating adoption, each individual involved must utilize hope to go beyond fancied ambitions and recognize a personal responsibility to shape his own ongoing story.

1

Above all, adoption is a consummate act of faith. Even after the decision to move forward is verified in a participant's heart, it may require resolute faith to proceed through the multitude of discoveries that follow. Faith cultivated through adoption will gradually attach itself to one's soul with permanence, lodging deep inside, enduring through every stage and circumstance.

Kevin is presently out of town teaching a seminar. His wife, Allie, is fine with suspending bedtime on this summer evening to talk with me. Their children play in the fading light while she tells me of her courtship with Kevin, recalling his surprising answers to her questions.

"'Who do you look like?' I asked Kevin a week after we met, 'your mom or your dad?'

"'Neither,' Kevin said, as he walked with me through Arcadia Park.

"'Then who do you act most like?'

"'Neither.' Kevin laughed. 'You see, Allie, I'm adopted.'

"'—Adopted! Kevin!'

"I stopped short," Allie tells me, "couldn't even keep walking. I always thought I would never marry anyone who was adopted," she says. *"I worried about the genes they might be carrying, whether they would have handicapped kids or kids without any morals.*

"I asked Kevin if he knew anything about his birthparents.

"'Nothing! Why would I want to?' he said. 'I had the best parents.'"

Allie gestures at their six-year-old, who is squirting water around the yard.

"When our little boy was born," she tells me, "we were walking through the hospital and there was a '70s type picture on the wall with fifteen babies in bassinets and nine nurses standing behind them.

"Kevin said to me, 'See, one of those babies is like me, probably born to some fifteen-year-old girl.'

"'Doesn't that matter to you, Kevin?' I asked.

"'Why would it?' he laughed, and grabbed a Twinkie.

"Then one night we were having dinner at his folks' place, twelve of us, including his sister who is still searching for her birthparents and always asking questions about them. It was the night of a big ball game. . . .

"Finally I said to his mother, 'Would it bother you if I asked about Kevin's birthparents? How old they were? Where he was born?'

"You see," Allie pauses to look up at me, *"Kevin had never wanted to know. His mom was totally okay with it. She explained that the birthmother was twenty and the birthfather twenty-two, university students who weren't prepared to marry, and since the father was gifted in science the agency had thought Kevin's [adoptive] parents would be a particularly good match—Kevin's father was already a chemistry professor at UCLA by then. But, the birthparents were students from the rival school!*

"Kevin winced when he heard that and said, 'this is really depressing' and went off to watch the game. That was all there was to it. Kevin is simply a happy, carefree person. He sang 'Don't Worry About a Thing' to me on our first date. He judges no one, has no anxieties. Playing ball as a kid he broke his nose in three places and doesn't care to have it fixed. I tell him he could use braces on his teeth but he says 'My teeth are me—my body's perfect the way it is!'

"He served a mission to Korea. Just the other day I read a letter from a stack in the basement that his dad wrote to him at the Language Training Center. 'Your mother and I can hardly believe you sit still and study Korean. You've always been a star, making plenty of home runs, but it's fantastic that you can let the Lord be star now, and run for him.'"

The doorbell rings; a child interrupts.

"Kevin is amazing with people," Allie continues. *"In a crowd he'll know everyone's name in five minutes; he can motivate anybody to do what he wants. Even though he was a science major like his dad, he's now head of all sales for American Express in Southern California."*

. . . It's a few days before I reach Kevin on his cell phone. "Adoption hasn't been an issue," he says. *"I've never cared about it one way or the other except to say I'm grateful to my birthparents*

for having the courage to give me up and to my mom and dad for
a great life."

The lifelong commitment to adoption feels remarkably different for the millions of individuals involved, parents and children alike. For many it is a comfortable fact. For others it can be intermittently stressful. Still others may struggle with the issue throughout their lives. Different reactions may have nothing to do with the virtue of the initial decision, the quality of parenting, or the eventual well-being of the matured child. But realizing that children can be vulnerable at different stages in their growth is crucial to easing the journey.

Consistent love and open communication between a parent and child generally assure an eventually stable relationship—that's the abiding comfort. And most newborn arrivals make a relatively smooth adjustment to adoption along the way, but not always. There are significant personal variables, in addition to temperament, which also affect the adjusting process: self-esteem and a sense of control, social experience at home and with peers, biological inheritance, level of family commitment, and many more. A sense of inspired destiny, when child and parents feel a strong spiritual confirmation that they belong to each other, also influences attitude.

Some children struggle with the idea of adoption by demonstrating negative behavior. These children may have been generally comfortable with the idea when told of their adoption at a very young age and in the warmth and security of a good family. But a child's feelings of loss are often latent during the preschool years. Adverse reactions may evolve later, after the child seems already to have made the adjustment, taking unprepared parents by surprise. As the child progresses through the typical pattern of intellectual development and begins the process of gaining knowledge and applying it to life's problems, a comprehension of abandonment or fear may emerge.

ADJUSTMENT STAGES

Psychologists became aware of Jean Piaget's theory of cognitive development during the 1960s.[1] It dramatically influenced the field of child psychology. Piaget believed that children's abilities to think and to reason progress through stages as they mature. Babies learn they are separate from objects, then that they are capable of action. Preschoolers learn to use language but are still egocentric. As children move into elementary school they learn to think logically, and they can analyze events when they are seven or eight years old. At that age a child who develops negative reactions to the idea of adoption may, for the first time, manifest obvious adjustment challenges.

What adults may then perceive as wrong, disobedient, or at least ungrateful actions in some children who were adopted, may actually be a reaction to the loss that these children now feel because they more fully compute what being adopted means. When some children comprehend that they have lost their biological parents, that sense of loss affects their feelings of closeness to their adoptive parents.[2]

Individuals who react negatively to loss react much as they would to grief.[3] One approach for dealing with sorrow is to act up outwardly, to begin taking others' possessions, or to run away. A child who is projecting outwardly might also act angry or aggressive, or begin to lie. Negative reactions from some children are manifest by reacting inwardly; they blame themselves and become depressed or isolated. Parents of these children may have done nothing wrong. In fact, they usually have done all they knew how to do that was right. They have taught their child correct principles and loved him completely.

Other children might not react at all while they are young. Then, during adolescence, when a sense of loss *is* realized by a child who is being raised away from his birthparents, the grief may deepen as the child's knowledge of the world continues to increase and he develops the remainder of his adult thought processes. This individual can reason and conjecture. One who already feels vulnerable may struggle even more as a teenager with questions such as, "What would it have been like to be raised in a different family?" He may resent the circumstances of the adoption—over which he had no control—

and rush off trying to demand control in other aspects of his life before learning which of his actions will work for his good.

"During the grief process," says Vera Fahlberg, M.D., in her book *A Child's Journey through Placement,* "a tremendous amount of psychological, and sometimes physical, energy is diverted into coping with strong emotions. Less energy is available for day-to-day relationships and the tasks associated with normal childhood development."[4] So the journey of a vulnerable child on the way to achieving a healthy independence and a consistent pattern of good choices may be more roundabout.

POSITIVE FORCES

Psychology is especially affirming when it catches up with the Lord's knowledge of his children's mortal development. Back in Abraham's time the Lord targeted the age by which children could understand the consequences of their acts and take responsibility for them. "Thou mayest know for ever," the Lord told Abraham, "that children are not accountable before me until they are eight years old" (Joseph Smith Translation, Genesis 17:11). Though children's mental capacities are ready for challenges with eternal consequences at age eight, the Lord provided a way for them to correct the errors they all would make afterwards due to their lack of experience. Hence, he commanded parents to teach their children "of repentance, faith in Christ the Son of the living God, and of baptism and the gift of the Holy Ghost" before they are eight years old, lest the sin be upon the parents' heads (see D&C 68:25). Sometimes when parents have diligently taught gospel principles to their young children, they become disheartened as they watch their children make inevitable mistakes. But the mortal learning experience allows children to grow stronger by working their way through the correction process.

Recent intelligence tests show that even Piaget may have underestimated children's abilities to compute information. Professionals who now use a broader measurement for mental abilities—tallying analytic, practical, *and* creative intelligence—still agree with Piaget, however, that cognitive growth is sustained by interaction between a child's biological development and his environment. Children accumulate knowledge in elementary school to the point where they are capable of realizing that to be adopted they first must have been relinquished. They can assimilate the fact that some families are made up of people who choose to live together, but most are made up of people who share biological ties.

A vast number of children who were adopted grow up fully comprehending the facts of adoption without being adversely affected in any way. Their experience never becomes much of a story because it is simply a fact. So it is not surprising that many parents focus earnestly on building their own eternal family and find it difficult to imagine the possible struggle of their growing young person. Furthermore, the timing of potential grief in parents and child is off. Birthmothers tend to grieve earliest—while the child and even the adoptive parents may be unaware—and most poignantly during the first two years, until they can settle into the next phase of their lives. Adoptive parents on the other hand, like most new parents, finally relax into satisfaction with their role about the time a vulnerable child begins to feel loss. So the susceptible child has no ready audience to share grief with as in other forms of family adversity. When a child has parents who die or divorce, there are other relatives and friends mourning with them. A child who feels grief for not being born into the ideal family usually grieves alone.

As with other life adventures, parents need not search for problems in their children, but must still make ready to meet them if they develop. And although it is important to understand adjustment, everyone realizes sooner or later that the greatest joys and sorrows transcend all aspects of adoption. Adoption is sometimes an enigma. One learns to compose himself in the face of it. It is a matter of contemplation and decision, but even more so a matter of soul. The person who seeks to do the will of God concerning another must retain perspective. Parents are strengthened when they envision their part in the larger plan of happiness for children; they may calculate the cost to themselves but will never be able to compute the advantage they pass on to the adopted child and to the birthparents. And as significant as adoption is in completing the Lord's eternal purposes, it is when adoption seems insignificant that participants may be closest to achieving their ultimate goal.

I call Laura's mother at 8:20 a.m., before music lessons begin for the day.

"I'm looking for the perfect adoption example," I say. "Where is Laura living now? May I get her phone number?"

There is a pause. Laura's mother is busy and efficient in the mornings but now she hesitates.

"Laura doesn't talk about adoption," she says, " . . . never. She is a gentle perfectionist," her mother adds slowly. "She has created a dream with her husband and their two little boys. Her three-year-old would never think to eat before blessing the food."

"Didn't Laura have the typical challenges with adoption growing up?" I ask.

"Oh, but that was when she was a child," Laura's mother says, not defensively but with clarity, reminding me that the past has traveled on.

Adoption has dissolved for Laura. She once felt the concerns common for children who were adopted. But as she moved through a variety of developmental stages her concerns were addressed and she advanced, leaving them behind. Adoption is not relevant now, even in recalling what she has learned in her lifetime. All Laura's memories are void of the concept.

I ask Laura what has made her happiest in life.

"Well, I've always wanted to please my parents. Most kids don't like their folks to attend parent-teacher conferences," Laura says, "but I loved them to go because I knew it would make them happy. I was just a typical kid. When my parents told me to do something I didn't want to, maybe I argued with them, but then I did it. I could never understand my siblings who disobeyed."

Reopening the issue of one's personal adoption to someone like Laura may be insensitive because it is not only inapplicable to her present life but clashes with her beliefs. Laura can talk about adoption in the abstract and discuss ways to help other adopted children who are still struggling. But for her the situation no longer exists. Laura has not fallen into what a psychologist might term "denial." Her adoption has simply been superseded by her gift of faith. Like the scriptural concept of adoption, where we may become spiritually begotten to Christ through faith on his name, Laura is begotten to her parents "because of the covenant" and delights in being obedient (see Mosiah 5:7–8).

On the opposite end of the adjustment spectrum, however, there may be children with just as much faith who desire constructive connections with birthparents. Other connections must be carefully considered and are not categorically bad. In fact, children adopted past infancy generally bring with them previous attachments, weak or strong. Even though separation from their birthparents was necessary, they may continue to grieve over the loss of those relationships during an adjustment period. Understanding the difficulty of the transition is effective. "Adults need to be supportive," Dr. Fahlberg explains, "as the child talks, cries, rants and raves, or just sits. It is the adult presence combined with emotional acceptance of the child's pain that is much more important than actual words."[5] The fact that a child was once attached to birthparents or foster parents, and consequently needs understanding through a transition stage, should be encouraging for parents who adopt older children. It's the unattached children, those who never felt love or connection to anyone, who are the hardest to help.

REALISTIC EXPECTATIONS

For individuals who finally decide to participate in adoption it feels not so much like a matter of choosing to adopt as it does a matter of accepting the inevitable. In *Kinship with Strangers,* Judith Modell concludes from her anthropological study that the "opted-for kinship" of adoption in the United States "has simulated a destined parenthood. 'Falling-in-love' and 'meant-to-be' convey the inevitability of the adoptive relationship—as if natural."[6]

Individuals with strong character feel after their own destiny and finally do what they must do. The actual decision to participate in the adoption circle makes them feel better, yet perplexed that so much of eternal significance is beyond their control. Gratefully there are ways to calm the anxiety, to sample the rightness and permit the placement to take on a specific shape, where fewer and fewer of the consequences feel outside one's reach.

An individual's exploration into adoption possibilities can penetrate to the outer reaches of human need. One can search deep and wide for intelligence and wisdom. One can prepare with the diligence of a graduate student researching his thesis topic, and no aspect of the preparation will be wasted. The more information people acquire on adoption, the broader their inspired options. The Lord works best through prepared minds.

Participants can expect surprises. They can decide to enjoy the discovery process, reverence the waiting, and cherish the uniqueness of their situation. Even if the motivation for adoption is out of their control, the outcome of their contribution and happiness is not. Alternate dreams need be no less rewarding. The very harshness that may have redirected one's original plans often yields a kind of beauty the unstretched self could have never imagined.

Finally, adoption can compel one to kneel more. It is the uncharted course that prompts the best of people to pray their way through, to be receptive to divine guidance. While searching for direction there is more reason to be silent, to listen. Every step that is cloudy and unclear illustrates that people are nothing by themselves; only the meek can search for knowledge open-mindedly from the Father of all. And each sought-after decision contributes to a lifetime practice, a perfect design for endless growth.

NOTES

1. Jean Piaget, *Judgment and Reasoning in the Child* (Paterson, NJ: Littlefield, Adams, 1964).

2. David M. Brodzinsky, "A Stress and Coping Model of Adoption Adjustment," in *The Psychology of Adoption*, ed. David M. Brodzinsky and Marshall D. Schechter (New York: Oxford University Press, 1990), pp. 6–7.

3. Ibid., pp. 7–14.

4. Vera I. Fahlberg, *A Child's Journey through Placement* (Indianapolis: Perspectives Press, 1991), p.165.

5. Ibid., p.173.

6. Judith Modell, *Kinship with Strangers: Adoption and Interpretations of Kinship in American Culture* (Berkeley: University of California Press, 1994), p. 229.

And there are diversities of operations, but it is
the same God which worketh all in all.
1 Corinthians 12:6

2
THE PENDULUM
OPEN ADOPTION

JoAnn and her three-year-old son, Ben, snack on peanut butter
sandwiches at the kitchen counter, bare feet dangling. Ben is one
of JoAnn's last two children received through an open adoption
procedure. JoAnn's husband, LeRoy, is on duty as an emergency
room doctor at Glenwood Hospital. They have other children who
are at school. Ben slides down next to his fire truck on the floor.

"The birthmother has the hardest part," JoAnn says, "because
she has the loss. I had ovarian cancer when LeRoy and I had been
married four months. I thought my grief was as great as someone who had lost a baby. I know now it wasn't the same." *Her*
voice is mellow, liquid. She pushes her hair behind her ears.

"The majority of birthmothers out there love their babies—
only a few are jaded—and my children are proof of that love. Love
makes birthmothers willing to give the baby a chance. My heart
aches and breaks for these women, but they are strong and aware
that placement is the right thing. They also understand the practical part of child rearing; they have to think of themselves too
and know it will be hard to get childcare.

"When grandparents discourage them by saying, 'I can't let
you give that baby up,' I want to say, 'Let her do what's best.'"

Ben crawls onto JoAnn's lap, whispers in her ear, then disappears down the hall.

"I grew up believing it was a woman's purpose to have children. *After my cancer surgery we started going to adoption agencies, but they wouldn't consider us until we'd been married several years. Then they wanted me to promise in writing that I wouldn't work outside the home; I was still teaching to help LeRoy through medical school.* Maybe his profession will prove divine, *I thought;* something will work out because LeRoy's becoming a doctor. *Nothing happened.*

"Then a friend of my sister's daughter got pregnant. She wanted her child to be raised in a family like my sister's, so my sister encouraged her to come visit me. I took the young girl to doctor appointments, on errands. I thought she was wonderful even before I realized we might adopt her baby. After the decision was made I was sure she'd change her mind. When the baby was born, she invited us to the hospital. That was ten years ago, when the tradition of keeping everything closed and secretive about adoption was still hanging on.

"A year later," JoAnn says, *"we saw that birthmother at a wedding reception. She greeted me with a big hug.*

"'How are things?' she asked me. "That woman had the maturity not to break down while I talked a bit. Last week I visited the city where she lives and I know she wanted me to call her, but I chose not to. She's got sort of a clingy personality; if I initiated something it would open the door for more and more contact, and we do fine without that.

"LeRoy wasn't skeptical about openness like I was," JoAnn says. *"A few years after our first open adoption, friends approached us when they learned their daughter was expecting. This young woman was Ben's mother. I have known his birthmother since she was a small girl.*

"This placement is too close to work, *I thought.* Maybe it would be best to find a couple she didn't know. *The girl was only two months along at our first meeting, with a long time left to change her mind. I didn't want to get my hopes up if it wasn't going to pan out."* JoAnn glances around the carpeted play area.

"But I was a different person by the time Ben was born. I was *calmer because I was older, more experienced. And Ben's birth-mother had much better family support than the mother of our first open placement. The circumstance was more public—all sorts of people knew. We met periodically with her to make sure we all felt secure. LeRoy only joined us the first time we talked—it just worked out that way and was actually more comfortable for him. After she learned that her baby was a boy we decided together to surprise LeRoy, knowing how happy he would be to have a son after our daughters."* Ben is back at JoAnn's feet toppling blocks. JoAnn is smoothing his hair.

"In his birthmother's mind," JoAnn says, *"it was the right thing to have us present for the delivery. We just stood to one side, talked sometimes when she wasn't hurting. It was relaxed—lots of smiles—crying when there was pain and laughing in between. The actual birth was a bit awkward; it's hard to know someone going through agony and not have anything to offer in return."* Ben climbs back on her lap.

"At the moment of delivery we had to restrain our excitement," she smiles, *"and LeRoy is very restrained, but he grinned when he saw it was a boy! The doctor gave her the baby, she held him, kissed him, and then gave him to me. But we didn't take him home with us; she wanted a couple of days in the hospital with her baby. The birthfather spent time with them. She told us it was really hard for him. I began having doubts again.*

"Even after all that waiting," she says, *"I still wanted what was best for Ben's birthmother. I didn't want to have her baby unless she wanted me to, and I also knew she wanted what was best for Ben. But I couldn't be the one to actually take Ben from her; LeRoy went by himself."* JoAnn speaks gently and Ben is content.

"During that first week Ben's birthmother called," JoAnn says, *"lonely for her baby. When she came over, I left them alone; after a while she carried Ben back to me. She called and came again. I believe she thinks of Ben as our joint venture. I send her pictures when I remember, and tell her about his progress. I talk to her on Mother's Day and it's very comfortable. It works for her and for me. I would never be afraid of her coming to see me. I can do things for her I wish I could for the birthmothers of our other children who weren't open placements. It's important, not only for*

*her, but I want Ben to know—I want my other children to know—
that they were cared for enough to be given what their birthmothers thought was best." Ben fidgets, pulls JoAnn's head down
next to his mouth.*

*"I know it's still hard for her," she says, peering up from his
firm grasp, "because she hasn't attended some of the functions
where we would both have been invited, but the thing I like best is
that when I see her she doesn't single him out; she pays attention
to all of our children."*

The pendulum of the adoption procedure has swung wide.
Open adoption currently encompasses all continuing contact
that is mutually acceptable to both sets of parents. It always
includes a face-to-face meeting of birthparents and adoptive
parents in order to exchange identifying information. The
birthparents relinquish legal and basic childrearing rights, but
both sets of parents retain the right to continuing contact and
access to knowledge of the child. The frequency and content
of ongoing communication depends on the needs, desires, and
specified relationships among those involved.

Even conventional or traditional adoptions are now open
enough to allow all nonidentifying and medical data to be
exchanged between adoptive and biological parents through
the agency. Birthmothers may play a role in picking the family
but agencies discourage them from contact after placement—
at least until the child turns eighteen and both express a wish
to meet. Secret or closed adoptions, where no information at
all is exchanged between birthparents and adoptive parents,
have not been part of good agency practice in recent years.

A MODERATE OPTION

Some advocates for both open and conventional adoption
cite principles from a study supporting semi-open adoption by
Ruth McRoy reviewed in *Openness in Adoption*.[1] Semi-open
adoption assures a continuing relationship mediated by the
agency—including face-to-face meetings—but with no identifying information exchanged. Semi-open adoption purportedly
has the greatest benefit and the least risk. McRoy, who completed the study at the University of Texas, summarizes the

advantages: birthparents have the security of knowing about the child, adoptive families are more stable without regular contact from the birthparents, and the children have sufficient information to develop a positive sense of self but are not subjected to a confusion of roles among the two sets of parents.

LDS Family Services utilizes the semi-open adoption arrangement, which has been recently modified to allow the exchange of parents' first names. The birthmother (and birthfather if he chooses to participate) selects the adoptive parents from autobiographical accounts and personal letters to her. All her preferences, including matching of general physical appearance if desired, are honored. Prior to the face-to-face meeting with the prospective adoptive parents—a meeting, which she may elect to have before or after the baby is born—she also sees a collage of photographs. All these individual decisions are accommodated ahead of placement. Afterwards, all communication is exchanged through the agency. Routinely, all non-identifying letters, and even photographs of the child, are forwarded through the agency for the first five years. Thereafter, correspondence collects in the file until requested. The flow of communication tends to perpetuate itself: adoptive parents often writing letters of gratitude as well as providing information on significant dates, birthparents sending remembrances. From both sides of the adoption experience come confirming expressions by those who choose to work with LDS Family Services: "We can feel the other family's love and support" and "It is their faith that sustains us."

GENESIS OF THE CURRENT MOVEMENT

Openness suddenly increased when the large number of unmarried birthmothers, influenced by the women's liberation movement of the early 1970s, started caring for their babies instead of making adoption plans. After a few years some of these birthmothers were unable to continue parenting. Because they had already ruled out the traditional manner of adoption and developed an emotional relationship with their children, they were trapped.

"Rather than see those children enter the foster home system," explain Annette Baran and Reuben Pannor, early instigators of the open concept, "we offered these parents the option of open placement. [The relinquishing parents] would help select the [adopting] family and be part of the child's move and initial adjustment to the new home."[2] Concurrently birthmothers and professionals, who agonized over the practice of suddenly and completely severing the ties between a birthmother and her child, began to trust that a more open and gradual transition was not only possible but also kind.

The open movement caught on and swung forward aggressively in an atmosphere of reform, gathering behind it individuals from all sides of the adoption triad. Some adults who had been adopted were hostile for being denied access to information about their origins and identities. Some birthparents asserted that secrecy made their loss more complex and difficult. Some adoptive parents expressed frustration at an inability to help their children connect with a biological heritage. Social workers gradually realized that many of their standard adoption practices were indeed, or at least perceived by some others, cold and coercive.

Spurred on by coverage of open adoption in social work journals and popular magazines, the 1987 American Adoption Congress announced that it "unanimously supports the policy of open adoption as standard practice," permitting "adoptees, birth parents and adoptive parents to make decisions about the kind and extent of relationships they desire."[3] The Child Welfare League issued a similar endorsement, adding that the level of openness was to be based on the consensus of all participants, including the child, if possible. Consequently, several adoption agencies gave up their long-standing commitment to confidential placements in order to win back their mediating role between birth and adoptive parents.

Meanwhile, competing lawyers and new adoption agencies used open adoption as a vehicle to increase their clientele. They promised birthparents that they were only relinquishing responsibility and could remain active in their child's life. Since there is nothing legally binding in open adoption commitments between parents, the reality was that the promises often disappeared after the adoption was finalized. "When we developed the [open adoption] concept we were very idealistic about it," Baran said. "What's happened is that the entrepreneurs, motivated by profit, have insinuated themselves into the open-adoption system. They are empathetic, but into business. The opportunists are leaving us idealists gasping for breath."[4]

Over the last fifteen years more and more agencies have specialized in open adoption, educating and counseling both the birthparents and adoptive parents so that they can make enduring, successful commitments to each other based on shared integrity. The power of these commitments emanates from the conviction that open adoption is best for all children (not just older children but newborn infants too). The advantages may seem reasonable: adoptive parents have constant access to information about the child's background, birthparents can see in person that their child is well cared for, and a child can know from the lips of both parents why she was adopted.

DECISIVE FACTORS

Individuals have different capacities for handling unfamiliar, unprecedented relationships. Consequently, the similarity of birth and adoptive parents can become a big factor in placements that depend on trust and common sense. When openness is desired and both sets of parents have comparable values and selfless dispositions, open arrangements may work out successfully. In open adoptions it is typical for adoptive parents to receive their child right from the arms of the birthmother. There are even a variety of "entrustment ceremonies," where a formal transference of the baby is celebrated with all kinds of relatives invited to share the creation of a new family unit—a large, blended one where members in both families have a continuing role. Correspondence and occasional visits continue as the parents desire. Many children are growing up in adoptive homes where they keep photos of their birthparents on the dresser. "Cooperative adoption is not meant to be co-parenting," affirms Sharon Kaplan-Roszia, a professional with thirty years experience. "The adoptive parents clearly are the parenting parents and the legal parents. The birthparents assume the role of special friends or that of an aunt and uncle."[5]

The strongest and most extreme proponents of open adoption encourage even disparate sets of adoptive and birth-parents to stay connected "for the good of the child." They urge all adoptive parents to muster the courage and gain the compassion to lead out in nurturing less secure birthparents. They trust that all people are capable of learning appropriate interaction—to communicate honestly, openly, and to respect clear boundaries. Though birthparents may start out poorer or less educated, supporters remind, in ten years the situation may totally change. "And if the relationship is not nurtured," says James Gritter, author of *The Spirit of Open Adoption,* "it may become closed—then the present will no longer exist for the child."[6]

When adoptive parents in a New England study[7] were given freedom to arrange their own form of openness with birth-parents, the most striking feature was diversity. Nearly all the adoptive parents expressed initial reservations: reluctance to deal with the birthmother's pain, concern that the birthmother would want her baby back, and pervading anxiety of too many unknowns. Despite the initial fears, however, none regretted participating and later identified a variety of advantages: some knowledge and control over which birthparents they could work with; information about the birthparents' personalities and medical histories with which to answer their child's future questions; and assurance that the birthmother had chosen adoption freely and felt good about the decision.

All disadvantages to open adoption in the minds of the adoptive parents were centered around uncertainty over the long-term impact on their children. "Everyone's just flying by the seat of their pants," one parent said. Other couples with no misgivings felt like they were having to cope with their families' and friends' anxieties. "They fill you with all their fears. You not only have your own to deal with." One father acknowl-edged he thought it was conceptually better for the child but, "I'm nervous about it actually because our son's birthparents are from a completely different social and educational class, and I have a fear in the back of my mind that he'll want to identify with them."[8]

Social work professionals who conducted the New England study concluded that openness should be offered to all parents, that the process should be shaped by the parents rather than the professional, and that the parents should write out together (before placement) how often and what form of future contacts will occur—with a mechanism for renegotiating their plan if desired.

The future will tell a lot more about the long-term results of open adoption. Results from one of the first longitudinal studies are starting to come in. The study is being conducted in New Zealand by Mary Iwanek, manager of Adoption Services in Wellington, among seventeen families in which the oldest adopted child is now twenty-one. In an open arrangement, Iwanek concludes, "the more interaction there is between the adoptee, his adoptive family and his birthparents, the more successful the adjustment is for all of them. It's a mixed bag," she says, "when adoptive parents still harbor personal issues or endure some of the disruptions of modern life [divorce, death, moving away] just as it is when birthparents never truly give up the child in the first place." In 1985 open adoption in New Zealand escalated as all adoption records were opened to adopted children age twenty and older. "Now 90 percent of the people involved in adoption make a commitment to ongoing interaction right from the beginning," Iwanek says. "Nevertheless, we have a few adoptive parents who can't cope and some birthparents who don't want their circumstances known. On the whole, however, we have a society that feels the need for connection."[9]

In the United States there continues to be a serious debate over the practice of open adoption. There are well-qualified professionals who are very cautious about any ongoing contact between adoptive parents and birthparents. Their biggest concerns center on adequate bonding between the adoptive parents and the child, and the child's personality development that is especially tenuous during the teenage years. Other experts are more concerned about contact between disparate adoptive and birthparents, thinking that interaction may exacerbate the relationship between them and ultimately confuse the child. Alfred Kadushin, who has conducted extensive research on adoption, suggests "The real problem of open adoption, despite its increasing popularity, is that children ultimately have to resolve identity issues of who they really are and loyalties to each set [of parents]."[10]

Other potential drawbacks to open placements were itemized by social workers with St. Mary's Services in Chicago. They observed that birthmothers who don't think of their child as gone often fail to move on with their lives. Adoptive parents who perpetuate a strong relationship with the birthmother may jeopardize the strength of their relationship with the child. "As for an adopted child," the study concluded, "there are risks of 'serious interference' at every stage of his development."[11] The child may feel a lack of permanence within her adoptive family and grow anxious about the birthmother taking her back or about the adoptive parents abandoning her.

"The only thing I can say after a conversation with Reggie is, 'Thank goodness I was adopted!'" Jill sits erect in an overstuffed chair. She is short, shapely, and blows her long curly hair out straight, bunching it in back with swank clips. Jill was adopted as an infant and searched out her birthmother at age fourteen.

"It seems crazy to me now," Jill says, "that as a teenager I couldn't appreciate my adoptive family. It's not that I regret getting in touch with my birth family—I was one of those kids who had to—but afterwards I was torn between the two families. They are so different.

"Reggie called to say that he's out of jail, his marriage is on the rocks, and he is still angry," Jill says. Reggie is a younger son of Jill's birthmother by another man.

"Reggie cursed my parents, my whole adoptive family," she says. "My adoptive parents haven't had any contact with my birth family recently except to invite him and his father for a barbecue five years ago—which turned into a slap in the face. That day his father cornered me after dinner and got into this heredity thing. He talks loud and my parents were in the next room."

"'You're exactly like your mother and my wife,' he said to me. 'You don't belong in the adoptive family. Haven't you read the latest? Heredity is up to 90 percent of a person's makeup—and that's you!' It took me three days to come out of the dumps after that one." Jill spins a key ring around her index finger. Her birthmother later married Reggie's father, an extremely intelligent man who was horribly abused as a child. The father used abusive patterns on Reggie, whose jail sentence was the result of abusing his own wife and children. Jill's adoptive parents are nurturing, stable, and receptive to new insights about adoption.

"When my birthmother died—" Jill's key ring drops to her lap, "—I was almost relieved." She pauses, staring at the carpet.

"But I was still caught in that rebellion thing where I couldn't listen to my adoptive parents. It took me a couple more years to finally understand that I couldn't live like my birth family or with them. Now I have to stay on my guard—too much communication with them levels me." Jill is compassionate beyond her strength, keeping in touch with all her relatives. Her eyes blink moist.

"I want to help my birth family because their lives are so difficult and it's not all their fault. I keep hoping that they will want to change when they see the way I live, that they may even accept the gospel. I love them but I'm afraid of them.

"I can't understand," Jill says, "why when we're all adults they're still trying to pull me away [from my family]."

The quality of life is linked to the quality of the people living it. The same seems to be true of open adoption—it may be as successful as each participant's ability to engage in creative, mature, and responsible problem solving. For all the debate, there have doubtless been net gains through relaxing the strict closed policies of the past. More birthparents are currently choosing the adults who they feel will best parent their child. More adoptive parents are not just acknowledging but appreciating the role of the birthparents and wanting to share background information about them with their children. More children are free from mysterious secrets about their past and consider that having birthparents is a simple fact of life.

RESPECT FOR PREFERENCES

A major incentive in the open adoption movement has been to enhance the rights of birthparents; yet it is an unequivocal fact that a significant group of them continue to choose confidentiality. Keeping the placement of their child quiet is sometimes simply a personal preference, other times a choice they perceive to be best for a child born of an extramarital relationship. The preference for confidentiality may also be fueling huge and growing numbers of international adoptions. Though some adoptive parents of foreign-born children wonder how they can compensate for their child's lack of connectedness, others are grateful to have chosen international adoption to avoid the risks of openness entirely. "Witness the increasing number of both birth and adoptive parents who adopt independently to avoid agency adoptions," adds E. Wayne Carp in *Family Matters,* "which increasingly follow the CWLA's [Child Welfare League of America] recommendation to practice open adoption and make no promises of confidentiality to birthmothers. It is estimated that one-third to one-half of all nonrelative adoptions today are independent adoptions. It is hard not to conclude that there will always be some adoptive triad members with a claim to privacy."[12]

Regardless of different opinions on the subject, H. David Kirk, the "father" of open communication between adoptive parents and their children (which he has publicly clarified is not the same as open adoption) believes we should all agree on at least one thing—"give priority to our grown children's interests. All others come second."[13] Adults who were adopted can speak to their unique and valid desires. Then, it is the parents' chance to stand back and trust their child, as they expected their child to trust them.

Even in the LDS Church, where children who are legally adopted by worthy parents are usually sealed in the temple, LDS Family Services is sensitive to the needs of adult adoptees and their rights to nonidentifying information about their birthparents. But more significant than "rights," the Church teaches, are promised blessings. At a missionary meeting in Hong Kong in 1996, President Gordon B. Hinckley said, "We are a covenant people in a relationship with God our Eternal Father, eternal and everlasting if we live worthy of it."[14]

The sealing covenant of parents to child is deemed as strong as if the child had been born to the adoptive parents, even for purposes of tracing genealogical lineage. It makes no difference to the Lord whether one is born or sealed into a family, just as it makes no difference whether one is born or adopted into the House of Israel.

"People used to argue as to whether the Chinese were literal descendants of Israel. I do not worry about that. Whether they get their blessings by inherited birthright or by adoption, the end result is the same—they become partakers of the everlasting covenant between Jehovah and Abraham, which extends to all of his posterity, whether by literal descent or by adoption."[15]

Manny was adopted by a couple in their forties who own a bookstore. He is polite and charming on the job. He helps a lady who needs a refund, a drink of water, and a book on comic art. While he is leading me to the used book collection, we happen onto the subject of adoption.

"I was kind of a gray-market placement," Manny jokes. He walks upstairs to book aisles on the north edge of the store. "My adoptive parents pulled a few strings, forged a few papers— because they were slightly too old. But maybe I got a better shake with older parents. I had a lot in common with children from broken families raised by their grandparents—that bi-generational kind of relationship," he smiles, "augmented by my mentors employed in the store. But my life was essentially books! I was into adult-level literature at age eleven; peers didn't influence me, I influenced them—with all the answers they wanted. I'm one of the luckiest people I've known!

"And I just heard from my birthmother, Charlotte," he says. "She wants us to meet soon, which is fine with me; I think she is dying of cancer. After we visit it's my impression that Charlotte would be happy to talk with you too. She is scrupulously frank."

Unquestionably, the growing popularity of openness has

increased the number of adoptions that were originally closed and have now become open. Open advocates claim that this fact validates the process of openness from the beginning. But in practice, explain Kathleen Silber and Phylis Speedlin in *Dear Birthmother,* the bond that children feel with their birthparents is sometimes "merely an intellectual curiosity about their background, while others verbalize an emotional drive to have physical contact with a blood relative."[16] Silber and Speedlin also explain that the birthmother has been customarily the brunt of most adoption myths, such as "the birthmother obviously doesn't care about her child or she wouldn't have given him away," and "both the birthmother and birthfather will forget about their unwanted child."[17] Consequently, older birthparents watching the open adoption concept growing more popular sometimes feel stigmatized by the lingering stereotypes—so foreign to their honest feelings—and initiate the opening of a closed adoption with their adult child.

"Manny is living my lifelong dream," Charlotte tells me. "I love books dearly and always dreamed of opening a bookstore-coffee shop." Charlotte is wrapped tightly in a terry cloth robe. She fiddles with a plastic vial of pills.

"When I got pregnant with Manny during my senior year at Loyola University, my Peruvian boyfriend wanted to marry me but I couldn't handle spending the rest of my life in South America. I eventually married a chemistry professor who was not able to age gracefully. After seventeen years he took his life and within a year after that I was robbed, raped in the middle of the night, and found out my mother had Alzheimer's. And the tremendous guilt I felt in giving up Manny never went away."

"I was tortured," Charlotte says, "because I couldn't visualize what Manny had become. I hear about people who can do that, but it's impossible for me to believe." Her voice halts, . . . "So it bothered me deeply; I could never be reassured he was okay.

"I've not thought a lot about mortality until lately," Charlotte says. "Once I realized I was going to die I felt that I couldn't finish my life without knowing about Manny. In the end, my motivation to find him was for my own peace of mind.

"I was still afraid—that I might disrupt his life, or be rejected. But people eventually do things because of the way they feel," she says. "I had copied his adoptive parents' address down years ago from a hospital file and it had never changed. My best friend helped by calling Manny, then Manny phoned me. I don't know where the energy came from while he visited here. I am very emotional, but Manny is the same way—it made our meeting very easy. Now nothing is left unresolved. When it was over, I literally crashed." Charlotte breathes deeply.

"Manny suggested I go meet his parents, but I have no desire. I don't think it would help anything," she murmurs. "I'm at my worst." She pauses, shifts in her chair.

"The reactions from my family were not all positive. When I told my brother, who has adopted a son of his own, about Manny—that I met him—he cried. I think my brother was frightened. He thought it was selfish of me to contact him."

The expanding world, full of daily reminders that things will never be as they were, demands our scrutiny. We are bound to explore. We must discover whether openness, for instance, is a popular idea or has lasting value. We need to learn how much adoption policies are shaped by economic needs or psychological proofs. We must comprehend the extent to which personal preferences or varied circumstances justify a procedure. Then we must pray for guidance.

UNRESOLVED CONFLICTS

Confidentiality was originally instigated to provide children with opportunity, birthparents with anonymity, and adoptive families with equality. All states approved sealed-record provisions and eventually passed laws to amend children's birth certificates. Agencies served the interests of adopting couples—the ones who paid their fees. Because standards, safeguards, and requirements focused on confidentiality, it was possible for agencies to escape the continuous evaluation common in other areas of social work. The pendulum had swung too far.

When the scarcity of babies became the new pattern, birthmothers were more valued and agencies focused on serving

their interests. In today's climate, pregnant teens who are willing to accept services that provide counseling and information
on adoption are almost seven times more likely to choose it.[18]
These birthmothers may then attend support groups in order
to make all the informed choices about adoption and prepare
for their continuing role as a birthmother. After the baby is
born birthmothers may receive therapy and post-placement
counseling to develop an appropriate relationship with the
adoptive parents, assimilate their loss, and move on with their
lives.

Some women who agreed to adoption for their children
years ago are left confused by the openness movement. They
were given quiet assurances by agencies that have now
changed their approach. Some of these incognito birthmothers
wait, overwhelmed with fear, wondering if they will be forced
to face old heartaches.

"I made a mistake when I was young," one tells Dear Abby,
"and I suffered for it. I can appreciate people's curiosity about
their biological parents, but I beg them to consider our right to
keep this part of our lives private. Revealing past confidential-
ities can do incalculable damage to the present." Such a birthparent is part of a tender, quieter segment of the adoption
triad. To such a person "open" means exposed or public.
"Closed" expresses a continuing preference for privacy.

In contrast, a group of vocal women who relinquished children in the past have banded together in a national organization (Concerned United Birthparents) as political advocates for
adoption reform, including openness. These birthparents
(most of them women) feel they were coerced into relinquishing their children. Research done within a self-selected group
of birthmothers shows a significant correlation between the
primary reason for placing a child for adoption and the birthmother's desire to search.[19] Individuals who reported that relinquishment of their child was due to external pressure (family,
social workers, or lack of money) were significantly more likely
to have instituted an active search for their child in later
years than individuals who reported internal reasons for their

decision such as age, unpreparedness for parenthood, or desire to complete schooling.

The way birthmothers in the past perceived their choices is as pronounced as the arguments over what to do with birth records in the future. Some contend that since open adoption is a standard practice, sealing original birth records will no longer serve any purpose. Then, swinging far out, they project that there cannot be acceptance of open adoption placement in the future without acceptance of opening records of the past. Others poignantly plead, "No! States can protect the confidentiality of past adoptions and still open records from this time forward."

MIXED VIEWPOINTS

Meanwhile, there can be rousing support for the couples standing outside the hospital nursery who chanced to discover—because the adoption was open and both families chose to meet—that the baby being placed had a common grandmother of both an adoptive and birthparent. "We would never have learned that without openness. The placement was supposed to be!" Other birth and adoptive families gather for joint birthday parties as the child grows. Adoptive parents exult over the clothes, blankets, rings—an ongoing string of tokens sent by birth families to their adopted child, demonstrating a continuing love.

But there can also be compassion for the birthmother who went on to marry and raise a family in the Church and then was contacted just before Christmas by her daughter, born before her marriage and placed independently for adoption. "She asked to come visit," the birthmother said, "And I thought, sure—I've resolved this issue in my own mind. I shouldn't be afraid of opening up." However, the uncanny genetic likeness, the revelation that the daughter now had a same-sex partner, the subsequent announcement to her other children and eventually to her grandchildren, and the desire of the recently introduced daughter to be included in every family gathering with her partner, left her gasping, "Who is this helping?"

And surely there should be sensitivity in today's open climate to feel the frustration of a grown adoptee, in a previously closed placement, who was later hounded by his birthmother. She called, visited him at his job, and sent boxes of memorabilia to his house with the message, "My hope is rising that you will want me." The son who was adopted says, "She thinks I should move thousands of miles to live near her—and be part of the clan." The son is now a huge grown man—majoring in electrical engineering—who stands holding her Christmas card gently in his hands. "I'm content with anything," he says. "But I wouldn't hurt my adoptive parents—I owe them everything. And when she called our child 'her granddaughter,' that was the last straw for my wife." He looks up, helpless. "Now, any contact bristles."

Finally, there can be deep gratitude for the strength of a child—placed for adoption after a few years in foster care—and her adoptive parents. The child steps out of the family car, presses the wrinkles out of her sundress, and then holds tightly onto the hand of her adoptive mother. They walk together, resolute, the child intermittently looking up to catch her mother's eye, waiting for her reassuring smile. They progress steadily through the prison gate, steel doors, and concrete corridors on a visit to the birthmother, hoping to bring some light into her life.

The clear focus of reformers has been the child who was adopted. The child was supposedly "reborn" in the days of confidentiality, and open advocates now say that on behalf of the child the birthparents must be available. But focusing on whether a child wants that openness is the only way the one can be benefited. Imposed openness denies individual choice as much as imposed secrecy. Wayne Carp, an adoption historian, concludes, "Extreme positions rarely work in a situation with as many diverse motivations, interests, and rights as those occasioned by adoption."[20]

There is sufficient research to show that openness in adoption can present many unanticipated challenges and should not be embraced lightly. Birth and adoptive families may be abrasively dissimilar or individually discreet. Privacy is not pathological, as some have claimed in regards to conventional placements.

LDS Family Services has maintained moderation in its adoption policy. Its semi-open approach insures against the risks inherent in open adoption. Exclusive communication through the agency after adoption can protect participants from infringing on each other's agency. But there are many infants and children in need of good homes who will never come into the LDS Family Services program. Adults who feel inspired to find them may be searching through a variety of other individuals with powerfully different viewpoints. The type of adoption one pursues is not an issue for conversion, just inspiration.

NOTES

1. Ruth G. McRoy, Harold D. Grotevant, and Kerry L. White, *Openness in Adoption* (New York: Praeger, 1988). Also summarized in Jerome Smith, *The Realities of Adoption* (Landham, MD: Madison Books, 1997), pp. 58–61.

2. Annette Baran and Reuben Pannor, "Open Adoption," in *The Psychology of Adoption*, ed. David M. Brodzinsky and Marshall D. Schechter (New York: Oxford University Press, 1990), p. 316.

3. Ibid., p. 318.

4. Annette Baran, as quoted in Lincoln Caplan, *An Open Adoption* (New York: Farrar, Straus, and Giroux, 1990), p. 93.

5. Sharon Kaplin-Rozsia, as quoted in Jeanne Warren Lindsay, *Open Adoption: A Caring Option* (Buena Park, Calif.: Morning Glory Press, 1987), p. 234.

6. James Gritter, "Commitment in Open Adoption," speech presented at First Biennial Conference on Open Adoption Families, Colorado Springs, Colo., June 18, 1998.

7. Deborah H. Siegel, "Open Adoption of Infants: Adoptive Parents' Perceptions of Advantages and Disadvantages," *Journal of Social Work* 38 (January 1993): 15–23.

8. Ibid., pp. 19–20.

9. Mary Iwanek, telephone conversation with author, July 13, 1998. See also "Open Adoption: An Evolving Practice," 1994 Australian Adoption Conference, Post Adoption Resource Centre, 1994.

10. Alfred Kadushin in Smith, *The Realities of Adoption*, p. 42. Also, telephone conversation with author, September 21, 1999.

11. Caplan, *An Open Adoption*, p. 89.

12. Wayne E. Carp, *Family Matters* (Cambridge, Mass.: Harvard University Press, 1998), p. 232.

13. H. David Kirk, "Looking Back, Looking Forward," address for Adopted Families of America in Dallas, Texas, July 2, 1995 (Indianapolis: Perspectives Press, 1995), p.18.

14. Gordon B. Hinckley, *Teachings of Gordon B. Hinckley* (Salt Lake City: Deseret Book Company, 1997), p. 148.

15. Ibid., p. 147.

16. Kathleen Silber and Phylis Speedlin, *Dear Birthmother* (San Antonio, Texas: Corona Publishing Company, 1982), p. 91.

17. Ibid., p. 11.

18. Steven D. Mclaughlin, "Evaluating the Adoption Component of AFL Care Demonstration Project," *Final Report to the Office of Adolescent Pregnancy Programs*, DHHS, March 1991, in "Facts on Adoption," the National Council for Adoption, pp. 27–28.

19. Anne B. Brodzinsky, "Surrendering an Infant for Adoption: The Birthmother Experience," in *The Psychology of Adoption*, p. 301.

20. Carp, *Family Matters*, p.233.

Ye might be partakers of the divine nature.
2 Peter 1:4

3

FOOD FOR THE SOUL
NATURE AND NURTURE

The soul, the eternal spirit within the mortal body, is invisible and scientifically undetectable, yet essential to understanding the unique possibilities of each person. No individual, adopted or not, is simply the result of heredity and environment; a person's capabilities can grow beyond both. All mortals bring with them a divine origin and possess a divine destiny.

These spiritual aspects of human beings go beyond the study of psychology. But there are other aspects—genetic nature and the nurturing quality of environment—which clearly fit into it. Joseph Smith berated himself for "the foibles of human nature" that led him into temptations—not a disposition to commit any great malignant sins, for "such was never in my nature," he affirmed. "But I was guilty of levity, and sometimes associated with jovial company, etc., not consistent with that character which ought to be maintained by one who was called of God as I had been. But this will not seem very strange to any one who recollects my youth, and is acquainted with my native cheery temperament" (Joseph Smith—History 1:28).

This candid disclosure in Joseph Smith's personal history is a helpful model for understanding the balance between human nature and the soul. As the Prophet grew he schooled his nature with his powerful soul. And his innate cheerful disposition strengthened him to endure persecutions that might easily have stopped the progress of another man. Such honest disclosure reinforces the obvious: that within all human beings are differing natural traits that affect that person's behavior. In addition to natural tendencies, a variety of environmental influences may have a similarly strong impact. The loving, nurturing family in which Joseph Smith grew up was more conducive to his success than a dysfunctional one.

FOUNDATIONAL DEBATE

By the late 1800s Charles Darwin's studies had persuaded scientists that an individual's biological tendencies affect their development more than does their environment. Darwin's cousin Sir Francis Galton believed that an individual's nature prevails enormously over the environment in which they are nurtured. "The one element," Galton concluded, "which varies in different individuals, but is constant for each of them is the natural tendency; it corresponds to the current in the stream, and inevitably asserts itself."[1]

By the 1900s, however, the position of environmentalists was stronger. John B. Watson argued that if he took a dozen healthy infants and brought them up in his own specified world, he could guarantee any one of them would become whatever specialist he might select—"doctor, lawyer, artist, merchant-chief, and, yes, even beggar-man and thief, regardless of his talents, penchants, tendencies, abilities, vocations, and race of his ancestors."[2]

In 1966 Leonard Heston published a study[3] in Britain linking children who were reared in foster homes with the psychiatric disorders of their biological mothers with schizophrenia. Extensive studies followed that connected genetic factors to behavior but also established the significance of both genetics and environment on human behavior. Debate continues over the contribution and interaction of each.

For many adoptive parents, knowing a child's biologic heritage is a positive factor. They believe that if they can adopt a child with "reasonable" intelligence and "normal personality" they can help shape beliefs and attitudes. Like the majority of children, most children who were adopted grow up finally to accept their parents' value system, which many good parents hope will include embracing the gospel.

Brynne hikes with our family to Cascade Canyon the summer after her third year at Antioch College. Partway around the east side of Jenny Lake she learns that one of our children was adopted. "I'm always saying I'll adopt," Brynne laughs. "It's a lot less painful."

"Are you serious?" I ask.

"Well, it simply doesn't matter which way children come into a family," says Brynne. "And it's been so exciting for me. You know, I'm adopted."

"Then adoption really isn't an issue for you," I say.

"I think it is an issue but not in the way most people think. I have mystery behind me—I feel like I was sent from God to earth. I know that sounds weird, but it has given me confidence, like the Lord was saying, 'You are meant to follow your own spirit, to stand on your own two feet.' I'm my own person. I am a child of God. That gives me a foundation—the beginning of who I am."

The trail winds to the east, ascending underneath one of the Teton Range's highest peaks. Brynne is short and slender. Hiking is effortless for her; she competed as a speed skater in high school.

"Some people come up to me and say, 'You don't look anything like your mom.' And I say, 'Well, I'm adopted and that's probably why.'" Brynne is laughing again. "At first they think I'm joking because I have no reservations.

"But some people will say," Brynne continues, "'You and your mother have the same smile,' and I think that's what's really neat. My genetics aren't the same. But I have the same mannerisms as my mother and my father, and in that respect I'm really part of them. I'm built of the strength that they have. And that's why I am their daughter—it's not the genes that count."

Around a bend in the trail we stop in full view of Hidden Falls—broader, higher, and more powerful than we had imagined. The trail climbs steeply, with frequent places to stop and soak in

*the view. "I think the various goals and drives we had in heaven,"
Brynne says, "come with us, and I think they're the 'underdrive'
of everything we do. When people say, 'Your birthmother gave
you away because she didn't love you,' I say, 'No, you're wrong.
Because she loved me so much she gave me up. She knew I wasn't
her child but was here to live with another family—with my own
parents.'"*

"Do you feel any connection to your birthmother?" I ask.

*"Yes," Brynne says. "I pray for her—that she can be happy and
know I'm happy—but my role and her role are different. She filled
her role. The idea of having a baby and knowing it's not yours
when you're having it, and going through with the adoption in
spite of other people's ridicule—that's incredible, that's inner
strength! Sure, my birthparents made one wrong decision, so
what. They made the right one by fixing it."*

*Brynne is ahead of me now, hiking with the younger set. She
smiles back, gesturing at the total expanse of the lake below. By
the time I catch up, she's refreshed, relaxed.*

*"My role is to be grateful," she says. "I've known since I was a
child that I am where I was meant to be. I think that without a
Church adoption it is a bit harder. All I have is a 3- by 5-inch
card—Watson baby: nearsightedness, hay fever, Swedish background—and that's it. I don't think more information would be
helpful to me. It might be too tying."*

SOUL INPUT

Genes don't dictate people's behavior, they only set up the
probabilities. Environment may then impact the extent to
which a person's genetic potential is expressed. Most significantly, each individual soul, with conceivable power to direct
its nature and environment, must make final choices for itself.
But these choices may also be affected by biological limitations or environmental background. This intangible combination of factors—nature, nurture, and soul—may result in some
unexpected events. One thing is certain, adoptive parents with
a noticeably dissimilar child may learn sooner an essential fact
of all parenthood: No parents own their children. Parenthood
is stewardship, not ownership, and parents of children with

special challenges have an especially fertile context in which to learn respect for another soul's individuality.

"We knew we had a pistol when we left the hospital," Gwen says. "When Melvin was hungry, he was mad. He was determined by nature and had a much stronger personality than I did. Just keeping track of him was a full-time job."

Gwen and her husband, Russ, live in a fertile farm area of the southeast. They have extra land to grow okra, turnip greens, and black-eyed peas. Russ is a big man with large hands, happier in his garden than at work for Grumman Aerospace. Gwen is a musician and a seamstress.

"When Melvin was two," Gwen says, "we didn't have a fence. There was a stream back on our property and Melvin wanted to be outside all the time, so I bought a harness that I could tie to a rope on the clothesline post. Melvin had a lot of area to play in while I tried to give piano lessons. It was such a wonderful idea! The first time, and every time I tried it, he ran to the end of the rope and screamed." Gwen's laughter makes tears; then earnestness settles in her countenance.

"Melvin was never content with the moment. He always had to be one step beyond where I was. I made preparations for a birthday party; all the kids came. When it was time to play games, Melvin wanted to open presents. When it was time to open presents, he wanted to be eating refreshments. I just kept saying, 'the problem is me.'

"Russ was bishop at the time. Melvin began running away. By age thirteen Melvin was skipping school. We had to pick him up after being in fights, and we were getting phone calls from the hospital saying they had him. He always had to be in charge of everything, then worked so hard that he burned out in a few days. He couldn't keep a job.

"Melvin married a girl when he was seventeen; they either adored each other or fought. I came in on them one day after they already had two kids—a third was on the way. They were chasing each other around my table with eyes as big as saucers, calling names. My first idea was to phone the police, but I shocked 'em by just standing there.

"'What's going on?' I asked. They were full of accusations. 'Well, let's sit down a minute and see if we can talk this through.' I kind of asked questions, 'What's your feeling on this?' and, 'what's yours?' When it was over Mel gave me a big hug. 'Mom, you should be a marriage counselor.' They went home arm in arm." Gwen smiles to herself.

"It was about this time that I got a phone call one evening from his birthmother, Olga. I felt like every muscle, every bone in my body tightened. Russ was out in the garden planting the last of the beans. I hung up the phone and went out to tell him. We decided maybe it would give Melvin stability to meet his birthmother—knowing his roots might help him handle his troubles. He did have a job helping retarded children at the mental hospital but he wasn't dependable.

"'Yes, I'd like to meet her,' Melvin said. 'But you'll always be my parents. She'll never be my mother.'

"The day Olga arrived from New Jersey, Melvin picked her up at the airport in Atlanta. It was an unseasonably cool day in April. She burst into the house, sweat standing out on her brow, with gifts for everybody. Her suitcase was full of food—cabasa packed in dry ice, all kinds of bread, homemade horseradish, and sauerkraut. She was from a wealthy Czech family who had lost everything when they moved to New York City before World War II. Olga was a chain smoker, a strong Catholic, and very respectful. She used the Lord's name in every exclamation, and 'Bless his soul,' over her father and brother. For two weeks we did things together.

"We went to see the new temple in Atlanta when it was open to visitors. As we approached the gates, there were hecklers passing out literature. They handed it to her and said something negative about Mormons. Olga got real mad.

"'You have no business being here. Why this is these people's religion and it's their right. Now you just get on.' She grabbed the pamphlets, walked in the gate, and threw them in the garbage. And that's just the way she was. Olga and Melvin related real good. They enjoyed each other but that's where it ended. There was no emotional attachment. They've had no more communication with each other.

"After Olga's visit, Melvin's brother, who we also adopted, became adamant that he never wanted contact with his own birthmother. 'It kind of messed Melvin up,' he said. 'Now Melvin thinks he's inherited her craziness and he's pretty much given up trying to improve himself.'"

But for Gwen the reunion was helpful. "When I saw Olga, I saw Melvin," she says. "She was the same impulsive type of person. Then I knew the problem wasn't just Russ and me. Had Olga raised Melvin, he would have been brought up pretty strict. It was his nature to buck authority. He would have bucked her. We've never doubted our decision to adopt Melvin. Olga may have had more trouble with him than we did."

Gwen and Russ chose to adopt Melvin over another available infant who they helped place with friends in their ward two blocks away. The other adopted child was easy to parent, achieved with the slightest encouragement, and is currently in medical school. And Gwen and Russ wouldn't consider trading places with his adoptive parents. "We're happy for the other family's successes but they haven't been without their own problems. Working out problems is what life's about."

ASPECTS OF PERSONALITY

Olga fits the textbook definition of an individual with an antisocial personality. Such people behave impulsively, seek immediate gratification, and cannot tolerate frustration. A genetically antisocial parent is much more likely to have an antisocial child. Remi Cadoret, who has done two significant studies linking genetic inheritance to antisocial behavior in adopted children, says this is especially true among predisposed children during adolescence. Cadoret explains in *The Psychology of Adoption,*[4] that antisocial and alcoholic behavior in parents may also be linked genetically to their children's hyperactivity and attention deficit disorder. "It is apparent from a large number of studies of twins and adoptees," Cadoret concludes, "that behavior ranging from personality traits and intelligence to psychopathology, such as substance abuse and manic-depressive disease, have at their base a genetic factor."[5] Genetic inheritance can increase the possibility of alcoholism, bipolar illness, schizophrenia, and obesity.

No matter how individual inheritance is assembled, all infants show recognizable differences in temperament during the first weeks of life. Those differences were defined by psychologists in the 1980s. They include activity level, rhythmicity, intensity of reaction to change, and quality of mood. Specific combinations of these factors can make up the "difficult" child, who has intense reactions, negative moods, and a lack of rhythmicity or a predictable schedule. Characteristics of temperament predispose infants to react in certain ways, but scientists are beginning to discover that genetics and environment work together to determine personality.

RISK COMPONENTS

An example of the "nature" versus "nurture" interplay is illustrated by Jerome Kagan's study[6] of the personality trait of shyness. Kagan, a Harvard professor, has monitored 500 children with inherent shyness for seventeen years and determined that children can outgrow a predisposition to shyness if the parents gently but firmly desensitize them. Though shy children's hearts beat much faster than other babies in the womb, Kagan found that with constructive assistance no more than 20 percent of the children remain shy by age four. A study of the same genetic predisposition to shyness in humans is being conducted with rhesus monkeys at the National Institute of Child Health and Human Development. The shy monkeys, when raised by a foster mother who is an expert caregiver, will not only outgrow shyness but become a leader among peers and in turn teach her offspring to overcome the same predisposition.

A constructive role in adoption can be to give children who are adoptable and who have a higher percentage of risky predispositions, a chance to develop normally in an environment away from the problem. Integrating people with similar genetic weaknesses can exacerbate the behavior. Cadoret supports selective placement for children with high-risk backgrounds into homes where there is no evidence of similar problems, while giving the adoptive parents sufficient information to make an early diagnosis if necessary for suitable treatment.

Awareness of risk can be constructive when it fortifies parents with realistic expectations during a possibly difficult process, but not when the knowledge is misdirected to overanticipate problems. The interplay between physical and temperamental aspects of development in the first years can confound parents and professionals. Some difficult babies grow out of discomfort while some easy babies grow more challenging. Mature adoptive parents, like mature biological parents, can handle a difficult child with greater endurance if they comprehend their role early. There is an unpredictable element—though greater in adoption—which still exists in every child born. Because the gene pool is so large and the veil of heaven so opaque, parents never know exactly what they're going to get. Initial assurances that an adoption decision is right are not invalidated if a poignant struggle follows. The Lord inspires mortals with his intrinsic understanding of endless time, which may seem incomprehensible in this sphere. Bewildered parents may respond to the Lord as Nephi, "I know that he loveth his children; nevertheless, I do not know the meaning of all things" (1 Nephi 11:17). Parents' commitment to whatever kind of child they receive activates a ceaseless wonder.

Jeanne and Martin Pearson adopted two daughters, Shari and Krista, both in private placements at birth, from parents about whom they had very little background. Shari had a calm disposition. She was responsive to her parents' care and generally obedient. Her even temperament enabled her to take advantage of all the opportunities they offered. Shari graduated from college, found a good job, and recently married in the temple. Though she has pleased her parents, the wonder to others is that Jeanne and Martin love Krista—who did little they desired—as dearly. The ability to love is inextricably connected to the process of giving care. A difficult child needs abundant caring.

"Krista was a beautiful baby and cried actively when I changed her clothes in the hospital," Jeanne says. "In the rest room at the

airport I tried to feed her for the first time. She would not soften—she could not mellow. She arched her back and hurled her limbs. In ensuing days, whenever I held her, she fussed and would not feed.

"The attorney told us she was the 'product' of a professor and a student from Berkeley. This was in the mid-sixties. The birth-mother selected me because I was her same age, twenty-six, and we both already had little boys.

"Krista wandered as soon as she toddled. Neighbors who helped me search said, 'Are you sure she's not downstairs, or in the yard?' She always went far away. In middle school, we got calls from the principal long after school was out—'Krista's still here.' She hung around with friends to smoke pot and ran away once at age fourteen. When she ran again in high school, an unidentified caller phoned us in the middle of the night from a cafeteria downtown. 'Is this Krista's mom?' I sat up, turned on the light.

"'I don't think she comes from the kind of family that would expect her out on the street,' he said. 'She reminds me of my younger sister.' By then Krista was on speed. She reentered deten-tion, pregnant with Zach.

"I went to see her regularly when she moved into an apart-ment. I was very observant of Zach," Jeanne says. "He seemed happy. I brought him home with me frequently and he could never get enough to eat. Zach was sitting at my kitchen table, finishing cookies and milk, when he told me, 'Mom puts needles in her arms like doctors.' I learned that Zach had missed twenty days of school, was arriving late, dirty, and one day had left to find food.

"'Would you like me to help you?' I asked Krista. The state was ready to take custody of Zach. That was three years ago.

"Krista was on cocaine and heroin the last time she got preg-nant. 'We will support you,' I told her, 'when you decide to give this child for adoption.' Krista enrolled in a teen mother program. Every week we went to a substance abuse meeting held in our ward chapel; it helped her feel a sense of self-worth. She returned on Sundays—sat near the back, crossed her legs, and cried. After the birth I held her addicted baby girl while we waited for the adoptive parents to come from Oregon. When I wrapped the baby

up tightly and hugged her in my arms, I could stop the little thing from shaking.

"When the hospital staff told me there was only a 2 percent chance of Krista ever getting off drugs, I had to be satisfied with any progress in her life. Now she is relatively clean—stabilized on pot. Krista lives with her current boyfriend in a house trailer in Texas."

I visit Jeanne and Martin at home. Zach is in the kitchen flipping a pog on the sideboard. White countertops sparkle under fluorescent lights; a row of glass canisters banks his shots. Martin watches Zach. A smile breaks over his face as the pog ricochets off the cookie jar, past the canisters over to the toaster. "I look at Zach like I looked at Krista while she was growing up," he says. "If we can't help these kids, who else can? Three years ago Zach had lots of fear. He had to sleep by our bed for months. He couldn't pass food around the dinner table without taking some. But we have hope that Zach can be the one to break the addictive cycle."

"Krista called this afternoon," Jeanne says. "She and her boyfriend can't find work so they'll be coming through on the bus in a couple of weeks, en route to the northwest. They will have a forty-five minute stop here."

"Will you take Zach to see her?" I ask.

"Yes," Jeanne says, "but before we go I'll tell him—'Remember how we talk about Mommy on drugs and Mommy off drugs? Sometimes she can hug you, but sometimes the drugs won't let her.'"

Breaking the addictive cycle is momentous, everlastingly crucial. Parents striving to save a child know they are instruments in the Lord's hands. As Jeanne and Martin continue nurturing Zach, Krista not only survives but grows through their faith. Even as the propensity for an addiction can pass from one generation to another genetically, faith can pass from one generation to another spiritually, assuring an eventual triumph.

INFLUENCE OF DRUGS

Drugs alter heredity and environment. Any child—adopted or not—may be vulnerable to drug use. Addictions are developed in society but are perpetuated by a propensity carried in a gene. Millions of babies in the United States are damaged in utero by a mother's drug and alcohol consumption. Those exposed to cocaine or crack, particularly, show abnormal physical responses to basic needs and environmental stimuli resulting in attachment problems. The developing fetus of a mother who drinks may have mental retardation and facial abnormalities. Increasing responsibility on the part of birthmothers nationwide is reflected in the sharp decline of drug, alcohol, and tobacco consumption during pregnancy but generally after the first trimester, by which time the damage has often already occurred.[7] Most birthmothers infected with HIV/AIDS in this country are now voluntarily tested and receive perinatal preventive treatments, cutting in half the rate of transmission to their babies.[8]

There are adoptive parents who will raise some of these children with caring and hope. Other children will languish in foster care, and still others will remain in homes where they will be neglected by their birthparents. The Lord loves *all* these children.

Parents who adopt a child that is biologically or genetically at risk, knowingly or not, can grow to comprehend the larger scope of their child's divine nature. As parents seek inspiration to assist their child, they gain a better view of their own role in the Lord's plan. As parents follow the spiritual guidance they receive, temporal concerns are quieted, personal frustrations calmed, and sweet assurances uttered "that all these things shall give thee experience, and shall be for thy good" (D&C 122:7).

Individual human beings have heart and soul. Even parents who struggle with disadvantaged children to the point they can no longer expect them to function constructively in society continue to hope they will. Hope can grow in the soul—resilient and enduring, perpetuating itself through an eventual resolution of the toughest challenges.

NOTES

1. Sir Francis Galton, in Karl Pearson, *The Life, Letters and Labours of Francis Galton* (Cambridge: University Press, 1914), p. 8.

2. John B. Watson, *Behaviorism* (New York: Norton, 1930), p. 104.

3. Leonard L. Heston, "Psychiatric Disorders in Foster Home Reared Children of Schizophrenic Mothers," *British Journal of Psychiatry* 112 (1966): 1103–10.

4. Remi J. Cadoret, "Biologic Perspectives of Adoptee Adjustment," in *The Psychology of Adoption,* ed. David M. Brodzinsky and Marshall D. Schechter (New York: Oxford University Press, 1990), pp. 29–39.

5. Ibid., p.28.

6. Marc Peyser and Anne Underwood, "Shyness, Sadness, Curiosity, Joy: Is It Nature or Nurture?" *Newsweek* (Spring-Summer 1997), pp. 60–64.

7. United States Substance Abuse and Mental Health Services Administration, "Women of Childbearing Age," which can be contacted at http://www.samhsa.gov/oas/nhsda/ar18t047.htm

8. National Center for Health Statistics, Centers for Disease Control and Prevention, "Maternal and Infant Health Surveillance," "Status or Perinatal HIV Prevention U.S. Declines Continue: Hope for Extending Success to Developing World," http://www.cdc.gov/nccdphp/pregnanc.htm

Ye were also in the beginning with the Father.
D&C 93:23

4
BEYOND HOUSEPLANTS
DEVELOPING IDENTITY

The discovery of one's identity is the great revelation in life. People who complete the quest find their own unique purpose and thus become at home amid the world's challenges. Such individuals recognize that personal growth is an ongoing responsibility and they are not only secure within themselves but are also motivated to help others.

The restored gospel of Jesus Christ reveals our rich heritage in the premortal realm. All people on this earth had their own spirit identities as sons or daughters of the Eternal Father. Everyone worshipped him and accepted his plan: to obtain a physical body and gain earthly experience. But that knowledge is verified only through individual faith, developed as one calls upon the Lord and receives personal assurance of his love as well as direction for daily life. So the mortal journey of getting to know our Heavenly Father (away from his direct presence) is also a process of re-revealing ourselves to ourselves— harmonizing the spirit we were before we came here with the person we are becoming through the experiences of mortality. Eventually, if one lives a virtuous life he is promised that "then shall thy confidence wax strong in the presence of God" (D&C 121:45). One of the great purposes of life is to achieve not just a secure identity in this world but one that will give us confidence going into the next.

ADOLESCENT CHALLENGES

The search for identity becomes urgent and significantly personal during adolescence. Most adolescents make positive, healthy, emotional and social development during the teenage years. And although an adolescent's reactions may vacillate with their changing hormones, they have no more psychological disturbances than the rest of the population.

Teens who have been adopted generally respond like others. Janet Hoopes, a psychologist who has conducted her own studies on adoption and the development of identity, says, "It appears that satisfactory family relationships could perhaps effectively mitigate or even eliminate the 'intensification' of identity concerns."[1] This is the overall picture. But even a constructive pursuit of identity may be difficult for a youth to achieve, and some studies suggest that adopted children may have a higher risk of facing identity concerns.

"There was not a single stage in my life that was affected by adoption," Henry says. Henry is 6'3" and weighs over 200 pounds. He's mostly East Indian. "Looking unlike the rest of my family was kind of fun, only I never sunburned."

Henry is in the aviation school office at 4:30 P.M. on every good weather day. "It's 27 knots out there," he says. "I don't take people out over 10, maybe 15 if they're experienced."

"On which aircraft are you qualified to give lessons?" I ask.

"All of them," he says. A rental price list on the desk shows eleven options from the tiny Cessna 152 to the Piper Seneca II, with two engines. Henry leads the way to an adjacent hangar.

"I work for a fixed base operator some days," he says. Just inside the hangar a Gulfstream G-3 dominates, but Henry goes over to the Citation Jet beyond it. "This one I co-pilot for two local corporations. See the T-tail curved up high? That's so the exhausts don't burn it." He waits, allowing time for me to examine the craft on all sides.

"I like to explain things to people," he says, "help them in any way. It's easy now, maybe impossible when I get on with a

commercial airline." Henry extends to his full height, leaning back on his heels.

"For now I work days as a policeman. Law enforcement is the kind of job that grows on you," Henry continues. His voice is full of energy. "Just like flying!" He steps ahead, cautioning me about a protruding antenna.

"I like it so much I can tell I'm going to have to keep a reserve position on the force in the future, even when I'm not full time. But there are some characters around, in aviation and law enforcement, who try to get me in trouble. With my broader back-ground I get more requests for help than they do." Henry is comfortable being the polished gentleman.

"Are you under attack because of discrimination?"

Henry smiles. "No, the sergeant over me is black and female; she's not the problem. It's the older ones, with fewer credentials. Maybe they're just bored." He walks back toward the office.

"But just like with adoption, it's no big deal," he says. "Remember, there are a lot of adopted kids out there that no one ever knows about, because they're the same race as their parents, well-adjusted, and don't care about differences. Have you talked to . . ." Henry lists several of his friends who grew up in a residential suburb of Las Vegas.

"Henry is one-fourth Mexican-American too," his father, Carl, says. "But he did not have Spanish friends in high school—he did not befriend or join that group. On the contrary, he tended to pal up with the 'aristocracy,'" Carl laughs. "I don't really know what that means."

Henry's father works in administration at the University of Nevada. Both he and his wife are Caucasian.

"Henry is wonderfully bright," Carl says. "In some ways, the view he had of schoolwork was a sign of his intelligence. He figured out how to barely pass classes. He started at the first of each term with an A or B on a test and then said, 'Well, that's too good. I certainly don't need to work that hard.'" Carl laughs heartily.

"Henry cruised through high school with a 2.0 average. We had him tested at age twelve to see if he had a learning disability. The psychologist came back shaking his head, saying he was giving

more perceptive and thoughtful answers than most adults. He had an IQ of 154.

"Now I don't understand that!" Carl smiles. "I was the kind of person who never missed a class—sort of a compulsive-obsessive type. Discipline wasn't an issue in my family. My father looked cross-eyed at me, and that was all I needed. I mean he never touched me, never threatened—it would have been absurd. He was always my friend and I did anything to stay on his good side.

"Henry was completely different. He got to the point where he simply wouldn't obey. He was exercising his independence. My wife had run-ins with him over music lessons. When he was sixteen and bad about curfews, my wife pushed hard, got really angry because he wouldn't obey the rules, and frustrated with me for not enforcing them. I said, 'What he's doing is not really terrible, and how do we enforce penalties on a kid that big anyway?' I was careful to sit down with him, try to cajole a little bit . . . not, 'Do that and you're out of here!'" Carl chuckles, dropping his chin.

"You know how it is with your own kids—you might get mad at them and yell at them but they do exactly what you did when you were fourteen or sixteen. You kind of recognize what they're thinking and why they feel that way. With Henry, I didn't know or understand.

"But Henry was never significantly involved in alcohol or drugs, doesn't smoke. As a teenager he developed a pretty neat way of operating; he is meticulous about his room. He does a fancy job of detailing cars, lifts weights twice a week, runs. He has 1,500 to 1,600 hours flying time and is extremely careful going through his checklist. The disappointments are things like his early divorce and the Church—he simply has no interest yet."

DEVELOPMENTAL STAGES

Young adults who have established their human identity are recognizable. They are like Henry. In spite of disappointments, Carl's description of his son reveals a psychologist's definition of optimal identity in Henry, publically described by Erik Erikson in the early 1960s as "a feeling of being at home in one's body, a sense of 'knowing where one is going,' and an inner assuredness of anticipated recognition from those who count."[2] Henry exudes self-esteem and competence that neither minority race nor adoption seems to have diminished. He achieved a solid identity during adolescence—which is only one stage, however critical, in the continuum of development. The full maturing of identity can be as much a lifelong process as assimilating adoption.

Erikson divided the human life span into developmental stages that describe the resolution of an individual's challenges from infancy to old age. Psychologists generally accept Erikson's stages, called the "Ages of Man."[3] Each stage describes environmental crises that all individuals face, which must be resolved in order for an individual to fully mature. In the first year of life, a child learns to "trust" or "mistrust." In the second year the challenge evolves into a sense of "autonomy," which vies against feelings of "doubt." By kindergarten, a child should have developed "initiative" instead of "guilt." And if the child continues to thrive, by puberty he will have mastered "industry" over "inferiority."

Erikson's fifth stage is the one that occurs during adolescence, triggered by the "identity" versus "confusion" crisis. Erikson believed that the major task for an adolescent is to resolve the "identity crisis" successfully—to confront the issue of "Who Am I?"—to explore alternatives, and commit to a set of values. Individuals who grow past adolescence without distinguishing their place in the world become confused with an adult role; they are unable to cope with full-blown demands and to form mature relationships with the opposite sex.

"But achieving identity is not where the impact of adoption begins or ends," says Richelle. "I majored in child psychology. My challenges were not addressed during the critical stages of development, and, more importantly, my emotions were not allowed to be expressed either. My mother was also adopted."

Richelle is bright with enthusiasm. She brings her mother and her two young sons to the park. We sit around while the children play in the sand waiting for Audrey, her mother, to speak first. But Audrey stares into space for a while, and when she finally talks her voice is flat, toneless.

"My parents were both Jewish," Audrey says. "My father was

a citrus farmer; he grew lemons, oranges, and grapefruit. As the years progressed, he also marketed orange blossoms that people wanted to buy for receptions and weddings. He was an alcoholic and was smoking up to four packs a day of the harshest cigarettes when he died. His name was Richard and that's how Richelle got her name. I like to play with names like that." Audrey wears tiny ruby earrings and white walking shorts, stretching her legs out in front of her on the bench.

"Your birthmother looked just like you," Audrey says to Richelle, "except for a slight gap between her front teeth. I looked her over at the attorney's office while she asked me questions. She wanted to know if I would be home with you, if I would raise you Jewish." Richelle's attention is riveted on her mother's apathetic account. She savors every word, smiles a lot, and dispenses snacks and winks to pacify her children.

"You ought to find her, Richelle," Audrey says. "If I could find my birthmother, I would." Audrey looks away into the distance and Richelle taps her sandals on the ground.

As we walk together toward the parking lot, Audrey rouses, becoming enthused for the first time as she talks about food; "Every morning I mix orange juice, nonfat milk, one banana, and a chunk of tofu in the blender. You should try it."

"I keep telling Mom," Richelle says, "she ought to move closer to us."

Within days after our conversation in the park Richelle contacts her birthmother and they decide to meet. Richelle describes their reunion.

"When I walked into her apartment," Richelle says, "the first thing she said was, 'You didn't get the nose—the Bernstein nose! Oh, you're beautiful, so tall—just like your dad.' Her kitchen was full of deli food. I liked it all. I kept wanting to give her more hugs. We both love eating and cooking and I spent six-and-a-half hours with her that first day. She gave me a book about her grandparents. Her grandfather had studied to be the Tzaddik, the teacher of the Talmud and Hebrew in Poland. When he married at age eighteen he was drafted by the tsar. In order to evade the draft, Siberia, or execution, he moved his family to America in 1901."

Richelle races through the story but doesn't slight a detail. She has become imbued with her newly discovered heritage. Her birthmother, Janet, appeared to have a stronger identity than her adoptive mother, Audrey. Intellectual and personality patterns, as well as clearly established values, were obvious strengths in her birth family, the same characteristics Richelle recognized in herself and missed in her adoptive family.

"People think about adoption reunions as so simple for everyone," Richelle says. "But after my visit with Janet, she literally crashed. Janet's a professional woman. She has lived with the same boyfriend for fourteen years—he didn't want children and her lifestyle never changed. She got depressed after realizing what she had missed. And suddenly it hit her that, 'if I have grandchildren I can no longer deny I'm really in my forties.'

"And when I described the meeting to Audrey, she said, 'Well, maybe you don't need contact with me anymore.' I wanted to say, How dare you do this to me? You're the one who hoped I would find my birthparents. But I stayed calm. 'If that's the way you'd rather have it,' I said. 'I love you very much—my kids and husband do too—we would all be devastated.'

"'Well, no—' she said, '—but Janet is young and thin and has lots of money.'

"So now I have to be on my guard with both of them! Janet told me right from the first, 'I couldn't have taken it if you had made contact and told me you had this horrible childhood.'

"'Don't you want me to tell you that part?' I asked Janet.

"'What?' she shrieked.

"'Just kidding,' I told her.

"The truth is my adoptive parents divorced and Audrey remarried when I was six. I was molested for the next three years by my stepbrother, and again when I was eleven by my grandma's boyfriend. I didn't understand until one day it clicked: he was doing wrong.

"Not once did I feel desirable. 'What are you crying about!' I was told many times. 'You have it so good.'

"The Jewishness, which I can see now as part of my birth family, was never taught in my home. We performed the rituals—lit Sabbath candles, celebrated the festivals—but we didn't live the ethical part. I was not taught values. No one ever said, 'Don't drink. Don't have sex, lie, or steal.' They kind of thought we were houseplants. They fed and watered us, and supposed we would grow into adults.

"By the time I was a teenager I rebelled against everything, but that assumes there was some value structure in place which never existed. I didn't realize I was bad, because I wasn't as wild as my friends. I had absolutely no sense of boundaries—nothing was too strange or absurd. I'd hang out on Sunset Strip with the rock stars and go to parties in Hollywood. I ate pizza with Guns and Roses, dyed my hair a different color every week, and wore ear-rings all around my ears." Richelle fingers her close-cropped hair, "But I always dressed tastefully," she laughs.

"One day I remember thinking, in ten years I'm going to be like my friends—the people around me are formulating where I'm headed. I wanted to be married by then—at home with a bunch of kids—not like any of those people.

"I started investigating churches," she continues. I found the LDS church with a whole new way of life, full of values. My dad hired a de-programmer. I passed through the teenage crisis stage, was married in the temple, and had two kids, before I realized I still had huge unresolved problems. One day I couldn't stop crying. I took both kids with me and found my husband in the computer lab. He was working full time and carrying fourteen college credits at night. I had nine. Our preemie baby wouldn't take a bottle so I wore a beeper to school; when he got hungry I would race home and back.

"After that crash, I had to go for counseling. I realized that I couldn't worry any more about everything looking perfect—the house, the car, the kids, the grades, even me. The memories of my childhood that I had carried for so long came out. I remembered my brother and me playing in my parent's dresser—we took all the clothes out. My dad came in, slammed our hands in the draw-ers, and then slammed my brother's ears and head in, thinking he was teaching us not to play there. I needed to deal with the guilt I had for the way my brother had been abused. I remembered the sexual stuff that I had repressed during my mother's second marriage. I had to deal with the fear I had that my stepbrother still molested others—I never reported him.

"Finally, I was able to address my relationship with Audrey, to deal with the continuing anger I had towards her as my mother. I learned to identify every time she upset me, and how it made me feel. Audrey would say, 'You bathe your kids in the morning, I always bathed mine at night.' I was feeling, You must not think I'm doing a good job if you say that, when all she innocently meant was, Oh really?

"The feeling I had when I first made contact with my birth-mother, Janet, was she's such a wonderful person—I'm going to run away with her and not see the rest of my adoptive family any more. That really scared my husband. I just meant that I was really comfortable with her, as if I had known her all my life.

"And when Audrey started manipulating me after I met Janet I cried, 'You have pulled this selfish, "poor me" crap every impor-tant time in my life.' But then I said a prayer, and wrote Audrey a letter—four pages front and back. I told her I thought God wanted me to be her child. It was the first time I ever paid Audrey a com-pliment without qualifying it.

"I later explored, as I wrote in my journal, what was really happening between my birthmother and me. I was wanting from her all the emotional nurturing that I hadn't received from my mom. But I also realized that I couldn't get what I needed that way. The relationship had to change between Audrey and me. I realized I would have to nurture Audrey and teach her how to nurture—she'd not yet learned." Richelle slows to a smile, relax-ing her shoulders.

"Now I enjoy Audrey's company. She's content with herself and pleasant to be around. Conversation flows freely between us. Addressing all the earlier developmental stages," Richelle says, "has finally made emotional intimacy possible with my own mom!"

ADULT ADJUSTMENTS

Erikson calls the early adulthood crisis "intimacy" versus "isolation." Richelle was in this sixth stage—married and a mother herself—when she was forced to address the unresolved problems in earlier stages. Not only did Richelle successfully smooth out earlier developmental deficiencies during this stage but she commenced a new relationship with her birthmother—taking a conscious step away from isolation. Though the meeting triggered negative reactions, Richelle was then confident enough with her own identity to meet this additional challenge by helping Audrey to feel secure—a course that allowed trust between adoptive mother and daughter for the first time.

Most people don't simultaneously achieve an identity in all areas. One might develop a facet of ethical identity separate from one of occupational identity, sexual identity, spiritual identity, or political identity. To achieve a full identity, an individual must integrate these various aspects of the self with each other over different points in time. For some who were adopted there may be another element too. The self as a family member is an important component of identity, but the adopted child may feel connected to two families: The one she lives with and one she may only imagine.

When one acknowledges the reality and longevity of the human soul, in combination with the gradual development and attainment of identity, there is no place for distinguishing between opportunities afforded adopted and nonadopted children—and eventually even for children who viewed their childhood as traumatic. Unquestionably, a child's success is enhanced by enlightened parents and assorted mentors, and one's early childhood profoundly affects her adolescent adjustment. But ultimately each person faces adulthood and must assume the responsibility to outgrow the traumas of her past.

Earnestly studying and living the gospel can heal any soul. Jacob, the first to be born in the wilderness to Lehi and Sariah, is a classic example. In his childhood he witnessed abuse and suffered through affliction and sorrow that would have wounded the strongest of children. But he turned to the Lord for comfort and received *compensatory* blessings. The Lord actually consecrated his afflictions to his gain (see 2 Nephi 2:2), which fortified Jacob to dedicate his whole adult life to the service of God. According to President Boyd K. Packer: "True doctrine, understood, changes attitudes and behavior.

The study of the doctrines of the gospel will improve behavior quicker than a study of behavior will improve behavior."[4]

Secure in one's identity there is still the challenge, throughout the rest of life, to maintain impetus. "For that is what is lost in so many lives," says James Hillman, "and what must be recovered: a sense of personal calling, that there is a reason I am alive."[5] In his book *The Soul's Code,* Hillman—himself an internationally prominent psychologist—describes his belief that the key to sustaining one's identity is within the soul and its urgings, attributing the continuing drive in productive individuals to their having had exposure sometime in their life to a uniquely suited ideal which calls to them. What Hillman describes as a personal calling of the soul is clearly manifest in a loyal member of the Church who is motivated to follow the promptings of the Holy Ghost. Lifelong vitality is strong evidence of spiritual identity.

EVENTUAL REWARDS

Individuals who secure both a human and spiritual identity have amazing resiliency. Richelle now has little ongoing association with her birthmother, but the introduction was instrumental in her finding a wealth of genealogical records that will bless countless others. Richelle is aware that her adoptive line is her genealogical line, yet she accepts these additional connections with the reassuring knowledge that "all of you are children of the most High" (Psalm 82:6). Her birthparents are more like friends: a newly discovered sister and brother in the Lord's great family.

The fact is that any or all factors contributing to the achievement of identity are relevant, for parents and children. It is the result of the search for identity—the solid, consistent, united self-concept that is important and apparent. And the adopted person who has successfully navigated through the process has unique experience from which to benefit others. An aspect of Hoopes' psychological study concluded with the twist that "adoptive children were more able, for the most part, to successfully influence members of their family."[6] They did not attempt to do so more often, but when they did, their attempts were more successful.

Other rewards of full identity achievement for children who were adopted may be elusive and random. Remarkably, it is not just the quality of people and circumstances involved with adoption that shapes successful identity. It's the intensity and longevity of the roles being played that give incentive toward resolution. In a paper delivered to the American Psychological Association, Barbara Goebel and Sandra L. Lott pointed out that perhaps adoptees work harder at the task of achieving an identity and so master it better than the non-adoptee.[7] The difficulty of a situation may create a stronger desire for achieving resolution.

NOTES

1. Janet L. Hoopes, "Adoption and Identity Formation," in *The Psychology of Adoption*, ed. David M. Brodzinsky and Marshall D. Schechter (New York: Oxford University Press, 1990), p.163.

2. Erik H. Erikson, *Identity: Youth and Crisis* (New York: W. W. Norton, 1968), p.165.

3. Erik H. Erikson, *Childhood and Society* (New York: W. W. Norton, 1963), pp. 247–73.

4. Boyd K. Packer, *The Shield of Faith* (Salt Lake City: Bookcraft, 1998), p. 26.

5. James Hillman, *The Soul's Code* (New York: Random House, 1996), p. 4.

6. Hoopes, "Adoption and Identity Formation," in *The Psychology of Adoption*, p. 158.

7. Barbara Goebel and Sandra L. Lott, as cited by Hoopes, "Adoption and Identity Formation," in *The Psychology of Adoption*, p. 166.

All things must needs be a compound in one.
2 Nephi 2:11

5
FUSION
CURRENT PSYCHOANALYTIC INSIGHTS

Whether one contests or esteems Sigmund Freud, his concept of the unconscious mind underlies almost all modern approaches to understanding human behavior and motivation. Freud created a whole new field of science. Before him, man had been defined as either political, religious, or economic. Thereafter, man was psychological. From the psychoanalytic perspective, adoption is an issue for nonadopted as well as adopted children.

Even though other aspects of Freud's theories have been rejected with time, one enduring aspect is the existence of ambivalence in parent-child relationships. All people feel love and hate and are motivated by wishes and fears. Typically, a child matures by directing these feelings toward a set of parents. But a child who was adopted may fantasize that his biological parents are better or worse than his adoptive parents. Two sets of parents may make it easier for a child to avoid working out the relationship with people toward whom he may at times feel both love and hate.

INDIVIDUAL AGENCY

Gaining experience with opposites has been an eternal part of the Lord's plan. As Adam started his life in the temporal world the Lord explained to him that when his children "begin to grow up, sin conceiveth in their hearts, and they taste the bitter, that they may know to prize the good" (Moses 6:55). Innocent infants gradually grow into testing toddlers—constructive progress in the Lord's growth plan when the children have parents who teach and direct. The freedom to choose is itself a gift "given unto them to know good from evil; wherefore they are agents unto themselves" (Moses 6:56). But a child left without the care of parents has been the theme of poignant stories told throughout the ages. Moses was rescued, floating in a basket among bulrushes, by the daughter of Pharaoh. Cosette was saved from hunger and abuse by Jean Valjean. Superman was raised by a couple who found him after he landed from outer space.

In psychoanalysis, Freud attributed public interest in children who are separated from their parents to a universal tendency among all human beings to do the same thing; to strive for independence and begin distancing themselves, at least psychologically, from those who gave them birth. Freud said, "It is a commonplace event that, as the latency child begins to separate himself from his parents and become critical of them, he develops the idea that he is a stepchild or an adopted child."[1] Freud maintained that the fantasy of being adopted, which is not uncommon for an unadopted child, was the craving of an older, more critical child for his perfect parents—as they appeared to him when he was younger:

> Indeed the whole effort at replacing the real father [with] a superior one is only an expression of the child's longing for the happy, vanished days when his father seemed to him the noblest and strongest of men and his mother the dearest and loveliest of women. He is turning away from the father he knows today to the father in whom he believed in the earlier days of his childhood; and his [fantasy] is no more than the expression of a regret that those happy days are gone.[2]

According to psychoanalysts it is during the elementary school years, when children become less concerned with their bodies and focus on the skills needed for coping with their environment, that they begin to separate from and become more critical of their parents.

Beth and her husband Darrell own a clothing store in Scarsdale. They inherited the business from Darrell's father.

"The night we decided to adopt a child," Beth says, "I started to wonder if Darrell's father might also have been adopted—he got so emotional over our decision. When we went to Lake George the next summer I had a few minutes alone with him. He's big like Darrell, one who enjoys being the boss of his own territory and you always know what's on his mind. In that private setting he acknowledged that he had been adopted and showered praise on his adoptive mom; he was so respectful of her. Then I told him, 'You know I'm also grateful to our baby's birthmother.' His mood switched; the tender, 'quick to tears' side of his nature evaporated.

"'If I found my birthmother,' he said, 'I would tell her to go to hell! I do not claim her—I never want anything to do with her.' Beth's eyes bulge.

"I was shocked," she says. "The conversation was over. You see, otherwise he is a warm and gentle man. But no matter how good adoption was for our son, Peter, Darrell's father had no gratitude for his birthmother.

"'It's abandonment!' he would say.

"'Don't ever tell Peter that!' I told him. Beth chuckles, chafing her shoe on the floor.

During Peter's growing-up years, his grandfather gradually mellowed. By the time Peter married, his grandfather could talk about his own birthmother without getting angry. He told Beth, "'She gave me life, and hopefully she loved me enough to know what was good for me!'"

REALITY GAP

Ambivalence is as much a challenge for adoptive parents as for their children. There can be a gap between the real and the imagined child. That same gap may exist between biological children and parents. Psychoanalysts believe that it is not just the children but also their parents who have to create a "fusion" of feelings. Tangentially, it is unwise for adoptive parents to disown certain aspects of their child—commonly the aggressive acts. Some parents openly claim that these embarrassing aspects are not "theirs." But no one can know for sure what behavior is inherited; and blame is a dangerous approach. This kind of attitude puts the child in a cruel corner, where he must either disown his own bad behavior (which may indeed be an integral part of his "self" during a particular stage) or disown his relationship with his adoptive parents. Adoptive parents have a particular need to work out a constructive relationship in which they may feel both love and hate for aspects of their child's behavior.

If adolescents decide they do not wish to be like their adoptive parents, they may logically go one step further and decide whether they wish to be like their biological parents. Adolescents, adopted or not, often challenge parental values and authority as they attempt to define their own identity. Children who were adopted may need to go through a more involved process.

Beth and Darrell's son, Peter, is now an adult and has a child of his own.

"When I was sixteen," Peter says, "I hated the differences I had with my parents. I asked them to help me find my birth family. They leaned heavily on me to leave the issue closed—'You really don't know what you'll learn. You may uncover things that you wouldn't want to know; there could be adverse effects.'

"So I was a hellion," Peter says. "I used adoption as an excuse. I have genuine hurt for what I put my parents through. I tell other adopted kids how obnoxious I was. 'Did you do the same thing?' I ask, and they give me that knowing smile.

"There were the negative things between my parents and me that separated us, like my temper, but we were different in many more ways. I didn't see it then but my wife can now. I'm more mellow. I don't care so much about wealth—I don't need to accumulate money. As long as my wife has a car, I can take the bus. Animals are important to me, but when I was growing up everyone else in the family had allergies. Now I have a dog and two cats.

"Last year, before my wife got pregnant, I was apprehensive

*that we might have to adopt. But that's strange too, because I feel
entirely a part of my adoptive parents."*

Paul M. Brinich, author of "Adoption from the Inside Out: A
Psychoanalytic Perspective," explains that there are many reasons for becoming parents: "In creating and loving our children, we re-create and love part of our selves. We give to our
children the task of fulfilling the dreams that we were not able
to satisfy, and insofar as they are able to achieve what we have
wished for them, they gratify our own wishes."[3]

Living childhood dreams through one's children can be constructive as parents become the leaders, supporters, and
guides. Parents can indulge in their favorite childish fun again
with their own children. Brinich lauded the gratifying, repara-
tive, and creative functions of parenthood and added, "Like
Voltaire's God, adoption is an institution that, if it did not
already exist, would have to be invented."[4]

OPEN DISCLOSURE

Honesty is the effective fiber of adoption. New adoptive
relationships flourish, psychoanalysts concur, when participants are willing to acknowledge their losses. But honest
recognition of one's limitations is far more valuable than clinicians claim; humble acknowledgments benefit the soul. All
partners in adoption can exercise personal valor by accepting
the fact that the child loses biological parents, the adoptive
parents lose a biological family, and the relinquishing parents
lose their offspring. But these losses are not tragedy; on the
contrary, they can be the motivation to seek out direction in
life—to find in one's soul that life is a serious matter. Adoption
prompts individuals to confront reality.

Prominent psychoanalysts have pointed out that Oedipus was
adopted. In Sophocles's play *Oedipus the King,* adoption saved
the abandoned child from the death that his birthparents had
chosen; the oracle at Delphi had predicted that he would marry
his mother and kill his father. Tragedy ensued, not because he
was adopted, Brinich points out, but because his parents "did
not tell him he was adopted."[5] People who grow up without
comprehending their larger identity (some individuals now in

their fifties and sixties were raised by adoptive parents advised
during the 1930s and 1940s not to tell) may inadvertently face
exposure. "Even in families that try to keep adoption a secret,"
say David Brodzinsky and Marshall Schechter, "the truth almost
always comes out eventually." Brodzinsky, a clinical psychologist, and Schechter, a child psychiatrist, have treated participants
in adoption all their professional lives and concur that when hidden truth about adoption is discovered "the adoptee's sense of
anger and betrayal can be nearly crippling."[6]

*"I had no clues that I was adopted," Joe says. "I found out quite
by accident." Joe is the oldest volunteer at the children's hospital;
everyone calls him Grandpa Joe.*

*"I was walking by the library in Springfield a few years ago,"
Joe tells me, "when I passed my uncle. He was in his eighties, an
immigrant from England.*

"'Hello, Uncle George,' I said. He stopped to examine me.

*"'Tell me who you are.' He was getting old then, like I am now,
so I tried to help by reminding him.*

"'I was called Joey when I was younger, Joey Finlinson.'

"'Oh, you're the adopted one.'

"'Really?' I said, 'I didn't know.'

*"'No,' he excused himself and looked away, 'I've got you mixed
up with someone else. I don't recognize you.'*

*"About a year later I was in New Canaan. My favorite aunt
lived there. Whenever she came to visit us in my youth, she and
my mother had acted like a couple of giggly schoolgirls—
vivacious, full of fun. Mother has since died. Aunt Bea went with
me to the grocery and she sat on the passenger side of the front
seat; I was driving.*

*"'Aunt Bea,' I said, 'am I adopted?' I glanced over at her. She
was dumbfounded.*

*"'Why do you ask?' I told her about my experience with Uncle
George. Everything was quiet.*

"'Finally,' she said, 'Yes you are, and I'm your mother.'

*"Aunt Bea had been a young girl at the time she got pregnant,
a baby tender of the man who was the father; he offered to pay*

*for an abortion. So her sister and brother-in-law had agreed to
raise me.*

"*I was stunned. 'You may have given birth to me,' I said to her,
'but Elizabeth is my mother!'*

"'*That's as it should be.' She didn't resist, or act hurt.*

"*But I wasn't satisfied: I went to a lawyer. In front of the judge
I said, 'I have been raised as Joe Finlinson. I want to be officially
adopted.'*

"*The shock passed gradually. I still go to see Aunt Bea once a
year. We have a ball. Even though she's my favorite aunt, I am
glad my parents are the Finlinsons. I learned that I didn't come
to them until I was two years old—on the Greyhound bus in a
sailor suit. When I was six, osteomyelitis affected my right hip
and left shoulder. Every time my parents thought to tell me about
my heritage they lost heart. In those days, if you put a skeleton in
the closet, you kept it there.*"

BIRTHMOTHER CHOICES

Society is opening up. Just as it is important today to let children know early about their adoption, it is also wise to treat
their birthmothers with respect. Judgmental clinical and social
attitudes about unplanned pregnancy have been on a steady
decline for the last twenty-five years. The current atmosphere
of acceptance and understanding for unmarried mothers has
prompted many women who have previously relinquished
children for adoption to come forward and express grief over
the way the adoption issue was handled with them. These
birthmothers believe their poignant feelings were ignored.
Such candor has increased public sensitivity to the complex
dilemma faced by every birthmother.

Today, when abortion is available and most unmarried
mothers keep their babies, the young women who consider
adoption for their child generally weigh the decision carefully.
Clinical studies substantiate that the women who finally relinquish their babies usually do so from a position of strength
rather than weakness; they are seeking what is best for them
and their child. The choice is difficult since the mother who
carries a baby in her womb to term usually feels heart-
touching ties. These mothers are doing what the leaders of the

Church urge when they select a faithful, stable mother and father for their child. They are enhancing the prospect that the gospel will bless the lives of all concerned, but their action requires tremendous courage.

"Part of me cannot believe that the pregnancy even happened," Cheryl says, "because I can't imagine living through it. I acted of my own will, but I could never do it again. There was a force, a power present that helped me." Cheryl wears jeans and a navy sweatshirt; her feet are bare. Hundreds of children's photographs cover the bookshelves of her library.

"On Memorial Day weekend a month after my wedding, I was desperate—caught in a losing situation. I was newly married, forced to move out, and told I was pregnant all in the same lump of time." Cheryl runs her fingers through her blond curly hair.

"My family's view on this whole thing is that I didn't try hard enough. Preparing for the wedding had been the social event of the year. The invitations were ordered, I'd had umpteen showers and horrible misgivings. My fiancé urged me on, 'It's Satan who doesn't want us to go forward.' When the marriage broke up, family members said, 'What you are doing is wrong,' 'You will regret it,' and finally, 'Let us keep your child.' "I don't think anyone wanted a baby more than I did. I can't go through Marshall Fields Department Store without picking out a child's dress. And I can't understand the mind of the guy who snowed me. When we moved into our two-bedroom apartment after the wedding, I discovered that he had been married before, and that one room was ours and the other was for guns and ammunition. When he showed me the weapons he said, 'This is our savings account, our security, our insurance.' He kept a gun behind our bedroom door.

"Even though I had dated him for five years it was always, 'Hey, by the way . . .' and then he'd be gone for a few days. He trained SWAT teams, I think. After we were married he called from out-of-town to get me moved out. He called when he found out I was pregnant.

"'I can prove that you are out of your mind,' he said. 'I can take this baby. You will never keep it.' He called me, using different names, for years. A common friend went to lunch with him and *reported to me afterwards, 'He had a hard time not using the gun on you during the first week of your marriage.' I can't fathom what he would have done with a child.*

"I had an interesting doctor who said, 'Under the circumstances, we won't let you see the child—we'll put a towel over your face.' And I said, 'Excuse me, I will see the baby—this isn't the Dark Ages.' But he acted like hiding me was better. Who was he protecting? My mind was made up. I didn't waver in the hospital. All the details were handled by the agency. The birth wasn't announced in the newspaper; I wasn't put in the maternity ward. I shudder to think what would have happened had the new paternity laws been in effect."

"Of course, I 'mother' the children down the street." *Cheryl breaks into a broad grin.* "One street over there is a child born seven weeks earlier than mine—I watch her like a hawk. I've had thousands of 'my own kids' at school, in the ward." *Cheryl waves a hand at the photographs.* "My friends seem to understand what I missed. They share babies with me—not like push it on—but say things like, 'Cheryl wants to hold the baby.'" *Cheryl curls back down in the corner of the sofa.*

"I don't understand my family," *she says,* "that benefited from adoption and now can't support it. I was adopted when I was three. It was always okay with me until my teenage years, and then I had questions. I needed medical information but in my family we don't talk—I knew not to ask. In that way I'm different. My whole well-being, my health, depends on not hiding my experience. When I have had a chance to explain the situation, no one else but my family has faulted me for giving up my child. I've learned to trust myself. I haven't had to depend on people telling me that adoption was okay; it helps—but I still knew in my heart."

Edward K. Rynearson published a study in the *American Journal of Psychiatry* on birthmothers who had relinquished their babies fifteen to thirty years earlier. Nineteen of twenty women had developed very substantial ties with their infants. Rynearson adds that the strength of attachment persisted even though most had denied their pregnancy up to as far as the seventh month, all had general anesthesia for the birth, and eighteen of twenty were never allowed to see their newborn infants.

"This identification became more manifest in the second trimester with quickening. During this time the subjects established an intense private monologue with the fetus, including a rescue fantasy in which they and the newborn infant would somehow be "saved" from the relinquishment. The 19 subjects also decided on names for the developing baby and experienced the common apprehension that they might miscarry or that the baby might be defective."[7]

LIFETIME IMPACT

Psychoanalysts recognize the psychological needs of birthmothers as well as those of adjusting adoptive parents. Over a lifetime the experience of adoption, according to psychoanalysts' vast store of documented case studies, is not an acute stressor but generally and simply a circumstance.

NOTES

1. Sigmund Freud, "Family Romances," in *The Standard Edition of the Complete Psychological Works of Sigmund Freud,* vol. 9, ed. James Strachey (London: Hogarth Press, 1959), pp. 240–41.
2. Ibid.
3. Paul M. Brinich, "Adoption from the Inside Out: A Psychoanalytic Perspective," in *The Psychology of Adoption,* ed. David M. Brodzinsky and Marshall D. Schechter (New York: Oxford University Press, 1990), p.45.
4. Ibid.
5. Ibid., p.48.
6. David Brodzinsky, Marshall Schechter, and Robin Marantz Henig, *Being Adopted* (New York: Doubleday, 1992), p. 156.
7. Edward K. Rynearson, "Relinquishment and Its Maternal Complications," *American Journal of Psychiatry* 139 (1981): 339.

And the meditation of my heart shall be of understanding.
Psalm 49:3

6

THE PERFECT MATCH
ACKNOWLEDGING OR
REJECTING DIFFERENCES

Biological and adoptive families don't differ much—a perspective enhanced by the realization that husband and wife have no biological connection either. Each child in every family is singular. A biological child may manifest differences as powerfully as the most challenging adopted child, and an adopted child may feel she doesn't differ at all from her adoptive family. So the perfect amount of discussion for parents to have with their child about adoption defies generalities.

It is the amount of family commitment that's important, and ensuing unity may be tied to a force stronger and even more compelling than inherited similarities. Closeness of individuals within families could predominate by virtue of the connection between their souls. Clearly, it is the exertion of family members to nurture unity that builds character and steels love.

The June day is warm and sparkling. Suzanne's hair glistens—a whitish blond—the same color as her adoptive mother and father. She sits on the edge of a redwood deck that extends into the yard. "Because you wouldn't guess I was adopted, I've rarely discussed it with anyone. Please don't mention our meeting to my

parents," Suzanne says. "The last time they heard I talked about
being adopted it really belted them. They don't bring that subject
up with anyone. When I do, it gives them concern."

"Has that protected you?" I ask.

"I guess. But I knew about it for a long time, so I would advise
others with adopted children to tell them. Treat it the way my parents did; let the children know that adoption is the way they came
to their family, that they are their parents, and that they love
them."

The topic is simple for her. Suzanne is blissfully silent, pregnant with her third child. Her two towheads are playing in the
garden.

"Our family's open about all kinds of stuff," Suzanne says. "My
dad is a doctor. When I was growing up we talked about prostate
cancer at the dinner table and it wasn't an emotional thing. It
was the job. I can remember one Christmas morning hearing the
telephone ring. We were opening presents and my dad answered.
'Merry Christmas,' he said to one of his patients. 'What color is
your urine?'

"Adoption was no big deal either. I never thought about it,
never! I guess I must have always known I was adopted, but being
told made no difference anyway because I didn't care. I was probably thirteen when my mom said, 'Well, this is what happened
. . . .' That conversation was the beginning and end of any discussion of adoption in our home. My dad had been in residency
at a hospital down in Houston. My parents tried for years to have
children so I guess the hospital knew that and called them one
day to say, 'We have a baby here.' The couple who had me was
young and unmarried, from strong Catholic backgrounds. The
birthfather was connected with the hospital—probably a student
in medical school—and this was what both their families wanted.

"The only time I actually think about adoption," she says, "is
when I am asked medical questions. Now that I'm pregnant again,
I have to fill out lots of questionnaires. I don't have any information." She stretches her legs out into the morning sunshine.

"I watch the talk shows on adoption and for me it's an issue of
society, not a personal thing. Adoption is the opposite of abortion.

*I don't understand how people can have abortions when they
have felt something living inside."*

"Would you adopt a child?" I ask.

*"I've never thought of it because I've had children too easily. I
have the opposite problem my parents do." Suzanne smiles, relax-
ing into laughter. "There's one difference between us!*

*"My neighbor was adopted, and his birthmother came to visit
him a couple years ago. That's when I thought, what would I do if
the same thing happened to me? I have no idea, no desire to meet.
I don't think of anyone else as my parents. I don't feel like I have
any other connections at all."*

*"What about your musical ability?" I ask. Suzanne is an
accomplished pianist with uncanny ability to sight read.*

"Where does your talent come from?"

"Good question," she pauses.

"Does your family have it?"

*"Not really. We all took lessons but my brother and sister soon
quit. Mother learned to play the piano a little when she was
young but nothing more . . . and she's always said, 'Well, music
just comes naturally to you,' and it does."*

"Have you considered heredity?"

*"No," Suzanne says, "never before!" She's stumped, laughter
flows. She rubs her collarbone.*

*"Since I look exactly like my family, and everyone's shocked
that I'm adopted, I can only think that it was meant to be."*

AVOIDANCE OF EXTREMES

Adoptions with virtually no adjustment problems deserve to
be cheered. Success in adoptive families supplies a vision filled
with inspiration and imagination to others. The many adoptive
families who live and breathe contentment feel so typical they
can't comprehend those having challenges. Content families
may acknowledge their adoptive makeup amongst themselves
but never be noticed for that distinction—they blend into society. However, when dissimilarities between parents and children are blatantly obvious or become a source of contention
in adoptive families, there is reason to increase family discussion of the issue.

Apparent differences between parents and their children

who were adopted have been studied since 1964, when David Kirk published his book *Shared Fate*.[1] Kirk championed truth and openness when the prevailing attitude of the time was "rejection"—a refusal to consider any distinctions between adopted and biological relationships. Kirk believed that parents should openly acknowledge their loss of ability to procreate while helping their child resolve her loss of heritage to biological parents. Together, he believed they could build a unique family bond.

"Acknowledgment" caught on. Instead of hiding their children's adoptions, adoptive parents started giving them a brief sketch of their background—often all they knew. Subsequent studies confirmed the value of a forthright approach; lack of discussion about adoption was found to repress a child's normal curiosity.

But acknowledgment can become an unhealthy extreme as well. Once acknowledgment became the norm, some adoptive parents concluded the more the better. Excessive reference to a child's adoption becomes an insistence of differences—a very dangerous approach. Kenneth Kaye summarizes a psychologist's current view of a child's ideal adjustment: "Perhaps they, the moderately acknowledging, are the best adapted adoptees."[2]

KEY TO ACCEPTANCE

The current consensus among most psychologists is not only that openness of family communication about adoption issues is crucial, but also that the variety of strategies used is not always relevant. Even when parents don't emphasize differences, an adolescent with developmental difficulties will use the "acknowledgment" strategy on her own. And teenagers in adoptive families are generally like those in biological families—fairly independent of their parents' opinions.

Self-esteem is the clincher. Those with low self-esteem are also those who acknowledge more differences and disadvantages in adoption. Self-esteem is the biggest factor in the frequency of a child's thinking about her biological parents. All types of problems—physical, emotional, behavioral—can contribute to poor self-image.

Kenneth Kaye's conclusion is that "self-esteem and attachment are functionally inseparable."[3] A child who does not accept herself cannot accept her family. Adolescents lacking self-esteem in biological families may have somewhat similar feelings. But a child who was adopted has a real circumstance on which to blame the problem.

"I expected we would raise Marty like our other children," says Kate. "Whether or not we should tell Marty she was adopted was never an issue; we assumed that approach from the beginning. But acknowledgment of her differences seemed unkind. And when she couldn't make a good adjustment growing up, our challenge was to open a closed adoption. That took guts!"

Kate now lives in Boulder, Colorado. Her husband, Tom, works for Storage Tek. They adopted Marty after they already had two biological children, when babies were easy to locate.

"We went to an agency back then," Kate says, "and they discouraged us. 'You'll never find a match,' they said, looking at our daughters. We weren't searching for a match; we adopted Marty through a private attorney. I must admit, however, that when we went to Florida to pick her up, we were reassured that she looked quite a bit like our other girls. But she was different—her temperament, her development, even her body scent. I ignored the differences. When she was four we had her tested for learning disabilities. She had been given a small part in a Primary program which she couldn't memorize. She charmed the psychologist with her gregarious personality but was unable to grasp abstractions. The child specialist explained, 'You may be able to teach her reading through multiple senses, but she will always struggle with math.'"

Marty is now a satisfied and creative mother herself who keeps the records on her own cosmetic business. She climbs into Kate's van with her two children—their clothes, toys, blankets, cereal snacks—and we're off to a cabin together for the Memorial Day weekend. The old grandmother sits in the front seat opposite Kate. Pastures stretch to the south where cows chew amid their frisky calves.

"Last summer I passed a herd of cows just like that," Marty

says to me. Her brown eyes sparkle. "I rolled down the window and yelled my loudest—they ran like crazy!" Marty laughs. "My kids loved it." She glances at them in the back seat. She is fidgety, tapping her manicured fingernails against the window.

"I thought you wanted to talk about adoption," she says to me.

"I have some questions." It's warm, and with Marty so cheery I hesitate, then hand her a copy of the workbook, Filling in the Blanks: A Guided Look at Growing Up Adopted.[4] *"Turn to the chapter, 'How I Feel,'" I say, "and try talking through some answers with me."*

"When I think about my birthparents I feel . . ." Marty reads aloud. "I feel love and guidance—at least from my birthmother," Marty says. Kate shifts in her seat. Marty's birthmother contacted Tom when she developed emphysema—after she had settled into a stable marriage and given birth to two more children. Meanwhile, Marty had grown into a teenager who isolated herself from her adoptive family, insisting she was too different to fit in. Marty became especially hostile to Kate for filling the place of her birthmother. Kate and Tom agonized, resisted, and finally decided it would be best for Marty and her birthmother to meet. They spent a couple of extended visits together before Marty's birthmother died a year later. Then Marty became unruly at home and adamant about moving in with other members of her birth family.

"And I never found my birthfather," Marty goes on. "I tried calling the attorney, the hospital. I asked everyone in my birth family but no one would say a thing."

Marty looks back down at the workbook. "If I ever met my birthparents I would . . ." she reads. "I can only answer from the way I felt before going to Florida to meet my birthmother for the first time. I was excited but I was scared too. I had thought about her every time I was sad, for as long as I can remember. She seemed like the way out of all my problems. The crazy thing is I never pictured her as an adult. In my mind she was my age—young. I thought she would be easygoing and always happy. When I met her, I knew she loved me but she was much older than I had imagined and sometimes she got upset. I stayed scared."

Marty opens the ice chest and takes out cheese slices for the children. Kate is mesmerized. She seems to be hearing the unexpurgated version of Marty's teenage feelings for the first time.

"When I went to visit her in Florida," Marty says, leaning up by Kate's seat, "I stayed alone in my room a lot—just like I did when I was still at home. My outlet in those days was in front of my mirror. I talked to myself. I had conversations with people in my imagination. I did mock suicide. My birth family was afraid of me going off by myself like that. But I had to stay apart. They were chain smokers—I couldn't breathe around them with my asthma. We were so different."

Marty opens a box of crackers for the children. Kate talks over her shoulder. "Tom and I were glad you had a chance to meet your birthmother, Marty." *The children make the only noise in the car.*

"I've never really told anyone about what went on when I finally moved to Florida after she died," Marty says. "My step-father felt responsible to you guys for my safety and he was really strict with me. I couldn't go anywhere alone—not even home from school when I was sixteen! After a while I refused to stay with him and my half brothers but I still couldn't bear to come back home. That's when a cousin in my birth family and his wife offered to take me in. They were quick to see I had problems with depression, ignored my bulimia."

Suddenly the grandmother, still reclining in the passenger seat, is talking. She opens her eyes to say, "But Marty, didn't you know how much your parents loved you?" *Kate glances around anxiously. The grandmother's too-frequent reminders of love antagonized Marty during her teenage years.*

"But Grandma," Marty says, "you have to understand." *She slows down, speaks tenderly.* "I couldn't feel their love." *The grandmother quiets. Marty's eager to continue.*

"My cousin and his wife took me to a psychologist in Florida," she says, "programmed from their viewpoint. After five minutes with him, I refused to talk. I knew I had gotten myself into the fix. I had no place to go so I considered the street."

Marty's children are thirsty. She fills their cups with water.

"Then my birth family in Florida asked me if I would go through therapy with peers. I was fine with that. I assumed it

*would be an outpatient arrangement with sessions after school. I
was taken to the hospital and interviewed by a therapist who
knew nothing about me. I told him all my feelings. At the end of
the interview he stood up in his office and said, 'You will need to
be admitted.' I couldn't believe it. I was furious! When he opened
the office door, I started running.*

"Hate and evil had been coming out of me for so long by that
time," Marty says, "for months, maybe years. It started while I
still lived with you and never left all the time I stayed with people
in my birth family. But as I neared the front of the hospital, a
thought crossed my mind—maybe these people can help. I
stopped running, but it was still awful. I was put in isolation. It
took hours for me to calm down." Marty rubs her wrist. "I hated
to wear that plastic bracelet, especially to the beach." She laughs
and picks up the workbook again, tilting close to Kate.

"'If I had to describe my feelings in one word—'" Marty reads,
"'—adoption is—.'"

"Full of pain," she blurts out, "—all my pain, all my birthmother's pain, all your pain, Mom. All the time I was growing up,
I hated it!"

The words float in the air. Kate grips the wheel.

"Remember," Marty says to Kate, "you had to tutor me every
night because school was so much harder for me than the other
kids. It wasn't fair! What I hated was not being born into our family." Marty puts her hand on Kate's captain chair, pulling herself
as close as possible. "I thought if I had been born to you and Dad,
I could think more like the other kids in our family, more like
you."

Marty relaxes.

"As for my birth family," Marty says, "I feel sad. They didn't
have the chances I did."

"Then are you stronger, Marty," I ask, "because you were
adopted?"

"No!" she cries. "The stress of those horrible years weakened
me. I think some of my brain cells were permanently damaged.
I'm only beginning to learn like other people." A half-mile from
the cabin Kate slows for ruts.

"There's only one more question in the book," Marty says.

"'What do people say about adoption that hurts?'" The children are singing in the backseat.

"It's when people ask me if I would adopt a child or give one up—that makes me sick!"

Kate jerks. The children start screaming. As the van pulls into the driveway beside the cabin, raucous laughter erupts and Marty opens the van door to let them run loose in the woods.

Marty sits back down, quietly absorbed in her feelings. Grandma stays put. "I can't think of adopting," Marty finally says, "because I could never bear to raise someone like me!"

Late that night Marty sits on the edge of the hot tub, bundled in a robe with her feet soaking. Tom had driven up after work; Marty's husband will come the next day.

Tom's the first to speak after they've all luxuriated in the quiet darkness. "Mom said she enjoyed the conversation with you on the drive up this afternoon."

"It's good to talk," Marty says. "Being a teenager for me was like walking one of those high wires they have in a circus. . . . on tiptoes . . ." She stands and walks toward the screen door.

" . . . without a safety net!" Marty smiles. The screen door slaps shut behind her and no one speaks for a few minutes.

"Okay," Kate blurts out, "What should we have done? If we were starting over again, with the information available today, could we have shielded her and ourselves? What good would have come from acknowledging her differences earlier? It was the differences themselves that separated us. And what if during her teenage years I had given in to her demands, just to keep her living at home longer. What if I'd said, 'Yes, go out with your friends all night. Because you are different, none of the moral values that apply in our home apply to you.'"

Kate looks at Tom. He lies relaxed in the Jacuzzi's swirl. "I don't want to look at the past," he says. "I feel lucky. I lost hope when Marty pressed to move down to Florida. Now that she's happy to be back, settled, with a husband and kids, none of the rest matters."

PROBLEMATIC DEFICIENCIES

Marty's learning disability set in motion precarious development, complicated by severe asthma and uncommon good looks. She had boyfriends early, loners like her. Other girls were jealous. Marty's insistence on living with her birth family during the teenage years increased her vulnerability. She risked losing additional self-esteem to learn she was more different from her birth family than she was from her adoptive parents. But her adoptive family was waiting close by so that when she was finally able to achieve an integrated sense of self, they were there to perpetuate a strong sense of belonging. Marty has continuing communication with both families—though far more frequent with the adoptive family in which she feels most comfortable. It's the shared values that have created an impenetrable bond.

Children who have suffered prenatal neglect, who have a genetic predisposition for learning disabilities, or who become emotionally preoccupied with adoption may encounter significant learning challenges. In their book *Being Adopted,* David Brodzinsky, Marshall Schechter, and Robin Henig list the most common learning problems: dyslexia (impairment of ability to read or spell), dysgraphia (difficulty translating ideas or sounds into writing), dyscalculia (difficulty with manipulating numbers), dyskinesia (poor muscular coordination), dysphasia (difficulty in speaking or understanding speech), and Attention Deficit Hyperactivity Disorder (ADHD—unusually high energy and short attention span).[5] Learning disabilities can affect more than a child's behavior in school; they may impact the development of self-esteem, good judgment, and emotional control. Adoptive parents of children with these problems can help them to overcome their learning disabilities or compensate for them by first acknowledging the problem, then communicating understanding rather than frustration, and finally by continuing to work through all that is necessary for the child to succeed—however many years it takes. Given sufficient time, a child with learning disabilities usually grows to function normally in society.

SUCCESSFUL COMMUNICATION

Empathy and communication increase in adoptive families that moderately acknowledge their differences. David Kirk, father of four adopted children, published a book entitled

Adoptive Kinship, which disclosed the results of a large-scale study correlating the "acknowledgment of difference" by adoptive mothers with their higher ability to empathize with their children. Kirk also determined that the greater the mother's empathy with the child's situation the more she would communicate readily with her child on the subject of adoption and, in turn, the more the child would freely ask her questions about the birthmother. Family members who kindly and persistently work through their problems build enduring and constructive relationships.

Kirk's study was accomplished through an extensive questionnaire. One question was eventually disregarded because it showed no statistical correlation with parents' acknowledgment or rejection of differences in their children. Kirk had asked the question, "Since the child's legal adoption, have you: felt that God or fate had a hand in bringing you and the child together?" Kirk was surprised and at first disturbed to discover that the answers did not align meaningfully to the study. He conjectured that the acknowledgment of God or fate in an adoptive relationship was simply a needed myth for adoptive parents to feel entitlement.[6] No matter how Kirk or anyone else chooses to explain the indeterminate responses, they substantiate the common actuality that most adoptive parents feel a sense of joint destiny with their child—one that may greatly enhance their family ties.

VALUABLE DIFFERENCES

Even when members of adoptive families handle their internal differences appropriately, outsiders may accentuate differences categorically. The differences between adoptive and biological families became the object of public policy debates in Canada in 1985. Legislation was proposed (but finally rejected) that would have permitted biologically unrelated siblings, who have become siblings through legal adoption, to marry each other. Kirk argued against the proposals. "That [adopted children] should be allowed to do so precisely because they are different," said Kirk, means that "the ordinary rules for other humans evidently need not apply to the adopted. . . . It would thus not only undermine the institution of adoption as a variant of the modern family, but would like-wise undermine with it the social ground on which the adopted person's familial identity is based."[7]

A great paradox lies in the fact that it is the differences inherent in an adoptive family that can be used to fortify itself. Though society generally is shifting away from family values in favor of individual values, the adoptive family may be moti-vated circumstantially to cultivate an especially enduring bond. Each family connected by adoption may start out devised rather than traditional. "But then something remarkable occurs," Kirk says, "for the contractually formed structure of contrived kinship typically becomes molded into the nuclear family of everyday life."[8]

Families sealed in the temple may develop an even greater bond—both of faith and knowledge—that their relationship can be permanent. "Sacred ordinances and covenants avail-able in holy temples make it possible for individuals to return to the presence of God and for families to be united eternally," reads "A Proclamation to the World" by the First Presidency and Council of the Twelve Apostles of The Church of Jesus Christ of Latter-day Saints. Adoptive parents who understand and nurture these covenants grow closer to their children. Children who were adopted and embrace these covenants feel more clearly their individual worth. Within such a bond, dif-ferences tend to subside and souls are freed to flourish.

Five years later I talk with Marty. She is helping other parents in the ward with their daughter, who is currently preoccupied with her adoption. The girl calls Marty on the phone directly now whenever she wants to talk with someone she knows will under-stand.

"Other people can grow from my strength," Marty tells me. "I know how some kids who were adopted feel. The differences between me and my family left me feeling alone for years. But it's the gospel that has saved my life. My family believes in it, so they believe in me. They were always there when I needed them. They always kept in touch. I finally understood—this is a forever com-mitment.

"I believe sealings are necessary to keep a family together but I also believe we're personally responsible to accept the consequences of our actions. As I learned to forgive my parents for the way they were, I learned to forgive myself for the way I'd been. It's such a process, but all parts of the gospel interconnect. My feelings for my parents and sisters and brothers keep intensifying. I am constantly seeking to be with them, just like I was seeking to be with my birthmother as a child. I am drawn to their unconditional love, and I know they are drawn to mine. We have become a gift to each other. I can only liken it to the feelings I have about being with Heavenly Father, the longing I feel to finally return and live with him.

"Now I know why I was adopted. I know what would have happened without it, and I don't think I would have survived in the other situation. And this is a funny thing to say, but if I died before the others in my family, I know there would be a void—they need me. I'm the one who works hardest at keeping us all connected."

NOTES

1. H. David Kirk, *Shared Fate: A Theory and Method of Adoptive Relationships* (Port Angeles, Wash.: Ben-Simon Publications, 1984).
2. Kenneth Kaye, "Acknowledgment or Rejection of Differences?" in *The Psychology of Adoption,* ed. David M. Brodzinsky and Marshall D. Schechter (New York: Oxford University Press, 1990), p.140.
3. Ibid., p.142.
4. Susan Gabel, *Filling in the Blanks: A Guided Look at Growing Up Adopted* (Indianapolis: Perspectives Press, 1988), p.38.
5. David Brodzinsky, Marshall D. Schechter, and Robin Marantz Henig, *Being Adopted* (New York: Doubleday, 1992), p. 87.
6. H. David Kirk, *Adoptive Kinship* (Port Angeles, Wash.: Ben-Simon Publications, 1985), esp. p. 52.
7. Ibid., pp. 165–66.
8. Ibid., p. 39.

Govern your house in meekness, and be steadfast.
D&C 31:9

7

DAD'S IDEA
PARENTAL STYLES AND
POST-ADOPTION SUPPORT

The importance of parenthood is contested only by the cynical. Parents are engaged in the work that perpetuates life. From day one the job requires continuous effort and is accompanied by a mixture of joys and sorrows. The cumulative process tends to humble parents, either abruptly or gradually, and to moderate excessive idealism. All preparation is constructive—all learning, all observing. However, the voices of professionals might bewilder parents. Those who advise adoptive parents not to anticipate problems might be absolutely right, and those who encourage them to consider the additional risks might be just as correct. It all depends on the propensities of the parents and their children.

Family psychologist John K. Rosemond tells of a couple who brought their thirteen-year-old daughter in for counseling over a growing disagreement. "She wasn't angry at having been adopted," he said. "She was sick and tired of her parents' constant references to it."

"They want to talk about it all the time," she told him, "like it's something weird, you know? Adopted, adopted, adopted! I'm so sick of hearing it, I could scream!"

"You're lucky," he told the parents. "Despite the fact that you were encouraged to blow the adoption out of proportion, and did so with the best of intentions, your daughter has kept straight in her own mind that it's really no big deal at all."[1]

Parents trying to fix a problem that doesn't exist may actually create one. Some children never struggle with adoption. A child is more an individual than he is an individual who was adopted; and all individuals are stronger than the stages they go through or the processes they endure. The individuality of parents is similarly powerful. Effective parental styles may be infinite in number and generally suitable for raising the typical child. But it's the atypical child, adopted or not, that can push parents beyond the broadest limits of their adaptability; and this is when they should probably seek professional help to avoid losing control.

"Adoption will be strengthened by the continued support of social workers," says Christopher Bagley, "and the parents should feel free, without guilt or stigma, to call on the agency for help and advice whenever this seems necessary. . . . There is an element of luck in adoption—if your child has a sweet temperament and adapts quickly and well, rejoice; but remember, if your child seems to have a difficult temperament, try and adapt yourself to the child's needs by finding a 'goodness of fit' between your temperament and his."[2]

"I ran a tight ship," Carmen says, "because I had to. My husband worked long hours and always carried heavy church responsibilities. I kept up the house, grounds, vegetable garden. I drove the kids to music lessons and supervised homework." Carmen leans over a cutting board heaped with chopped onions.

"Of course I loved my children. They could see it by how hard I worked for them. But when the children got out of line, I let them know. Sometimes I got angry. Yelling made my point clear," Carmen laughs. She is full of fun. She demonstrates how to clean a bathroom, then lets her kids take over. After jobs are done, she cheers while they make tree huts and hunt for water snakes.

"Marianne ended up all right," Carmen says. "I was able to open up the communication between us and calm down my parenting approach before permanent damage was done. But I could

*have saved a lot of misery if I'd understood earlier what I should
do. You see, Marianne was adopted. She was excitable, without
volume control, kicked goals from center field during soccer
games, and danced around the house like a Gypsy bride. In middle
school she became incorrigible. A boyfriend was more important
than any other part of her life. She wouldn't come home from
school until dark; any hint of criticism and she was out the door.
The day I found a razor blade on her dressing table I contacted a
psychiatrist."* Carmen drops the onions into sizzling oil.

"Initially, the psychiatrist met with us each alone," she says.

*"'Relax the pressure,' was his instruction to me. 'Allow excep-
tions to your rules, or lose her. And you cannot yell; it frightens.
She thinks you don't feel love for her.'*

*"I don't remember what he told Marianne before we left his
office. Even when he looked at her, he was still talking to me—
'she's very fragile.'*

*"I went home, stunned. Will our family disintegrate? How do I
let one child be an exception and not lose the rest? How can I
transform my personality? I collapsed that evening.*

"'How do I change that much?' I asked my husband.

"'Somehow,' he said, '—you have to.'

*"Even when I didn't yell, Marianne didn't improve. One
Sunday, after having been at a friend's house since the previous
Friday, she stormed in to say, 'You piss me off. You've always
hated me. I can't stand living here anymore.'*

*"I didn't raise my voice, but I started swearing in my mind,
mimicking her. My other children watched from the hall, with
sympathy. Then the crisis was over for me. My mind cleared. As
Marianne continued her tirade, I had a sense that endurance
would count as proof of my love, preventing a permanent rift.
And it did. We went together to therapy sessions with a social
worker. As I continued to mellow out it set a precedent for her.
Marianne has become our 'in-house' counselor,"* Carmen smiles.
"She's the best communicator in the family." Carmen pulls the
pan of onions off the stove and sits down at the table.

*"I felt noble for years after that—like I had endured a huge,
unavoidable trial. Once my children were all in school I went to
Middleton to do an internship in therapeutic family care. I wanted*

*to help other parents in the community who were struggling with
their children. I learned I had been foolish. The first day I was
told, 'Parents come in here convinced their kids are psychotic and
leave thinking their kids are normal.' The agency trains treatment
parents to run therapeutic family homes for disturbed children.
They also teach parent education classes on the same principles.
I learned about the problems and treatment of troubled teenagers.*

*"Trained treatment parents don't swear in their minds—they
know what to do and say without risk of emotional outbreak.
Even though they're not attached to other people's kids like their
own, I'm convinced their composure is a learnable model."*

ADJUSTING EXPECTATIONS

Christopher Bagley conducted a Canadian survey of children
in residential treatment centers which involved the most serious disturbances imaginable. There were distinct differences
between the adopted and nonadopted children. Adopted children came from more stable homes than nonadopted children, yet they had more psychiatric or behavioral problems
that developed earlier and for which they were given medication. The problems developed even though the adopted children were placed in infancy with seemingly normal parents.
However, the stresses of parenting a child with a difficult temperament seemed to have exacerbated problems. The adoptive parents had supported these children as best they could
but the mothers, especially, were often exhausted and
depressed.

"It could be that these parents were committed to an 'exclusive' parenting model for the apparently normal, white infant
they adopted," the project supervisor explained. "But attempting
to 'exclude' aspects of the child's behavior which were genetic
or organic in origin appears to have been an unwise strategy. This
exclusive process may well have served to impair parental adaptability in coping with the adopted child's needs. What evolved
was a 'lack of fit' . . . between the child's temperament and the
parental rearing style."[3] This might well have made the parenting of a behaviorally difficult child more difficult.

Adoption professionals now emphasize post-adoption counseling. This trend has been fueled by the increasing number

of special-needs adoption placements. Adoptive parents are typically part of the middle to upper-middle class in society; they tend to have high expectations for their children in terms of education and achievement. These expectations may be challenged by strong hereditary forces in their children who were adopted. If they ignore a child's biological heritage or, in the case of an older child placement, his background, then the adoptive parents will be less able to understand and assist their child's development. Lack of understanding creates in both parent and child a pervasive sense of powerlessness.

"Before my mom put us up for adoption, she would go off on three- and four- month jaunts. Geez," Troy chuckles, "while she was gone we'd stay over at Grandma's and get the tar beat out of us there too. I guess I was really ornery or something." Troy is now a six-foot tall navy mechanic stationed in Norfolk, Virginia.

"The best thing about adoption was settling into one family. My sister and me had already been in four foster homes and I was never sure where we were going next. My last foster dad was a truck driver; he carved a handle into a two-by-four. I used to get beat, punched, and dragged around if he was drunk, angry, or just wanted to take out his frustrations. I hid, scared because he was so big. My foster mom would jump on his back and drag him off. She was real nice. She cared a lot about us."

Troy was eight and his sister four when they were finally adopted by two educators, Shirley and Larry.

"'This is the end of the line,' Shirley said. 'No matter what you do or what you say, you'll not get me to send you packing.' She was always reassuring us that we weren't going to be moved again. I liked her reassurances but I had done everything on my own for quite a few years; I was already independent. I don't think my mom was prepared for that."

Shirley's a voracious reader, a humorist, and a meticulously groomed woman. Larry teaches drama at the college. The summer the children joined the family he had to leave them for six weeks in order to complete his doctoral thesis.

"That was a rough beginning," Larry says. "Troy acted out in all kinds of ways. He is very tenacious. Before that, I had never

known anyone more tenacious than Shirley. They both met their match. And it wasn't that the agency hid the history of Troy's abuse from us. They told us all they knew, and we had psychological help for short periods of time. But after the first year, when the adoptions were finalized, we were pretty much on our own.

"Shirley was a strong disciplinarian and determined to help the children; she made them toe the line. I had misgivings from the start, figured we were buying into serious psychological problems." Larry wags his head, speaking softly. "I think Troy might have done better in a less authoritarian home."

Troy summarizes his experience with adoption this way: "After living with Shirley all those years, I would choose physical violence over her verbal and mental abuse. I'd rather have gone back to being beaten. I didn't feel loved. The way I see it, my mom, Shirley, was trying to be perfect and wanted us to be just like her. She was trying too hard. If I had Bs or Cs, it was okay but it wasn't good—it wasn't the best. I could always do better. The things I was interested in—athletics, rebuilding motors—weren't important to her. That's the way I earn a living now, but I never felt like it was good enough for my mom. She wanted me to go to college—to be something that she wanted.

"Shirley thought if she showed us discipline," Troy continues, "that would take care of everything else, and that's where she was wrong. Keeping our background hush-hush wasn't helping me at all, because I thought about it quite a bit. I still do. My adoptive parents never really understood the extent of my sister's and my problems.

"I say that therapy should be mandatory. I think it would have changed my entire life. I could sit here and talk for hours about problems I had with adoption, even if I hadn't been physically abused earlier, all of which I've gotten over—it's no big deal now. But there's always the question that started before adoption, and continued after—was I really loved?

"After I got married my wife and I were having problems because of me. I came close to getting divorced before I went for help. Then a social worker started touching on feelings—just got them out of me—and I could see what the problem was and how

*to deal with it. After three months of therapy things were a whole
lot better."*

VARIETY OF APPROACHES

Life is a maze. Dead ends can teach us. Larry was a stable
male role model, Shirley a strong mother-hen type. Their decision to adopt was the first step on an imagined trail of success.
It impelled them to endure as they parented abused children
who had learned to manipulate adults. Troy asserts that Shirley
used the authoritarian approach, one of four very general
parental styles.[4]

Authoritarian parents are those who control the behavior
and attitudes of their children according to an absolute set of
standards. The approach is effective in crisis situations. In the
ghetto, children's lives are preserved by authoritarian parents.
Similarly, the children of authoritarian parents in impoverished
countries are more likely to survive. But in typical middle-class
America the method is not ideal.

Psychologists recommend the authoritative approach—
seemingly close, yet of polar effect. Authoritative parents also
exercise high levels of control, requiring their children to
behave in ways consistent with their age and abilities, but they
add warmth, nurturance, and two-way communication.

Another broad categorization of parental style is indulgence.
Indulgent parents tend to be accepting and responsive, placing few demands on their children. Parents who have anticipated adoption for a long time may be particularly susceptible
to indulging their children. Instead of encouraging a child to
grow deep and strong by working beside them, parents may
simply give the child everything he wants. A child who has no
chance to earn his privileges often grows self-centered beyond
his parents' wishes. When ultimately restrained, the child may
maintain that his parents have no right to discipline him.

Finally, there are neglecting parents who are uninvolved.
Neglecting parents usually face the greatest problems of all, for
they are too concerned with their own activities to pay earnest
attention to their children.

ADAPTING TO CIRCUMSTANCES

Children who are out of control at any stage can alter a parent's style. Authoritative and indulgent parents become authoritarian when their child runs onto a busy street; nurturing and accepting adults can go ballistic when their teenager runs away. Shirley may never have become an authoritarian parent if her children had been more manageable. The strict, private approach that Shirley and Larry tried, without training and support, is not recommended by professionals.

The older child often has a perilous background to outgrow. To help him go through a difficult adoption adjustment, professionals are trained to teach parents a variety of appropriate concepts. The object is to enable the parents to remain constructive and composed in the most exasperating situations and eventually outgrow the need for outside assistance. Parents can become the "caring leaders" who openly and regularly address anxiety in the family, as a therapist is trained to do. Fun activities have been created to cultivate family unity in a fragmented adoptive family: sketching a life map, drawing a family portrait, sharing private thoughts, playing charades, making a family collage, or even creating a sculpture of the family by placing each member in a characteristic position.

Children placed after infancy may more often see adoption as a mixed blessing; finding a permanent family signals an end to any dreams about their lost parents. A child who is grieving over his loss may need help finding new ways to perceive his past and tie it constructively to the present. Alternative behaviors and practical skills may be taught to these struggling children; healing cannot occur while there is preoccupation with emotional survival.

AVAILABLE TRAINING

Critical to smoothing a child's adjustment is the preparation of parents. Parents who realistically anticipate the changes that will occur in their family life can prevent crises from ever occurring. Parents embarking on adoption can be trained to view their family as a mobile; an older child coming into the family throws it off balance. Inherent difficulties are not indications of failure but part of a routine process to stabilize flux. Ellen E. Pinderhughes and Karen F. Rosenberg, in an article entitled "Family-Bonding with High Risk Placements,"[5] suggest that adopting an older child is more like getting married, or "getting married on a blind date!" Families go through the "Honeymoon phase," the painful "Ambivalence phase," then, gradually, feelings of mutual accommodation start to evolve. Although the child may still act out on occasion, parents have already learned to tolerate the behavior and, instead of feeling resentment, comprehend their child's feelings.

Research sponsored by the National Institute of Mental Health and the Bush Center for Child Development[6] found that only half of the families who were offered free preventive, post-adoption service accepted it. For those who did, the number of subsequent breakdowns were halved, and further need for therapy dropped considerably. The study concluded that adoptive families who really need a therapy program do not voluntarily participate without strong encouragement, and well-trained ordinary people with compassion usually succeed with even the most difficult offspring.

LIGHTENING UP

Maureen and Boyd are on the way from Boise down south for summer vacation. They stop at the old mill in St. Charles to give their four children a chance to stretch.

"I didn't want to do this last baby," Maureen says as she watches the other boys boost the little one onto the bed of a broken down truck. The "baby" is now almost two and is eager to be included.

"But Maureen started elbowing me in bed," Boyd adds, laughing. "'I'll bring home adoption papers,' I told her at three in the morning, 'if that'll help you sleep.'" Maureen and Boyd adopted two children through LDS Family Services, both Caucasian. Then two other children found their way to them—two boys of mixed race.

"I was frightened," Maureen explains. "You can't see it now, but our oldest son, Talmadge, was having health problems at the

time and getting so depressed. I thought our family was falling apart. So I was sure I couldn't open that door to adoption again."

"The best way I can describe our situation to you," Boyd says, *stretching his hands back behind his head, "is to say that when you have a child like Talmadge, who you're always thinking about and worrying about and working with—it sucks out all of your energy. So you feel kind of drained."* The boys have all crowded into the front seat now through the windowless opening in the back of the old truck.

"And with this new little boy," Boyd continues, *"who's from 'happy planet,' we've been renewed. Our batteries are charged, and everybody feels a little bit better."*

"Talmadge didn't want us to adopt this baby," says Maureen. *"But he went with us, all the way to Seattle to pick him up. And now, Talmadge has grown softer. He has reached out to this child and started to forget himself. Talmadge doesn't understand the process because he doesn't really interact with our youngest a whole lot; he'll do it more when no one is looking."*

The boys are whooping, mimicking truck noises, gearing up.

"Maybe it hasn't changed Talmadge," Maureen says, *"as much as it's brought love back into our home, and Talmadge feels that."*

"I'll give you an example," Boyd says. *"We try to read scriptures right after dinner, and this baby has disrupted scripture study so many times! We're trying to read and he's doing circles. He tries standing on his head, and everybody's just watching him and not paying any attention—"*

"—We're all laughing," Maureen chuckles.

"And," Boyd adds, *"that's just fine! Because if we can have that moment, that fun time together when everyone feels some lightness in a day, we're OK."*

Children remember feelings about the gospel far better than they remember facts. "Reading the scriptures shouldn't be like eating spinach," Elder Neal A. Maxwell reminds. Laughter, which reflects the incongruities of life, can be positively therapeutic. Parents can be inspired with ways to bring some bright spots into temporarily darkened stages in their children's lives. And striving to live the gospel has its marvelous surprises.

When we're relaxed enough to feel the subtle promptings of the Lord, we may also see the gentle ways he has eased our burdens and guided us through the hardest situations.

"The Lord's sense of humor surely is evident in our lives," Boyd concludes, *"sometimes while we're down here bawling our eyes out."*

MAINTAINING PERSPECTIVE

Parents who are stressed to the point they can no longer feel love in their family need outside help to restore perspective. There may be stages when a child's behavior is insufferable, but his soul is still worth saving. The Lord himself recognizes the need for discipline. He has delivered appropriate consequences to many of his disobedient children but his counsel to earthly parents, born of great godly experience, includes, "Reproving betimes with sharpness, when moved upon by the Holy Ghost; and then showing forth afterwards an increase of love toward him whom thou hast reproved, lest he esteem thee to be his enemy; that he may know that thy faithfulness is stronger than the cords of death" (D&C 121:43–44).

Rachel groans, crosses her legs, and looks down at the rug. She finished teaching music lessons at 7:00 P.M., then put her elderly parents to bed. It was after 9:00 when she finally arrived with her husband, Weston.

"I don't know anything anymore," Rachel says. She drops her head, evening out the gathers in her skirt. Weston sits tall on the sofa next to her, an estate planner who has taken early retirement. They have four adopted children. The three oldest are adults, living on their own now. Their youngest, Brian, is currently very challenging.

"I think kids who are out of control have an awareness that they need help," Weston says.

"And I could never underestimate the importance of good counseling," Rachel adds. "The right social worker or doctor or psychologist can bring someone to the point where they can resolve their own problems. It's just like a good teacher. They don't change the person, but a professional can act as a catalyst."

Weston leans back, running his hands through curly gray hair. "Kids aren't going to make it in this world until they learn to fit in," he says, "and some exhibit antisocial behavior."

"What about Brian?" I ask.

"We had him in hardiness training. It's a program run out of a home in Jefferson County. The attention is very individualized. We told them Brian had learning disabilities, neurological problems, hyperactivity, a little autism, and severe allergies.

"'We can work with all that,' they reassured us. After three months they said he was cured. Brian lasted back here for three days and took off again.

"'This is the only time in Brian's life,' I told the staff, 'that he's had a chance to stay in school. The insurance company has already agreed to work with us—I'll supplement if necessary. Please keep him, and see if he can make it through the year.'"

"We pleaded," says Rachel.

"After some considerable difficulty we rounded Brian up," Weston goes on, "and we got him back over there. In the meantime he had lost everything—a $600 dirt bike, guitar, watch, jacket. He has a few problems—"

"—I question whether he can ever live with us again," Rachel says.

"Brian's in high school now—"

"I'm just hoping he can learn enough skills that he can get along in society—"

"He has average intelligence," Weston says, glancing at Rachel. "I know I'm getting a raised eyebrow, but I have more hope, and Rachel is more realistic. Maybe that's a good combination. Brian actually reads on a third grade level—"

"—Sometimes he can read." Rachel grips Weston's arm.

"He will read one day," Weston says, "then not again for maybe a month. I don't know why. Nobody knows. Why are people wired that way?" Weston is winding up; Rachel is falling asleep.

"Brian's got to make a plan," Weston says. "He needs to be taught to get back on schedule when he fails. When he doesn't come home on time, he thinks he should never come home, that he's done everything wrong, and might just as well go out and

take marijuana. Somehow Brian has to comprehend what is hap-
pening in him, which is no uncomplicated problem.

"What's important for us, as parents, is to maintain a rela-
tionship with our children so when someone says, 'Who are the
people who really influenced your life?' they'll say, 'my parents.' I
believe in Brian, and I want him to know that I will stand by him.

"I pray every night," Weston says, "that someone will be put in
the path of all my children to help them."

Even the dysfunctions and immaturities of children are a
part of their uniqueness, their direction, their purposefulness.
Every child is a package—a peculiar combination of aspects
reflecting their genetic makeup, soul, and experience. Aspects
of the package may be abrasive, particularly in a child who
doesn't fit comfortably into society. When parents view such
a child as intriguing—off on an adventure with which they
might assist—then they keep the faith and imagination necessary to help him discover his niche. All of a growing child's
aspects, including the pain-causing ones, have constructive
potential.

Weston can talk like a psychologist now. He chose early
retirement in order to tutor Brian during his elementary school
years. Both he and Rachel have vision beyond the consuming
toll of the child-rearing years. Fortified by the pattern of their
older children, who are already settled into autonomous and
productive living, they continue to hope and plan for the independence of their youngest child. Above all, they stay close to
the Lord, having absolute trust that he understands their challenges and guides their decisions. They take courage from the
assurances they received when each child was sealed to them.
They have the comfort of knowing that they raised each of
their children to live and love the principles of the gospel.
Their faith is unshakable; they believe time will finally smooth
out the more complicated maturing process in their youngest.
They give all four children appropriate focus. However, their
own personal interests and spiritual commitments wisely off-
set their parental concerns. They are successfully preserving

their love of adult life amid the temporary confusion of the youngest child's life—a wondrous example for others.

───────────

NOTES

1. John K. Rosemond, "Questions and Answers About Adoption," *Hemispheres*, November 1994, pp. 120–22.

2. Christopher Bagley, *International and Transracial Adoptions* (Aldershot, England: Avebury, 1993), pp. 329–31.

3. Ibid., p. 300.

4. Rita L. Atkinson, et al., *Introduction to Psychology* (Fort Worth, Texas: Harcourt Brace Jovanovich College Publishers, 1993), pp. 500–1.

5. Ellen E. Pinderhughes and Karen F. Rosenberg, "Family-Bonding with High Risk Placements," *Journal of Children in Contemporary Society* 21, no. 3/4 (1990): 211–29.

6. Ibid., pp. 211–24.

Trust in the Lord with all thine heart.
Proverbs 3:5

8
CALM WATER
THE BIRTHPARENT EXPERIENCE

Birthmothers activate the hope in adoption. They personally confront questions with far-reaching spiritual implications. Forced to make crucial choices affecting not only their future, but also that of another soul, birthmothers can draw on power hidden deep within themselves. No wonder they may make courageous decisions that disarm onlookers; the Lord, who watches over all, is strengthening them!

Our straightforward society renders judgment on birthmothers. In doing so we all become involved and live together with the consequences. If we choose to esteem the young birthmother's relinquishment of a child for adoption, we save more women from the extreme of abortion and we save more children from the extreme of neglect and abuse. In 1960 only 5 percent of all live births were to unmarried women between the ages of fifteen and nineteen; the stigma drove most of those young women away from home to give birth in secret. By 1976 the proportion of unmarried teen mothers had grown to 26 percent but has since dropped to 13 percent because a third of pregnant teenagers currently have abortions.

Changes in sexual mores, social attitudes, and abortion laws have altered not only the number of unplanned babies born but also what happens to them after birth. Today, the disappearing stigma associated with non-marital births and the improving social conditions for single parents result in about 2 percent of young single mothers choosing adoption for their babies[1], a drop from 80 percent in 1970. The shift has also compounded the number of children being raised in poverty.

Kelly leans back on the couch and stretches her ringed fingers. Her dark hair is a teased mass, smoothed over and sprayed firm.

"*I don't think I was forced to leave,*" *she says.* "*When my parents found out I was pregnant my mom bawled for two days—could hardly talk to me—and my dad flipped. He wanted to know whose baby it was, what in the heck was I doing—blah, blah, blah—I never told them. Then it was, 'We can't have people around here finding out.' So my dad found me a place to live in another city.*

"*I grew up during the quiet days. I could count on one hand the number of times my dad said he loved me; he never opened up. I learned just six months ago—while helping him file for disabled veteran's benefits—why he and Mom adopted me. A grenade exploded in his groin during military training when they had been married a year. It wasn't my mom who couldn't have a baby!*

"*Here I am, forty years old, and I didn't know a thing about any of it, and that's the way I always felt about everything. In getting pregnant I wasn't trying to hurt my mom—she was gentle and affectionate. I was just looking for a love of my own in all the wrong places.*" *The words drawl out; it's late.*

"*Even after my baby girl was born and placed for adoption, I thought, there is a part of me that is fulfilled but I don't have anything to show for it. So I changed playmates, playgrounds, and found another guy.* "*Let's get married and have a baby,*" *I said. It seemed like a quick fix, grown-up thing to do. After a while he started beating me. When he hit the baby, I packed my stuff and boogied on home.*" *Kelly gingerly touches her forehead.*

"*After that it was like, let's jump out of the frying pan into the fire. I nearly ran out of the church during my next marriage. But I stuck it out for eight years and had another baby before a guy called to say, 'I just wanted to let you know I'm in love with your husband.' . . .*

"I felt lower than an ant under a snake's belly—the ultimate in my life. I knew I was a failure. With two little boys to care for, I was ready to cash it all in. But I had a friend who kept saying, 'what about all the people who care about you?'

"I settled into a good marriage a couple years later but was so physically, emotionally, and spiritually bankrupt that even though there really wasn't anybody to blame, I was still a blamer.

"'You can't blame God,' my therapist said. 'He didn't do it to you—you did it to yourself—you had to learn that way.'" Kelly stares at the carpet.

"When I was pregnant the first time, and living away, I would listen to my radio at night. There was a song—'Bridge Over Troubled Waters'—real popular at the time. That's what I am. For years after that I dreamt I was climbing a mountain, clawing to catch up with a child who was always ahead of me. I used to think I was dreaming about the little girl I put up for adoption. But I read that if you dream about it for a while the child is really you; I was clawing my way beyond the child in me. Now it's a relief that the whole thing is over. I don't dream it anymore. I don't live there anymore. All those relationships are gone." Kelly stretches her arms above the sofa.

"I don't really care to contact my birthparents, but if the daughter I gave up for adoption knocked on my door, that would be fine." She knocks her fist on the wall behind her, chuckling. "I have such a soft spot in my heart for other kids who are struggling. I see them doin' what I did and want to say, 'No, you don't have to do that. Just find someone to help you deal with it.'" Kelly stands up, rubs the wrinkles from her pants, and pulls her sweater down over her hips.

"I did the best I could," she says, "with the knowledge I had at the time. I know I'm a diamond in the rough, but that's okay. Too bad it takes so dang long to learn that."

INVESTIGATING THE OPTIONS

Presently, the most common profile of an unmarried, underage pregnant girl looks the same as decades ago: a teenager with an unresponsive or upset boyfriend, whose parents are initially angry but ultimately willing to help. There are also, however, a significant number of unmarried women in their twenties and thirties who face similar choices. And every year some married women encounter the same decisions during their pregnancies due to poverty, illness, marital difficulties, or their inability to raise an extra-marital or disabled child.

The difference today is in the variety of a birthmother's available options and the quality of feelings that accompany them. For all women involved, their eventual happiness depends on the amount of helplessness they continue to feel. Research by Michael D. Resnick and Robert W. Blum[2] found that women who abort their unwanted pregnancies score high on measures of helplessness. Women who are coerced into relinquishing their child struggle with feelings of helplessness as well. But the single teenage women who keep their babies confront the largest problem. They are the most likely to drop out of school, have serious employment and financial problems, experience unstable marriages, and become abusive to their children—a quagmire of helpless circumstances.

Helplessness often leads to depression. The way people regard their role in stressful situations is critical. When individuals believe they have created the problem, view the situation as unlikely to change, or believe that the circumstance affects most aspects of their life, they are more likely to feel helpless and to become depressed.[3]

Adoption counselors responding to birthmothers who are examining adoption may say "The last thing we want to do is pressure you into any decision. The decision must be something you feel strong and good about. Make tentative arrangements as soon as you can, but even after your baby is born, hold her, look at her. Make the final decision when you are certain you know what you want."[4]

SEEKING DIRECTION

To be free to choose the setting in which one's baby will be well cared for is a divine privilege. Such a huge decision needs careful preparation and brings with it profound responsibilities. For afterwards, all individuals affected must live out the results. Birthmothers and fathers may regret choices that put them in that situation. But they may also receive abundant guidance in deciding how to rectify it. The decision requires strength and wisdom beyond that which any individual could possess since it affects the needs of an additional soul, usually too young to represent itself. So, seeking confirmation from Heavenly Father, who knows the hearts of all participants, is an essential part of finding resolution.

The First Presidency has given directions for birthparents who cannot build a successful marriage with each other. "The best interests of the child should be the paramount consideration," they say. "Unwed parents who do not marry should not be counseled to keep the infant as a condition of repentance or out of an obligation to care for one's own. Generally, unwed parents are not able to provide the stable, nurturing environment so essential for the baby's well-being." It is reassuring to know that the First Presidency encourages unwed parents "to place the child for adoption, preferably through LDS [Family] Services. . . [which] helps ensure that the baby will be reared by a mother and father in a faithful Latter-day Saint family." They also affirm that "placing the infant for adoption enables unwed parents to do what is best for the child and enhances the prospect for the blessings of the gospel in the lives of all concerned."[5]

The birthparent who chooses an adoption plan will probably wonder at some point, "What's wrong with me? How can someone abandon her own baby?" The typical answer given by professionals is altruistic.

"You're not abandoning your baby. You want what's best for her. You chose to give birth when you didn't have to go through with it. And now you are giving your child a secure life. She will have parents who love her. You should never allow yourself to be ashamed of your decision."[6]

For the birthmother who determines to make an adoption plan for her child this answer is only as valid as she believes it to be, and only as practical as her opportunity to work through a full expression of grief, to experience support from others, and to refocus her life into purposeful and productive activities. Birthmother adjustment is a high-stress process.

Laurel found out she was pregnant one afternoon at the doctor's office. She had gone in with her mother for a first pap smear.

"'Your uterus feels large,' the doctor said.

"The doctor put this apparatus on," Laurel explains, "and let me hear the heartbeat. I freaked out. I learned I was seventeen weeks along; that was a weird day. I had already done a dance concert, gone snowboarding, all sorts of stuff. The doctor sent me on to the hospital for an ultrasound.

"'I'm getting an abortion,' I told my mom, 'and if you try and stop me I'll do it myself—I know how!' But when I saw the fetus was big, I knew I couldn't." Laurel stops her rapid-fire narrative.

"'Maybe,' I told Mom, 'we could find a family to take the baby.'" Laurel gives the words delicate expression.

"The birthfather was turning into a boyfriend when my mom went out of town. Of course I didn't know I was pregnant—guess I got really moody after that, which broke up our friendship. When I called to tell him I was pregnant and ask what to do, he was like, 'I dunno.' I finally decided, Fine, he's immature—doesn't know what's up. I was busy finishing high school—did a last dance performance where I had to wear a leotard.

"'They're going to know,' I said to my doctor.

"The last week of high school I went into preterm labor. When I finally got home two hours later, the baby had stopped moving and I was thinking, she's dead! My contractions were five minutes apart and I hadn't chosen a family yet. So I went on that anti-contraction medicine—the long muscles contract, the short muscles release—something like that, but it makes your brain contract too." Laurel is laughing. She props herself up on her elbows to breath.

"Ya know, my dad's never remarried since he and Mom divorced. A couple of times during the pregnancy he said to me, 'You might keep the baby, move in with me, and we could raise her.' Even a week before the baby came he asked, 'Are you sure?'

"What do you tell your dad?" Laurel asks me. "I didn't want his help raising my baby; he's a mean man. I wanted to pick a family that would be best for her, so I pretended to be a lawyer, out defending my child's rights. If I were a kid, who would I like my parents to be?

"People kept wanting to give me freebies like, 'We'll fly you here, we'll take you to this.' I refused any presents, didn't want to feel like my baby was bought. I drove to the homes and interviewed the families myself, even those out of state. I saw the bedroom where my child would sleep, the place where she'd go to school; I kept my emotions under control, asked all kinds of questions." Laurel beams at the green shoelaces on her twitching feet.

"I narrowed it to two families. The one mom is very much like me, a 'go-getter,' an advocate. She's a defense lawyer for abused children, and her husband's a child psychologist. The other mom is this sweet, nice, stay-at-home type. She and her husband own a river rafting business.

"'Which family should I choose?' I asked people I knew well. And they told me, 'The one most similar to you. For your child it will be like you are raising her.' But my decision flip-flopped. I decided on the professional couple many times, just didn't call them up. The lawyer mom got real forceful and demanding near the end.

"'We really need to know,' she said, concentrating on more things about the baby, always the baby. It got to the point where she kind of made the decision for me; I chose the other couple even though I didn't want their Mormon religion.

"'We want what's best for you,' the river rafting couple said. 'We know this is a really hard time. We'll take the baby even if you call at the last minute.' That couple was the perfect family!

"I asked to be induced so I could plan the arrival of my family and the adoptive family. I chose to be totally numb . . . when I have my own kid I want to feel all the pain so it will seem like my first. I was alone with my doctor for the birth, didn't even want the friend in there who'd gone to all the birthing classes with me. She and Mom stayed in the lobby . . ." Laurel pauses without taking a breath.

"Because it was between me and my baby," she races on. "When I got right down to it, having anyone else involved seemed like it would kind of taint the whole thing. The birth was easy; I didn't even have an episiotomy. I cut the cord. I felt great.

"'This is a piece of cake,'" I kept saying to my mom as they zoomed me down the hall. 'I could become a surrogate mom you know—I can do this!' My mother was quiet walking beside me.

"'No, I don't think so,' she said.

"During the night I kept the baby in my room. I was drugged but I kept thinking, I cannot go to sleep. I must stay awake with my baby all night . . . I must spend every second I can with her. So I stayed propped up; she was in this little bed by me and my mom was on a cot in the corner. During the night the baby got the hiccups, started crying that little baby cry, and I couldn't move." Laurel slows, speaking deliberately.

"My mom and I don't have a very good relationship. She's religious, likes things done properly, and I share little with her. But my mom woke up, picked up the baby, and stood there talking to her, comforting her. Those moments were the most precious in the whole world. And I just stayed there like I was asleep, while she did her first grandmother thing.

"But Friday morning when I woke up she was all nervous like, 'You have to go to court, do all this lawyer stuff.' She found a parking place far away from the courthouse and ran ahead while I hobbled behind. I felt a little sorry for myself.

"'We're going to be late,' she kept saying, 'I'm afraid we'll miss everything,' and then we ended up waiting for two hours before being called into the judge's private chambers. I looked like hell but I was not crying, still being happy. It was very formal, 'Your Honor . . .' the court clerk began her little spiel.

"'Do you understand,' the judge said, 'that you have no rights to educational, medical, legal . . .' she went on and on. I had no rights to things that I hadn't even thought of! And was like, 'Yeah, I understand.' She handed me a stack of papers, and that was when it hit me—but I still had to sign my name on everything. I was a mess.

"'Now, let me say something off the record,' the judge said. She turned around and leaned forward.

"'This is the most loving, caring, self-sacrificing thing you could ever do. I commend you.' The tears started.

"The couple was back at the hospital waiting for us, all cheery. 'Hi, how're you doing?' Seeing them was like meeting the Grim

Reaper. They'd bought all this baby stuff—must have gone to Costco—four kinds of seats, a video camera.

"'Well, tell me about her,' the mother said.

"'She likes to be held this way,' I told her, 'and she likes to drink this much.' But then I lost it and my mom . . ." Laurel sits up nimbly into a floor-dance position " . . . my mom bawled uncontrollably. That's hard to hear, because moms aren't supposed to. But she's the one who finally said, 'We've got to let her go.'

"Okay, I thought. I lifted the baby, looked into her eyes—those little kids know what's up—and handed her over while my heart went quuuump. I went home to sleep and woke up with more bleeding, milk oozing, and a stomach of flabby jelly. A hollow deadness just kind of walked around with me for a while.

"'I need a vacation,' I told my parents, so my dad promised me a trip in August for my birthday. That was something to look forward to. I tried to lose weight as fast as I could, get a tan, get on with my life. I started being friends with the birthfather again, to feel closer to the baby. He's like this wanderer and I have to keep tabs on him for the future."

Laurel reaches into her pocket and pulls out a photograph of the baby. "Isn't she funny? She's got a little attitude, I think. If she's going to come out half like me and half like him she'll be a wild woman—" Laurel's eyes sparkle, she giggles—"very free-spirited. See, the couple writes little notes on the back, sends me videos. The first time they called me it was really hard because I heard my baby on the other end. That's my baby, I kept thinking, but I couldn't do anything for her except cry on the phone. The separation felt like death, but with an angel still roaming around; you mourn them because they're gone, but then you get pictures in the mail and they're smiling. I went away to college carrying all this stuff with me. I got good grades my first year but hid the issue.

"When I switched to Rice University, the weight of everything came down on me. I had a poetry class and started to write a collection of poems to my baby, to Eve, but there was a whole questioning thing growing inside. Then I was sitting in my psychology class and all of a sudden the tears were going down.

"I made a mistake, I thought. I shouldn't have given her up. I'm

going to ask my psych teacher how to write a letter to the couple and let them know. My world collapsed. I went back to my room and lived in this funk for a good five weeks off and on, kind of chronically. Finally, I got to the point where I didn't let myself think that I had made a mistake; I knew that was not best for me or my child. So I said to myself, I made this decision and it's the best decision . . . at least I think so . . . and I'm not going to question it anymore.

"I dealt with it, got over it. I learned that you never let yourself get into that gray area or you'll go insane. And then there was this boy from my hometown who also goes to Rice—I've only told a few select friends about the baby—and when I told him he was like, 'How could you bring a life into this world and not take care of it!'

"I don't need this," I said.

"'You don't want to hear,' he said, 'because you know it's true!'

"I was crushed. He was the first to say point blank, 'You did the wrong thing.' But now I wonder what was gnawing at him . . . he was angry almost automatically.

"And it's not that I think giving up a baby is best for everyone. My doctor wanted me to convince a fifteen-year-old girl that it was the best thing for her as well and I thought, how do I know? While we talked together I learned she hadn't been able to think of herself as separate from her baby during the pregnancy. As she was getting down to the end and realized the baby was almost 'itself,' then she started thinking about its point of view, and that's when she could realize what was best for her too. But they'll have to rush that adoption, and the boyfriend's still sitting there asking, 'Even if we know we're going to stay together for the rest of our lives?'

"I can't judge that. If the boyfriend I loved desperately had been the birthfather, I might have kept my baby, I don't know. But it wasn't to be . . . babies go where they're supposed to. It's kind of this fate thing. I'm agnostic. I believe I will never be able to understand life no matter how hard I try, so I respect it and go with my gut feelings. The fact that my baby grew quietly inside me, in her little corner for four-and-a-half months and allowed me to get everything done—I didn't have to drop out of school,

*didn't have to not do any of my stuff —is like she was saying, 'I'll
do my own thing and you do yours, but please, just let me live.'*

"I didn't believe she was my daughter at that point. I believed
she was like my little friend . . . she had a life and needed someone to find her parents, and so I did that. I made my peace with
her and we said good-bye—there are horrible stories where the
mother and child can't do that—and she's my daughter now, but
not to keep. The open adoption saves me in that regard.

"At one point I believed the couple who have my baby were
breaking promises. They changed her name after we chose one
together and didn't tell me for a long time. But eventually it
worked out better. She's my kid and she's their kid. When they
talk about her she's Savannah, and I talk about my Eve . . . for
two kinds of relationships.

"So I'm not going to jump in and disturb her life while she's
growing up; it's only as open an adoption as Eve wants it to be.
And the way I see it, the adoptive parents are preserving everything I write, keeping close contact with me, and then they'll use
as much as they need. If Eve wants to see me, I'm here. When
she's eighteen I might look for her. She'll be seventeen years
younger than me, but I can imagine us becoming partners in psychological research or writing books together, taking a big trip."
*Laurel stretches back down on the floor with her tank top tangled
underneath. She balances Eve's photograph on her stomach.*

"I think about the time when Eve will come back and find me—
I want to make her proud. When she says 'You know . . .' and I
say, 'Yeah . . . I gave you up, but I became President of the United
States,' or 'I went into the Peace Corps.' When you give up something so precious as a baby to go on and live your life, you have to
make your life more meaningful. To justify giving her up puts a
lot of pressure on me, because I can't be left to say I sat on my
butt and watched TV for nine years. When I'm about to do something dumb I think, Eve would really be disappointed if she ever
found out." *Laurel's voice is steady, striding on.*

"There is a contract between us that drives me," she says, "so
sacred and yet so painful and awfully terrible and wrenchingly
agonizing, that it's beautiful. So I live in awe of this sacred thing."

Laurel's mother is a cultured, tenderhearted, devout Catholic woman. Even a year later, the birth is exquisitely fresh in her mind.

"I might write an article," the mother says. Her voice is soft, private. "Even though Laurel rejects religion, the birth was tremendously spiritual for both of us. She used to be liberal on abortion and now says things to me like, 'It's criminal to let women abort up to twenty-five weeks. The baby is a life by then!'"

Laurel's mother looks down at the lawn. "I believe going through the whole pregnancy process and giving up the baby saved Laurel's life. Before that she felt invincible, like she would never get pregnant. I think she would have gone on taking risks, experimenting. But Laurel paid such a high price. A person doesn't make the decisions she made and then screw up."

"And having the baby didn't just save her physically." Laurel's mother gazes around the yard. "Laurel was glowing after Eve was born, connected to God. I want to tell others who are facing the same situation, that giving away a child to another person is . . ." she pauses, tangled in emotion, *" . . . like the Eucharist."*

THE HEALING PROCESS

A comprehensive study of birthmothers by Robin Winkler and Margaret Van Keppel[7]—the first study to compare birthmothers with a group of other women experiencing stressful events—divided the post birth adjustment into two parts: the year immediately following the birth and all subsequent time. This is a helpful distinction because giving birth necessitates huge biological adjustments. A 500 percent increase of estrogen and progesterone during pregnancy drops dramatically below normal levels after birth, resulting in a chemical imbalance which ultimately corrects itself but leaves some women temporarily vulnerable. Regardless of whether a woman relinquishes her baby for adoption, without special medication 80 percent of new mothers become mildly depressed two to three weeks after the birth of their child and 10 to 15 percent experience severe long-term depression during the first year.[8]

The results of the two-part study showed that after the one-year point there was generally a gradual improvement in the birthmother's perceptions of her situation. But for half the women their sense of loss remained acute on the child's birthday and Mother's Day. One conclusion is that it may be an inappropriate goal for birthmothers to "put it all behind them." Another is that women who continue to experience excruciating pain for years on end have become stuck in the grieving process. Mary Beth Seader and William L. Pierce, speaking for the National Council for Adoption, acknowledge that an untimely pregnancy precipitates losses that cause pain. "However," they contend, "it is not a fact that individuals cannot recover from loss. Life is a series of losses, and if individuals could not recover from them, this would be a planet of basket cases." Seader and Pierce think birthmothers can be supported through their loss to a healthy resolution, not free from some regrets and moments of pain, but one in which "the individual can go on to lead a peaceful, happy, productive life."[9]

Anne Brodzinsky developed a practical approach for birthmothers dealing with the loss of their babies.[10] First, the woman needs a "safe" place following the event, relieved for a time from many of her responsibilities. In addition, she needs to be temporarily free to be less competent, to express her thoughts and deeply felt emotions without judgment. She also has a powerful need to be understood by familiar loved ones who can express simply through eye contact, touching, and being available, some measure of "knowing" what has occurred.

Brodzinsky suggests the adjustment can be further aided by creating rituals, reminders of the child's life that may include meaningful reading, the exchange of letters, candle lighting, the planting of trees, or virtually anything that represents vitality and growth. She suggests that inviting a church representative to an event connected with the adoption can also increase social sanction.

Such a forthright approach stuns some women who released parental rights to their children in secret years ago, trusting the word of social workers that they would forget about their babies. These earlier mothers believed that their decision gave them and their child a new beginning. Many of them proceeded to build full, significant lives within this construct and assurance. However, the capacity of individuals to resolve losses varies greatly, and for other birthmothers, who may have continued over the years to experience poignant anniversary reactions, Brodzinsky suggests that creating rituals even now might be appropriate for them.

A final aspect of birthmother adjustment occurs during the critical turning point when grief takes on direction and order. This renewal is made possible by working through the whole issue, releasing the anger, forgiving others involved, taking a hard look at everything that occurred, and coming to some understanding of the significant learning that has resulted. Reorganizing the experience constructively is a critical step in filling the gap and, best of all, it is a process that generates considerable productive energy.

So constructive healing is conditional not just on making the right decision but on persevering to make sure the decision works out right. Once a birthparent has received confirmation that an adoption plan is best for her child and has prayerfully selected the adoptive parents, then she must remember and cherish those feelings of peace. Going ahead with complete faith in the Lord's ability to forgive and in her own ability to repent has invigorating power.

Spiritual concepts lived out in a poignant context can make one more able to treasure their astonishing luster. The gift of repentance is the second most precious principle of the gospel. "For those who have been involved in serious transgressions," says President James E. Faust, "it is a lifesaving principle."[11] And its purpose is to cleanse and change one for the better. The purifying process of repentance includes suffering, an aspect that is circumstantially thrust on birthmothers. Yet real sorrow can bear delicious fruit—a broken heart and a contrite spirit—tenderly prepared to receive the love of the Lord. The Savior best understands a birthmother's sacrifice: he atoned to make the miracle of adoption possible. His never-ending forgiveness compels not only the birthmother but also her loved ones to forgive. The adjustment is gradual and necessarily difficult because it must be thorough and complete, but through struggle the birthmother can grow more than she ever dreamed. The heart-wrenching process of placing a baby for adoption can ultimately strengthen everyone involved.

"If we do something that hurts a lot, we tend to think the act must be wrong," says Jeanne Warren Lindsay as she counsels young women who have become pregnant too early. "Carrying out an adoption plan is an extremely difficult thing to do. If you decide to release your baby for adoption, of course you'll hurt," she says. "This is absolutely normal. It does not mean you've made a poor decision."[12] Current statistics substantiate that teenage birthmothers who plan adoption for their babies are far *more* likely to obtain higher education and better employment than those who don't, and are far *less* likely to repeat or abort an out-of-wedlock pregnancy in the future, a circumstance that isn't surprising for those who comprehend the power of repentance.

BIRTHFATHER AWARENESS

"Three of us were on the panel," Shane says, "at a university seminar sponsored by an adoption club on campus." Shane Edwards laughs, his thick mustache jouncing, "I'm sorry, but this is so amazing—two birthmoms and me each got a chance to tell our story in front of a group of college students. A girl in the audience raised her hand as we finished, anxious to be the first one to address her remarks to me.

"'Mr. Edwards,' she said, 'before I heard you talk, I never knew there was a birthfather!'

"Everyone laughed but she was serious, and her reaction is typical of the feeling I get from others most of the time." Shane has just returned from the store with a sack of groceries for dinner and sets it on the kitchen counter. He's wearing faded jeans and a sport shirt with sleeves rolled up to his elbows.

"I keep going to this adoption support group," he says. "I found my son almost four years ago but only recently am I finally getting my point across, that birthfathers do exist." Shane smiles. His speech is subdued, low-key.

"At a meeting recently, a young woman came running across the room to tell me, 'Because of you, I searched for my birthfather

and we have a great relationship!' One success like that keeps me going a long time, makes it all worthwhile." Shane looks down.

"Five years ago," he says, "I was just about to walk out of one of those support group meetings when this lady who does searches caught up with me. As luck would have it, the next day she found my son's name." Shane's teenage girlfriend had become pregnant when he was nineteen. He explains, "Young and in love, we formed big plans for a wedding, but her parents exploded."

"'She'll get an abortion—' they said. That meant flying to Japan because they weren't legal here . . . 'or put the baby up for adoption!' Within days the parents sent her away for the rest of the pregnancy," he says. "That was 1969 when birthfathers had no say in the matter. It ate me up throughout the years. I vividly remember crying myself to sleep, many times. I wanted to be part of my baby's life." Shane became a skilled carpenter, married, and started his own family with a woman who already had a child.

"My wife encouraged me to search but I didn't know how. Every year, during the week around my son's birthday, I used to get real hard to be with. Then I found this connection support group and searched ten months before I kind of gave up. But I still had this feeling of hope, or maybe just an awareness that it was possible we could eventually meet. When I actually had my son's name in hand I got these other weird thoughts: What if he was never told he was adopted? What if it hurts him? I imagined different possible scenarios. But when I heard his voice on the phone for the first time it was like ten times all the joy you feel with your first baby—no, more than that—I had been waiting twenty-three years!" Shane stands there unabashed, smiling until his blue eyes water.

"When I called to tell the birthmother I had found him she asked, 'Why would I be interested?' Shane chuckles, glances at the bag of groceries.

"Birthfathers suffer. Their loss is different but can be as great as that felt by birthmothers. I tried to start up a support group for birthfathers, to encourage them to search for their adult children. It didn't succeed; perhaps there's a reluctance in most men to get involved." Shane stretches tall, pushing his hands deep in his pockets.

"I realize that after birthparents and children find each other the novelty often wears off and both sides settle back into old patterns, knowing they need their space. But that's just not the case with me. My son decided to move up here from Virginia with his wife and kid after we met. He's still in contact with his adoptive parents, we're all friends, but my son and I are especially close. We simply choose to spend time together . . . every day."

Historically the biological father of a child who was adopted has played little role in the decisions surrounding birth and placement. Now the visibility of birthfathers is increasing as society is acknowledging their rights and responsibilities. But utilizing studies on birthfathers requires discretion, because those who participate tend to be self-selected. In one of the few studies on the topic,[13] half of the 181 men interviewed were involved in the adoption decision for their babies and were supportive of it. By contrast, birthfathers who were excluded from the adoption decision and felt it was arrived at under pressure from others were not only opposed to adoption but interested in searching for their child—not just for assurance that the child was alive and well (as is the case with most birthmothers), but for association. Many of these frustrated birthfathers had serious thoughts of taking the child back, a poignant reminder of the Baby Jessica case of 1993. Jerome Smith, a social worker who was called to testify on that case reminds us that "the higher courts [who transferred Jessica to her birth parents after living her first two years with adoptive parents] looked at the matter not in terms of the child's needs, but in terms of the constitutional rights of Dan Schmidt"[14] (the birthfather who never voluntarily terminated his rights).

THE FATHER'S RIGHTS

A birthfather's legal claim to his child was first established in the 1972 Supreme Court decision of *Stanley v. Illinois.* Subsequent decisions have expanded the support available to single fathers seeking parental rights; state legislation has focused in on paternal identification. The Family Support Act of 1988 requires states to obtain the Social Security numbers of both parents when a birth certificate is issued.

Several states have enacted legislation in the 1990s requiring the father of a child conceived outside marriage to be considered responsible to the same extent as the father of a child born within marriage. Putative fathers, as birthfathers are legally called, can assert paternity by registering at a designated state agency anytime during the pregnancy, or before the child is placed for adoption. Registering paternity establishes a putative father's rights to participate in decisions about the child's future but also obligates him to assume parental financial responsibility. Contested paternity may be confirmed or disproved by genetic testing.

Lawmakers envisioned that paternity legislation would make participating males more responsible, but two new problems developed. Some fathers assert paternity in order to manipulate the birthmother: "You must marry me in order to keep the baby or place it for adoption," they say, and then they ignore any financial obligations. In response, state laws in both New York and Utah, for example, provide that a man who is sexually intimate with a woman is deemed to be on notice that a pregnancy may occur. The absence of any manifestation of responsibility during the pregnancy by the father, including "I did not know," may eliminate the need for his consent to adoption.[15]

Other legal problems occur when the father has been deceived or misled by the birthmother. If she does not inform the father of her pregnancy, or leaves the state to place the baby for adoption without notice, the father may then claim to have been denied due process and try to undo the adoption. Since 1996 in Utah, however, in "recognition of the fact that mothers and fathers of children who are born outside of marriage often have substantially conflicting interests,"[16] the birthmother is entitled to privacy and is not obligated to volunteer information about the father. Standards vary *significantly* from state to state. In questionable cases, where an agency works only with the birthmother, it may hold the child in foster care for a certain period of time—sometimes with the prospective adoptive parents—while it petitions the court to nullify the potential rights of an absent or unknown father. Social workers and attorneys often check the state registry minutes before adoption papers are signed to be sure the father hasn't registered.

Birthfathers who leave the scene after their partner becomes pregnant do so for a variety of reasons. "To generalize that birthfathers don't care is a gross injustice to those who do," says Jeanne Lindsay. "Fathers are likely to experience denial of grief more intensely and for a longer period of time than do the mothers. This may give others (and themselves) the impression that they aren't experiencing any effects from the loss of the baby." Lindsay concludes that "the father may simply be behind time in his grieving. He may not experience the reality of the child until birth occurs."[17]

CONSTRUCTIVE RESULTS

Birthfathers and birthmothers may have the same opportunity to learn from their experience. Unintended conception pushes one into a stream—the current picks up and there's no turning back. Those who endure know there is a miracle taking place, even though they are unprepared for it. There is no point in struggling against those larger powers that should not be resisted. A new life has already been launched. As parents live with the growing fetus, they learn the art of waiting over an extended period of time. Waiting is preparing. One may move on, feeling alone, but the journey is a storing up, a reinforcing work of love. The expectant mother may ripen more in spirit because she is the one weighed down by the child in her body. She may take upon herself this new love, not as a burden of consequences but as a stimulus to progression.

The face-to-face encounter with her child is then more like a salute, praise, a cheer for one another. The exquisite binding followed by releasing, becomes resolution for life. The love remains so strong and powerful in a birthmother's memory because it is the greatest inward work yet done. And the huge sadness goes right through the center to change and enlarge her soul. Perhaps, if she could see further into the future, she might endure her sadness with greater confidence. But the birthparent is left to trust—trust that God can see clearly, trust that prophets speak truly, trust that other human beings are equally committed to the good of her child. The sadness passes because this new dimension of faith has calmed her heart. She gradually learns that a greater "calling" still lies ahead and she is now fortified with uncommon determination. Birthparents may develop early a rare form of courage. When they have been tested and their deepest spiritual senses activated, fear of the inexplicable disperses. Their relationship to God and their fellow beings has become true and real. Their lives will not cease to be difficult, but for that reason they will not cease to advance.

Adults who swallow their past mistakes and learn to acknowledge individual weaknesses enjoy life more. They accept their share of communal responsibility, not because their dreams are stifled, but because their dreams are enlarged. It is lending a hand to the next generation that sparks adults along; they find joy in giving the world something of their earned wisdom. Birthparents can contribute to society what they gain, enhancing the stream of history with valuable lessons. The maturity of the world will inevitably rise as people share with each other. Making an adoption plan for a child may be a supernally unselfishness act, one that deepens understanding and enlarges character forever.

NOTES

1. *Adoption Factbook III,* National Council for Adoption (Waite Park, Minn.: National Council for Adoption, 1999), p. 41. The national average obtained from the National Center for Health Statistics, "Report of Final Natality Statistics, 1996" was precisely 1.9 percent, but Utah was the highest at 6.9 percent of births to unmarried women resulting in adoptions.

2. Michael D. Resnick and Robert W. Blum, "Developmental and Personological Correlates of Adolescent Sexual Behavior and Outcome," *International Journal of Adolescent Medicine and Health* 1 (1985): 293–313.

3. Lyn Y. Abramson, Martin E. P. Seligman, and John P. Teasdale, 1978, as summarized by Anne B. Brodzinsky in "Surrendering an Infant for Adoption: The Birthmother Experience," in *The Psychology of Adoption,*

ed. David M. Brodzinsky and Marshall D. Schechter (New York: Oxford University Press, 1990), p. 305.

4. Gail B. Stewart, *The Facts about Adoption* (New York: Crestwood House, 1989), p. 26.

5. "Adoption and Unwed Parents," First Presidency Letter to General Authorities; Area Authority Seventies; Stake, Mission and District Presidents; Bishops and Branch Presidents, June 15, 1998.

6. Stewart, *The Facts about Adoption,* p.26.

7. Robin Winkler and Margaret Van Keppel, *Relinquishing Mothers in Adoption* (Melbourne: Institute for Family Studies, 1984).

8. Tom Verde, "Beyond the Baby Blues: Treating Depressed Mothers," Horizons, National Public Radio, 1994.

9. Mary Beth Seader and William L. Pierce, "Parent Access After Adoption," in *Debating Children's Lives,* ed. Mary Ann Mason and Eileen Gambrill (Thousand Oaks, Calif.: Sage Publications, 1994), p. 27.

10. Brodzinsky, "Surrendering an Infant for Adoption: The Birthmother Experience," in *The Psychology of Adoption*, pp. 310–14.

11. James E. Faust, in James P. Bell, *In the Strengh of the Lord: The Life and Teachings of James E. Faust* (Salt Lake City: Deseret Book Company, 1999), p. 404.

12. Jeanne Warren Lindsay, *Pregnant? Adoption Is an Option* (Buena Park, Calif.: Morning Glory Press, 1997), p. 181.

13. Eva Y. Deykin, Patricia Patti, and Jon Ryan, "Fathers of Adopted Children: A Study on the Impact of Child Surrender on Birthfathers," *American Journal of Orthopsychiatry* 58 (1988): 240–48.

14. Jerome Smith, *The Realities of Adoption* (Lanham, Md.: Madison Books, 1997), p. 127.

15. Aaron Britvan, "Birthfathers and the Law," and David M. McConkie, "Putative Father's Registries: A Balancing of Interests," in *Adoption Factbook III,* pp. 341–43, 344–48.

16. Ibid., p. 346.

17. Lindsay, *Pregnant? Adoption Is an Option,* pp. 71, 182.

He inviteth them all to come unto him . . . black and white
. . . all are alike unto God.
2 Nephi 26:33

9

MIDNIGHT
DOMESTIC TRANSRACIAL ADOPTION

The essence of a soul has no color. It is invisible. The soul has yearnings—feelings of uniqueness, intimations of greatness, sensations of restlessness. Most assuredly, the soul is individual and eternal.

Parents and children from a genetically related, nuclear family may think quite naturally of themselves as offshoots of the same family tree. The truth is that we all grow beyond our biological origins; physically, emotionally, spiritually we grow to become different, matchless individuals. Children are not learning at their parents' knees for very long. Parents eventually grow old and children grow up to take their turns shaping the world. It is the destiny and responsibility of each generation.

Adoptive parents whose child comes to them with remarkably different racial characteristics may learn sooner the equalizing lessons of life: Parents don't possess their children and they won't always control them. And a child whose physical differences from his parents are clearly manifest from the beginning may recognize earlier his own unique capabilities. Individuality is a kind of beauty, not when bound inward but when set free to invent, pursue, and satisfy the wondrously personal callings of the heart.

"I went to bed during pregnancy to save our two girls," Louise says, "but we lost our boy at 28 weeks from a cerebral hemorrhage. I lay in the hospital, engorged with breast milk, crying for an infant. Finally, I called an adoption agency to see if I could care for babies before they were placed, while paperwork was being done. I can handle that, I thought. I'm a nurse.

"The first one to stay with us was Adam," Louise says, "then Benito, and finally Chad. We alphabetized the baby's names." Louise is thin and of average height. Her husband Joel is a pediatrician two inches shorter than she.

"Adam came two weeks after I arrived home from the hospital. He was the color of dark chocolate. Joel walked in from the hospital on a break, gazed at him, and said to our four-year-old, 'Look how brown his skin is, Kimberly. God made babies just like the bears; there are brown bears, black, white.' There was nothing more to talk about, no value to associate with one color over another.

"As I worked with Adam," Louise says, "I wondered, What does this world have in store for you? He was placed with a couple from Wisconsin. The father started calling us every day and I didn't feel sorry anymore. He was a law student, a quadriplegic who had been a gymnast before his accident. I thought the baby was lucky to have that man to raise him, and when the child says, 'You don't understand how hard it is—you're white,' the dad can say, 'Yeah, but I've had hurdles too.'

"Benito was a Latin American baby, cocaine addicted and very irritable. I guess he was in a lot of physical pain, going through withdrawal. He'd cry himself to sleep just to wake up again. I had him seventeen days—I counted, and did not feel sad when he left. That little guy went to a couple in Pennsylvania who had adopted another Hispanic boy already. The mother called to ask, 'Is he really bad?' I felt sorry for her. Benito was a crab apple!—not comfortable in his skin at all. It was hard to feel affection because nothing I did made him less miserable.

"Chad was half black and half white. Three weeks later a social

worker called offering us the chance to adopt him. It didn't take
long to accept and change his name to Scott. The challenge was
with my parents. They were both raised in Chicago, where the
black population they knew lived in the ghetto. My mother said,
'Your grandmother is going to roll over in her grave. And the
child's going to end up right back where he came from.'

"'Scott didn't come from the ghetto,' I told her. 'My hope is that
the way we live will make him a stranger there.'

"'Why do you want to invite such pain into your life?' she
asked.

"'When the hard times come, we'll cry together,' I said. 'All I
can do is help Scott to love himself. I can't guarantee that every-
body's going to like my children whether I give birth to them or
not.'

"Then we needed money to complete the adoption," Louise
says. "If I had delivered at that hospital instead of the birthmother, the bill would have been completely written off. Joel was
doing his residency at Duke.

"'Nope, you get to pay,' was their response. Finally, the thought
came to me, why don't I sell Grandma's ring? She gave me her
diamond before she died in Arkansas twenty years ago. My mom
flipped out.

"'You can't sell the family heirloom!' Dad was the peacemaker;
he bought the ring. We took out a loan to cover the remaining
expenses.

"When Scott was two," Louise says, "I was weeding the rose
bed as he played in the yard. I looked at him and thought, he
needs a friend, a companion, someone who knows what it's like
to be black, to be a boy, and adopted in this family. So we applied
to adopt Andrew, who is now three. He's what Joel calls his 'can-
do' man, trying everything himself. In contrast, when you ask
Scott, who's now five, to do the simplest thing he breaks out in
tears, 'I can't do that.' We try to teach Scott how to do work in
small steps, but when a job doesn't turn out well he blames
somebody else. Scott said to me the other day, 'Mom, do you ever
have times where a line from a song just keeps going over and
over in your head and you can't stop it?'

"'You can't put another idea there?'"

"'No, it keeps going and going.' And I thought, oh Scott, you poor little guy. Psychiatrically speaking, schizophrenics have that problem and it's also a sign of obsessive-compulsive disorders. I feel a combination of compassion and irritation working with him. Since I experience some of those same feelings, they're very hard to accept in my child. I told Scott, 'Your academic work is very important in this family because good grades open opportunities and bad grades shut doors. But if you don't want to do brain work, you have to do body work.' Last week, he wouldn't concentrate on his spelling list.

"'Why don't you go outside and spray down the deck?'

"'Oh, Mom,' he grumbled.

"'Yep, go on.' He was happy as a clam out there, as if to say, 'I can do this. I like body work.' It may not be a white collar job he'll want."

"As far as adoption goes, Scott isn't conscious of it—he has more trouble with his skin color. He was waiting for a ride to his game at the community center when he said, 'I don't want to play basketball anymore, no one passes to me. I think it's because I have brown skin.'

"'What do you do when you get the ball?' I asked.

"'I try to make a basket.'

"'Maybe they don't want to give you the ball because they want to make a basket. Maybe it doesn't have anything to do with the color of your skin.' If he were older I could have said, 'Watch the pros, my dear.'"

Louise's husband, Joel, plays basketball every evening with Scott and Andrew on a shortie hoop in the front driveway. Lots of other children in the predominantly white neighborhood join in. He stands aside to talk.

"How do other people react to your adopting transracially?" I ask.

"Not one person I know has been discouraging," Joel says, "but I fear blacks don't like us very much." He smiles. "We go to an African American adoption support group; that increases our black awareness. However, I don't think about racial differences. I'm not convinced that dissimilar tastes in food, clothes, or music *are cultural pillars that affect happiness. We concentrate on building relationships with our kids."*

VACILLATING OPPOSITION

Joel is aware of the opposition to transracial adoption that has existed among black social workers, but he also knows there are thousands of black children who need adoptive homes. The demand for adoptive families soared in the 1990s, like it did in the late 1950s, when thousands of black children were being reared in institutions and foster homes throughout the country. In the 1950s, however, it was black community leaders who demanded to know why adoption agencies were not placing black children even though Asian and Native American children were being placed, without restriction, into good adoptive families. Hesitant agencies back then were consequently pressured to abandon adoption practices that smacked so strongly of segregation.

As a result, transracial adoptions increased in this country until white parents had adopted 20,000 non-white children. In 1972 scores of white couples were attending an adoption convention of the National Association of Black Social Workers in St. Louis when the president, William T. Merritt, accused them of cultural genocide. As recorded in the *Wall Street Journal,* "Their children, he charged, wouldn't develop black pride and a black identity, both sorely needed to grapple with society and racism."

"There was an incredible hurt in the crowd," one adoptive mother recalled. "I was in terrible pain." The article continued, "Mothers nearby, some of whom were taking hormones so they could breast-feed their babies, wept openly. . . . Others, fearful they would destroy their babies' lives, soon gave them back to adoption agencies."[1] In the years following, a virtual ban on the adoption of black children by white parents was instigated by agencies in many states.

"Martin Luther King Jr. b-e-1-i-e-v-e-d i-n e-q-u-a-1-i-t-y!" Julie says. He spoke to us for two-and-a-half hours and it seemed like three minutes. And it wasn't just the power of his oratory, it was

his message." Julie is a redhead with freckly skin, who went to college in the 1960s.

"It was the first time I'd been to a black Baptist church," she says. "My boyfriend and I were the only whites in the congregation. The choir started shaking and singing, 'Master, the Tempest Is Raging.' This is what you call joy in the Lord, *I thought. 'It's midnight,' Dr. King said. 'The Savior's coming at dawn and you'd better get ready!' We held hands out on the street, bowed our heads and made a human chain of brotherhood for what was going on—demonstrations, sit-ins, boycotts, and everything else that happened in '65 and '66 down South."*

"Since I was a little child," Julie says, "seeing people treated differently because of something they couldn't help tugged at my heart. I sobbed reading Uncle Tom's Cabin. *In high school I read every one of Frederick Douglas's speeches I could find; I was stunned by Ellison's* The Invisible Man. *It became more of an intellectual thing in college. Prejudice against blacks tied into the inequality of women's rights.*

"When my husband finished law school, we established residency but still couldn't have a baby. Friends said, 'Adoption is the very last thing to do. You should try everything else first.' Some neighbors wanted to start up a collection so we could go to a fertility clinic. But I had always wanted to adopt. Having pink skin, no eyebrows, and feeling so unattractive myself gave me this passionate thing about brown-skinned children. Our first child is Korean. Our second is African American-Caucasian—we adopted her in the '70s and the social worker said to us, 'We just didn't know where we were going to place this—she still called them "colored"—child.' I thought, how could I be so lucky? *The agency staff at that time had no training in transracial adoptions. They asked vague questions like, 'Do you have personal feelings against blacks?' 'How do you plan to enhance this child's identity?' Some African American children were placed with white couples who claimed that their adopted child was Polynesian!*

"Our home teacher came to comfort us. 'The longer they're in your home,' he said, 'the lighter their skin will seem.'

"'By hell,' I said, just to be dramatic, '—they'd better not change. I want them this beautiful color!'" Julie smiles. She now

works part-time for an adoption agency in Kansas City and studies sociology at night. Julie and her husband adopted eight children transracially before they divorced. Several have special needs and three of them are fourteen years old. We walk around Liberty Memorial Park together. Starlings screech overhead.

"This is a great place to raise black children," she says, "because there is such a variety of role models. My kids go to the Scouting program at the Baptist church where Emmanuel Cleaver attends. A black social worker who lives next door plays basketball with them. They have black friends at school. We go to black beauty salons, own all the ethnic literature you would want in the world, buy soul food at Ruby's, subscribe to Ebony and Jet, *and have shelves of rap music. My black friends say, 'You have more black identity in your home than we do,' and I say, 'You don't need it, you're there.'*

"All the major research on transracial adoption," Julie says, "concludes that there is no significant difference in grades, self-esteem, job acumen, and anything else about black children adopted by whites, as opposed to black children raised in black families, if the adopted black children have role models and are exposed to the black culture." Julie talks fast, her voice is subdued. "I have a real dilemma," she says. "Every weekend we have Darrin, a black-Korean who lives at Shawnee Mission Medical Center, come and visit. He's twelve and has been without a home since he was five. His caseworker told me last week that half a million dollars has been spent on him with all the testing, programs, institutionalization—and there's no adoptive family to take him. He's been Wednesday's Child in three states.

"So Darrin arrives at our home on Saturdays—this angry kid abandoned by his birthparents and his adoptive parents, sexually and physically abused, just about as mean a kid as you'd want to meet—and my kids say, 'Hey Darrin, hi bud, bro!' And they do his hair, play ball with him, hug him. My children are total knuckleheads in many ways, but in this one regard they are true geniuses. They welcome all people that come into our home and think they should be treated nicely. And I'm thinking, I should adopt him." Julie maintains her pace, breathless.

"Seriously," she says, "where else is he going to go? And then I

think, well, wait, look at all the two-parent families. Why aren't they applying to take Darrin? I may be dumb to consider it, but what are we going to do about this boy?" Julie is struggling financially, still hurting over the divorce from her husband and his family's lack of communication. Every day at her job she tries to find people to adopt children like Darrin.

"My ego couldn't have taken the beatings that Darrin's has— emotionally and socially. He has suffered, like all my kids, when prejudged by their skin. These kids resent that kind of treatment, but I have enough experience to get the issue clear. While my children are looking in the mirror, mad because they were adopted, or abused, or their moms used drugs, or their dog left, I say, 'What is the issue? I'm not sure what is going on inside you, but one thing I do know is that you've got to be in charge of your own happiness and you can't blame other things. Yes, Dad left. It nearly killed us, but you still have yourself. You still have people who love you. You weren't aborted, you were adopted. This may not be the best home but. . . .'

"You teach them to face their blackness," Julie says. "My daughter, Nannette, is still angry. She's the one of our fourteen-year-olds who's been a voracious reader. Every Virginia Hamilton or Mildred Taylor book makes her mad that she's being discriminated against by the white kids who live in wealthier neighborhoods and go with her to Indian Hills Middle School. Nannette can sing "Secret Garden" and "Phantom;" she's a fantastic gymnast, but she is clumped in with other children of minority race who are fine friends but pretty rough. Now she talks big like Queen Shineeka on Saturday Night Live, *mouthy as all get out, screams and yells. She's started to puff up her hair and spray it. Some of the kids she hangs out with get in fights. She was pushed around in the hall at school and got into trouble. Near the end of March she started saying, 'I'm so tired. My stomach hurts.' Now she won't go to school half the time. If she can't understand a homework assignment immediately she'll throw her books down. I'm not really in control of anything in her life anymore, but I need to know where she is. I called over to her friend Liberty's house the other night and the answering machine said, 'We've gone for the weekend to see Pink Floyd.' I asked Nannette, 'Is that*

their regular message?' Her little group is a microcosm of our society. Her friend, Liberty, is in a home study-school split; she recently tried to commit suicide. Another friend is living with an aunt while the parents battle over custody. The third one is living with a grandma, and the last one is a foster child.

"In my work I place a lot of African American children. Now there's kind of a movement swinging the pendulum back to transracial adoption as the economic realities of state care for displaced children are catching up. I favor family placements. No matter what color, a family is better than an institution or foster care. That's why I will place transracially. That's why I adopted. But I will always look for a black family first. I found fifteen of them last year.

"I fought the concept of white couples taking black babies until about two years ago. Then I said, 'What am I doing? I love these good people and in many cases that's the only way they can get a baby. They don't have the bigger bucks for Caucasian babies and if they already have more than two kids most agencies won't look at them. Even a non-profit organization will charge $4,500 for services to place a black baby in a white home. As a whole blacks are against that type of adoption because theoretically, they say, black babies could be placed in black homes for nothing, not for thousands. Many of the black birthmothers are on Medicaid and welfare without a lot of medical expenses, but adoptive parents who want a comfortably impersonal agency placement are charged $8,000 to $10,000, and they're willing to pay. You can go to Russia or China for a baby and pay that."

Julie paces back towards her car.

"Yesterday I saw a white mother," I say, "with a smiling black daughter in her grocery cart. It was in a mostly white neighborhood store and people paused to admire her child. She said it was her fourth black adoption and added, 'It doesn't really matter what's on the outside, it's what's on the inside that counts.' Do you believe that?"

Julie shakes her head. "The outside matters absolutely," she says, "because if black children haven't learned to feel the pride deep down inside about their blackness, when they get cursed the first time, can't get the job that was available until they walked

*in the store, or have to furnish double the references and a credit
line to buy a car, they're going to go crazy. Black children have to
perceive, accept, and love their blackness so they can be an advocate for themselves, strong enough to live in this world." A siren
starts in the distance. Julie leans against her car.*

*"Tell me we don't live in a racist society," she says. "From the
second row of bleachers I watched my son play baseball on
Saturday. He was up to bat, nervous and intent. The assistant
coach said, 'You struck out, you nigger.' I started to perspire. I put
my hands on my temples and tried to think, what would I do if I
were black? I knew the coach and the umpire. They told me later
I should have interrupted the game and the offender would have
been sent away for unsportsmanlike conduct. But that experience
illustrated to me that I must help my black children develop
'antennas,' so they can discern when they should stay to defend
themselves or leave to avoid danger. They need to have a sense of
their impact on others and how to deal with it, otherwise they will
be vulnerable in a partially hostile country."*

*The siren shrieks half a block away, and Julie doesn't notice. I
feel safe in her company. She has become strong, not bitter, facing
her problems.*

INSIGHTS FROM STUDIES

Studies on African-American transracial adoption picked up
in the 1970s and 1980s and showed there were no significant
differences in the self-esteem scores of black adoptees, other
nonwhite adoptees, and their nonadopted siblings being raised
by white parents. However, the adoptive parents tended to be
disproportionately higher educated, upper-middle class, and
liberal. Rita Simon and Howard Alstein contacted 206 transracially adopting families and were particularly interested to
learn that these "black children (in white families) perceive
themselves as black, as accurately as white children perceive
themselves as white" and do not attach any negative value to
that reality.[2]

William Feigelman and Arnold Silverman, who studied 713
transracial families[3] composed of black, Asian, Latin American,
as well as white children, determined that black children in
white families face more hostility than other transracial

adoptees, but they are also more clearly tied to their African-American identities. They concluded that the strong racial identity of black children was probably part of a greater commitment by their white parents to emphasize the children's background. Seventy percent of the transracially adopted African-American children expressed pride in their native heritage as compared with 57 percent of adopted Asian children and 50 percent of adopted Latin Americans. The white parents tended to be supportive of their children's identification with the African-American community and regarded their transracial children as African American in appearance. Most of their children attended integrated schools in communities that were predominantly, but not exclusively, white. As adults, their black children remained firmly committed to their white families—the only family they have and the only set of parents they want—but they identified with the racial backgrounds of their birthparents as well. Delay in placement was the most significant factor contributing to difficulties in adjustment.

Although two smaller British studies confirm the same positive outcomes for transracially adopted children, they do not confirm that most of these children identify with their biological race. Owen Gill and Barbara Jackson's study[4] of transracially adopted children with mostly Asian birthparents found the children saw themselves as white in every dimension but skin color, although few were confused about their origins. Society still tends to label children with only one black parent as black—since they are generally perceived as black. But according to a study by Christopher Bagley and Loretta Young,[5] about half of these mixed-race children growing up in white families see themselves as white. Though the British have a significantly different racial history, concerned professionals on both sides of the ocean wonder whether such children will be prepared to deal with racism and discrimination in the future.

Actually, the black population in the United States has never been uniformly opposed to transracial adoption. In 1992, *CBS This Morning* reported the results of its own poll,[6] which questioned nearly a thousand people on whether race should be a factor in adoption. Seventy-one percent of the participating African Americans thought race should not be a restrictive criterion in adoption placement while 70 percent of the white Americans who were polled agreed. Even in South Africa the law against transracial adoption was struck down in 1991, and the number of black women relinquishing their babies has risen dramatically while white families are stepping forward to adopt.[7]

A study of black childcare professionals[8] disclosed a marked division of opinion on the subject. Those with direct involvement in transracial adoptions tended to have favorable evaluations while those without experience were much more critical. Nevertheless, amid such vitriolic accusations many adoption agencies have been slow to change back over to placing transracially. In 1987 the National Association of Colored People adopted a resolution to support legislation and policies to place black children for adoption without regard to race, a resolution which they renewed in 1992. The Multiethnic Placement Act that went into effect in October, 1995, was designed to prohibit denying or delaying placement of any child because of racial or ethnic considerations. The Department of Health and Human Services says it is committed to vigorous enforcement of the act, that federal aid is conditioned upon compliance. Yet the new statute remains open to interpretation, including agency evaluation of the prospective adoptive parents' capacity to meet the needs of the child's cultural, ethnic, and racial background. The facts persist: matching race in adoption is statistically improbable in our country, where over half the children awaiting adoption are black and the black population is only 12.3 percent of the total.

Regardless of whether one resists or supports the official voice of black social workers, it is a fact that their ardor has triggered the awareness of more sensitivity in adoption placement policy. As a result, sensitive social workers of any color bridge the gap by personally encouraging recruitment of more black adoptive families. Black families are now adopting at a higher rate than white families. The government assists by subsidizing parents willing to adopt a child who is hard to place, when the parents cannot otherwise afford it.

CULTURAL AWARENESS

Transracial adoption issues in this country for the most part center on African American placements because they overwhelmingly predominate. According to figures collected by the National Children's Bureau, there are currently more than 44,000 African American children anticipating adoption who are waiting in foster care—over half of the total. Of the others, approximately 40 percent are Caucasian, 5 percent Hispanic, and 3 percent Asian, Pacific Islanders, or Native American. Consistently, the studies show that children of color placed into white homes have the same proportion of problems and successes as children placed into adoptive families of the same race.

Professionals in the field of adoption have generally divided themselves into three broad groups on the issue of transracial placements, according to John Triseliotis in *Adoption: Theory, Policy and Practice*: the integrationists, who stress the uniqueness of individuals and their capacity to move freely amongst cultural groups; the pragmatists, who seek adoption placement above all else for the many ethnically diverse children waiting in foster care; and the oppositionists, who maintain that every individual's identity is grounded in his cultural milieu and no placement should be allowed to separate one from it.[9] Most agree that it is best for children to be adopted into families of the same ethnic background. Since this is not always feasible, however, the emphasis of the arguments may shift as racism moderates.

History reaffirms that prejudice is changeable. An example is the history of adoptions in North America of Native Americans, which have not unfolded as favorably as that of Asian, Hispanic, or African American placements. When social workers in western Canada visited large numbers of native shanties during the 1960s and 1970s and found the adults stoned at midday, with their little children looking for food, they felt justified in removing these children. Yet the majority, who were then placed into white adoptive homes, maintained significantly poor self-esteem and a high tendency toward suicide. There seems to have been insufficient community support and role models; the white adoptive parents tried to instill a sense of native Canadian identity in their children but it was cancelled out by the negative effects of racism.

Christopher Bagley, from the University of Southhampton, in the Department of Social Work Studies, did a comparable study[10] on Canadian Native American children raised by their birthparents. Though living in the same general areas as native children who were adopted, the native children did not have the same difficulties and identity problems. A similar tragedy among aboriginal children adopted by white families in Australia occurred when the children, who were brought up to think of themselves as white, were ultimately discriminated against by most of the white culture.[11]

Although Native Americans have endured a tragic fate to which their children have been particularly vulnerable, the situation is currently changing. Some reservations have developed their own diversified economies; these are the tribal societies closest to organizing their own systems of child welfare and adoption. Support and respect for the Native American culture is growing. The popularity of native art and myth augments current literature, competes for museum space, and is thriving in retail stores—both the real thing and the "white man's" imitation. A respect for the earth and animal life have spread far beyond the reservation and are increasingly credited to their original source.

As a practical matter, the Indian Child Welfare Act of 1978 has made it almost impossible for white families to adopt Native American children in recent years. Children of predominantly native blood who end up in foster care cannot be placed with other-race parents without tribal consent. However, today there are many "part-Native American" children flourishing in adoptive homes, their identity being enhanced by the escalating esteem for tribal values and talents.

It requires conscious effort to understand and appreciate the attitudes of other cultural groups towards adoption. Adoption policies in the United States have been influenced primarily by Roman law, supporting an exclusive arrangement in a nuclear family. African, Native American, and Oceanic societies are tied to tribal customs that are far more flexible. It is not extraordinary in those cultures for people to love each others' children as their own, or 'unnatural' for an unprepared woman to give her child to someone who is. In some Polynesian countries, for example, those who can become pregnant may feel an obligation to consider offering their child to others who want to parent but cannot. The following story stretches beyond domestic placement to demonstrate the influence of tribal custom currently at work in the United States and to accentuate the pervasive nature of transracial issues that have international application. There is no clear boundary between most transracial and intercountry adoption issues.

"We watched Polynesian families give one of their children to aging parents just so their parents wouldn't be lonely!" Ron says. His hair is starting to turn gray around the temples, down into his beard. He wears a denim sunflower shirt.

"We had a house girl living with us on a plantation in Tonga who was large, maybe 300 pounds. She had a child out of wedlock. That baby, Mele, grew up with our kids. When she was three, the grandparents decided it would be best if we adopted her. They told Mele, 'Don't speak Tongan anymore. You are part of their family now.'

"Mele developed a mental block on her native language," Ron says. He looks up, smiles. Fishing hooks and dried chicken parts lay on a worktable in front of him. He ties black thread carefully around a tiny feather.

"When we moved to New Zealand," he says, "Mele spoke British English, and when we came back here to Montana, she mastered the rural dialect. In junior high school the principal called her in. 'Are you having any problems, Mele?' he asked. 'Is anyone unkind to you?'

"Mele told us: 'That was the strangest talk! I could never figure out what the principal was trying to get at.'" Ron laughs.

"Mele didn't date in high school but she played basketball and

volleyball. She was rebellious, hanging out with the rough crowd, but it didn't seem to be because of adoption or race. After she finished high school Mele visited her birth mom, who had moved to a Tongan community in Texas; that's when she was first shocked by racism.

"'They treated us like blacks!' she said."

"But Mele was never sorry to be Tongan," Ron's wife says. His wife talks comfortably from a recliner with her eyes half closed. "She always had contact with her original family; so did we. We were friends before, never expected to change that relationship after the adoption, and we never did."

"Mele's now settled into a second marriage," Ron says, "living with her birthmother and a lot of other Tongans during the start-up of a new travel business in California. She gave birth to still-born twins a few weeks ago. We talked to her by phone in the hospital the night the babies were delivered. At 11:00 P.M., her room was still full of Tongans saying, 'You should never have bought clothes for the babies, never have gotten a crib—it's taboo you know.' She had to deal with the whole bunch of them; the Polynesians safeguard their communal identity.

"'Get those people out of there!' I told her husband, 'so she can get some rest.' He did; they slept on mats in the hospital hall. The next day her birthmother's uncle died. The whole family was called together; the senior aunt made assignments. Mele and her husband had to buy the burial clothes (a suit, tie, and shirt for $50) while borrowing every penny for their own babies' coffin! But Mele has always had a place to live when things got tough. Her extended family is in and out of each others' homes all the time; it's the Polynesian way, even after they relocate in America.

"Mele claims she's stir crazy now," the wife says, "wants them to get a place of their own."

Ron stands up from his worktable, stretches his back. He strolls over by his wife's recliner. "Mele goes along with the island customs when she's living with her people," he says, "but on her own she's half and half. She's large like her mother now, and a super saleswoman. She brought her new husband here to visit.

"'I've made mistakes in my life,' she told us, 'but it wasn't your *fault. I would have had no advantages in this world if you hadn't adopted me.'"*

Adoption specialists, who used to worry that children adopted transracially would have the most difficult adjustment challenges during their adolescent years, now suspect that the young adult years could be an even greater challenge, when the shelter of their white home environment is left behind. Children adopted transracially, who have only white cultural skills, may have problems in adulthood integrating with their native cultural groups, problems which can be minimized if their adoptive families are diligent over the years in linking them with some associates of their own ethnic origin.

Dan O'Brien, winner of the 1996 Olympic decathlon gold medal at age thirty, was born to an African-American birth-father, a Finnish birthmother, and adopted by a white couple in Klamath Falls, Oregon. "In college, people thought of me as African American, and I tried to fit in, but it didn't work out. I failed. I wish I'd learned more about African American culture growing up. Over the last five years, I've become me," he says. "I feel a special connection to mixed-race kids. It's important for me to think I'm mixed-race. I found strength in others who are mixed-race or adopted, like Greg Louganis and Scott Hamilton. At one meet, a father brought over a four-year-old and said, 'Look, this is Dan O'Brien. His mom was white and his dad was black and he's okay.'"[12]

Race may be relevant only as a cultural concept anyway. Many scientists now conclude that race has little to do with genetics. The three distinct types of human DNA show no correlation with generally observed racial traits according to a study of millions of genetic sequences by Alan Templeton. For example, as reported by Templeton in the September 1998 issue of *American Anthropologist,* there are more genetic similarities between Europeans and sub-Saharan Africans and between Europeans and Melanesians than between Africans and Melanesians—peoples which seem to share similar racial characteristics such as dark skin, curly hair, broad noses, and other distinctive facial features.

Consequently, it is no surprise that transracial adoptions within the United States usually turn out well, and transracial living thrives naturally. A blond curly-haired mechanic married a Cherokee woman ten years ago and they are raising her sister's native daughter along with their mixed-race biological son. A white woman is raising her black grandson; he was born fourteen years ago to her son-in-law, who immediately left the scene. Adults come forward to assist a helpless child. Spontaneously, they rally and their ongoing responsibility becomes a personal call, a call to give advantage to another person. Of course, they say, it is the needs of another soul at stake. Such transcendent arrangements are oblivious to "race," blessedly color-blind.

PERSONAL ASSESSMENT

The significant results of a twenty-year transracial study by Rita Simon and Howard Alstein[13] concluded in 1991. Ninety-two percent of the adoptive parents said that with their hindsight and gained experience they would still go ahead and adopt transracially. Sixty-seven percent of those who were adopted transracially and are now finally grown say they would not have preferred same-race adoptive parents. Another 26 percent did not respond or know what to answer. In essence, the consensus among the grown children was, "My life has worked out very well"; "My parents love me"; and/or "Race is not that important."[14] Suggestions from the adoptive parents in this study to others who might be considering a transracial placement are: "Do it because you want a child and because you believe you will love that child as if you had given birth to it"; "Don't do it to show how 'liberal' or 'enlightened' you are."[15]

Transracial adoptive families stand out, not necessarily in a negative way but as a curiosity which involves constant explanations and justifications to others. Parents who plan to adopt transracially do well to assess how they may react to being a high profile family. Self-assessment questionnaires are available[16] to help people evaluate their natural tendencies in combination with the additional stresses of a transracial placement. Even a sensitive, non-judgmental person may be too private to comfortably parent a child of a different race. In addition, Triseliotis points out that "racism and discrimination are relative to the degree of pigmentation and physical difference displayed by the children."[17] Before adopting transracially parents need to consider not only their own feelings about race but also the sentiments of the people they live near and associate with. Studies about racial and ethnic identity cannot be generalized from one country to another or from one section of a country (or city) to another. Parents may also choose to move to a more integrated community or cultivate relationships with people of the same race as their child, friends who could serve as additional role models.

Distinctions between races are becoming increasingly blurred, a perpetual trend particularly noticeable in a predominantly white country like the United States. Someone today, looking toward adoption for the first time, may have to stop and think, *Would it be racist to look for a child of the same race, or racist to look for a child of another race?*

At one time predominantly white, The Church of Jesus Christ of Latter-day Saints is now flourishing in the aftermath of a revelation that extended priesthood blessings to all men, "without regard to race or color." On June 8, 1978, the First Presidency of the Church stated: "The Lord has now made known his will for the blessing of all his children." Particularly interesting is the explanation by the First Presidency of how the doctrine was received: "He [the Lord] has *heard our prayers,* and by revelation has confirmed that the long-promised day has come when every faithful, worthy man in the Church may receive the holy priesthood" (D&C, Official Declaration—2; emphasis added).

"Twenty years after the revelation extended priesthood blessings," Ned says, "almost to the date, I conferred the priesthood upon my own son." Ned and his wife, Vicki, have adopted four children of color. We spent an hour picking raspberries together, but now he steps aside to talk.

"It was as sweet a moment as I shall ever hope to have in this

life," he says. Vicki stands close by, but she's watching the children hiding in the canes.

"As I placed my hands upon Hunter's head of full Afro hair," Ned says, "I couldn't help thinking of the first converts in Nigeria. I could picture them in my mind. They had accepted the gospel twenty-three years ago without these blessings. The great privilege I was experiencing at that moment was a confirmation to me." Vicki turns to look at Ned, then faces me.

"You see," she says, "I've had a flooding of the spirit with each of these children. When I get that, I can move forward. I think Ned's more—"

Ned cuts in gently—"My experience is different," he says. "I didn't have a manifestation, a blast of revelation that adoption was right. It was more like, it probably would be a good thing, I feel good about it—kind of the same way you feel when you set foot in the mission field for the first time. You're not really sure how it's going to turn out but you move forward full of hope, and things work out."

The kids are over by the raspberry stand, watching the berries being weighed. Hunter comes back for the money to pay. We watch him return while the other children are cheering.

"We'll be OK," says Ned.

"He says that at times while I'm sobbing," Vicki laughs. "He's more faithful." She pauses, "I'm more . . . dramatic. When Hunter stepped out of the baptismal font I could visualize generations of his posterity doing the same thing."

The youngest, three-year-old Chloe, is now hugging Ned's knees, her fingers covered with berry juice. He spreads his hand over her thickly braided hair. "When Hunter's ordination was finished he was shaking hands with everyone, and then he came to Chloe, took her hand, and she turned his hand over to softly kiss it. As he passed the sacrament that first time, it was Chloe who reached out to touch him as if to say, 'I'm proud of you.'" The boys are lugging the berries towards their van. Chloe runs to catch up with them.

"I wonder if race is really important," Vicki says. "For so long there has been a separation of the races, and then look what *happens. In my craziest dreams I would never have imagined my life now. And the Lord kind of waltzed me into it."*

"When I heard people say," Ned smiles over at Vicki, *"'This white mama can't raise this boy,' I thought,* Guess what? His mama was a white mama, so you bet she can raise him!"

"That helped me," says Vicki, *"I felt a connection with the first two white birthmothers, but that was just the first step. He led us on to our full black children, and by then we were ready. I feel so close to this last one's birthmother. It's been a glorious experience. We went to meet her, and it opened up many doors to my heart that I didn't know were there."*

"Do you remember," Ned starts walking towards the shed, *"the black sisters who walked from Ohio to Nauvoo and ended up at the Mansion House? Jane, the one who stayed to live with Joseph and Emma was offered adoption by them. . . ."*

"I think she refused," says Vicki, *"but came on west with the Church, always stayed loyal."*

"Wilford Woodruff," Ned adds, *"adopted three Native American children, and Lorenzo Snow had one. We have good company!"*

Perhaps when all members of the Church, the nation, and the world catch up with the pure desires of prophets who plead to the Lord for equal opportunities to bless *all* people, this earth will feel a bit like heaven.

NOTES

1. Sonia L. Nazario, "When White Parents Adopt Black Babies, Race Often Divides," *The Wall Street Journal,* September 12, 1990, p. A1.

2. Rita Simon and Howard Alstein, as quoted by Arnold Silverman and William Feigelman, "Adjustment in Interracial Adoptees: An Overview," in *The Psychology of Adoption,* ed. David M. Brodzinsky and Marshall D. Schechter (New York: Oxford University Press, 1990), p. 195.

3. Silverman and Feigelman,"Adjustment in Interracial Adoptees: An Overview," in *The Psychology of Adoption*, pp. 198–99.

4. Owen Gill and Barbara Jackson, *Adoption and Race* (New York: St. Martin's Press, 1983).

5. Christopher Bagley and Loretta Young, as cited in John Triseliotis, Joan Shireman, and Marion Hundleby, *Adoption: Theory, Policy, and Practice* (London: Cassell, 1997), p. 169.

6. Rita Simon, Howard Alstein, and Marygold S. Melli, *The Case for Transracial Adoption* (Washington, D. C.: The American University Press, 1994), p. 61.

7. Marcus Mabry, "Whose Kids Are They?" *Newsweek*, April 14, 1997, p. 46.

8. Elizabeth Herzog, Cecelia Sudia, and Jane Harwood, as cited in Silverman and Feigleman, "Adjustment in Interracial Adoptees: An Overview," p. 191.

9. Triseliotis, Shireman, and Hundleby, *Adoption: Theory, Policy, and Practice*, pp. 178–79.

10. Christopher Bagley, *International and Transracial Adoptions* (Aldershot, England: Avebury, 1993), pp. 214-39.

11. Brian Butler, "Adopting an Indigenous Approach," *Adoption and Fostering* 13, no. 2 (1989), as cited in Triseliotis, Shireman, and Hundleby, *Adoption: Theory, Policy, and Practice*, p. 170.

12. Dan O'Brien, in Gail Steinberg, "Dan O'Brien—The World's Best Athlete: A Transracially Adopted Hero," *Up Close and Personal: Personal Profiles* www.pactadopt.org: Pact, An Adoption Alliance, 1998.

13. Simon, Alstein, and Melli, *The Case for Transracial Adoption*, pp. 71–104.

14. Ibid., p. 104.

15. Ibid., p. 95.

16. Pact, An Adoption Alliance in San Francisco has questionnaires available on the Internet at http://www.pactadopt.org or through mail at 3450 Sacramento Street #239, San Francisco, CA 94118.

17. Triseliotis, Shireman, and Hundleby, *Adoption: Theory, Policy, and Practice*, p. 195.

*In every nation he that feareth him, and worketh
righteousness, is accepted with him.*
Acts 10:35

10
LAYERS OF HOPE
INTERCOUNTRY ADOPTION AND
CONFLICTING VALUES

---

*Madeline studied in Mainland China while her grandpa taught
at a university in Xi'an during the 1993–94 school year.*

*"We walked together through the temple gates in Luoyang,"
Madeline says. "To the right was a line of people by the ticket
booth. To the left, lying all alone against a large wooden pedestal
was an infant girl. A bottle was tucked in her blanket, so I
guessed she hadn't been there very long. It was August, and this
little baby was dressed in layers of clothes, like the mother was
saying, 'Here's everything she owns—you won't have to buy
more.' My friend was traveling with us; she was very upset."*

*"'I could take care of the baby,' she said. 'I know my parents
would adopt her.'*

*"'Don't interfere,' Grandpa told her. 'It may be like a bird leav-
ing the nest, you could ruin the chick's future by touching. Let the
Chinese people handle it; they have their own system.'*

*"A large crowd gathered around us; the birthmother might still
have been watching. Afraid of becoming attached to the orphaned
baby we couldn't help, I walked on past a Buddhist statue into the
inner yard filled with little shops where people were selling*

incense and trinkets. Our Chinese hosts explained, 'Occasionally a boy is abandoned and he will be carried on into the temple and raised by the monks, but the girls are usually taken to an orphanage.'"

WORLD EVENTS AFFECTING AVAILABILITY

China's "one-child" policy left close to a half-million babies (mostly girls) in institutions or foster care.[1] Without compulsory abortions the number would be far greater. An overwhelming preference for sons, a reflection of economic need as well as traditional religious values, complicates matters even more. In 1995 China became the largest foreign supplier of babies to the United States, contributing more than 4,200 female infants per year, which is more than one-fourth of current international adoptions annually.

Fewer than 500 children from India—where 25 million children remain in institutional care—are adopted each year by parents in the United States. Muslim belief does not allow for children to be raised outside the faith. Hindu orphans can be adopted only by members of their own caste. There remain a quarter million children, mostly girls, in non-Muslim institutions who could be adopted yearly.

The situation of parents in China and India today is similar to that in Western Europe at the close of the thirteenth century, when the vast increase in population filled the cities and countrysides and drained their resources. Institutions were thus established for the care of abandoned children. Tragically, society held the naive assumption that children were well-cared for within these institutions. Social philosopher Jean-Jacques Rousseau explained in his *Confessions:*

> My third child was thus deposited in a foundling home just like the first two, and I did the same with the two following: I had five in all. This arrangement seemed to me so good, so sensible, so appropriate, that if I did not boast of it publicly it was solely out of regard for their mother. . . . In a word, I made no secret of my action . . . because in fact I saw no wrong in it. All things considered, I chose what was best for my children, or what I thought was best.[2]

Even more tragic, the establishment of these foundling hospitals in Western Europe facilitated abandonment. During the time that Rousseau lived in Paris, three-fourths of the children in institutions died before the age of twelve, as compared to one-fourth when reared at home. It wasn't that no one cared about what happened; few people knew. Ordinary citizens thought the disappearance of unwanted infants from view was a sign of social advancement.

In the eighteenth century death rates in America's foundling homes soared along with European figures to more than a 90 percent mortality rate. Charles Loring Brace, founder of the New York Children's Aid Society, believed that family life was a far better solution. "The best of all asylums for the outcast child," he said, "is the farmer's home."[3] He began the orphan train movement during the 1800s in which thousands of dependent children from eastern cities were transported by railroad to live with families in western states.

After World War I and the ensuing influenza outbreak, low birth rates in the United States activated private brokers to earn huge profits by arranging adoption placements; likewise, the number of adoption agencies increased to compete with the demand. Gradually, adoption was regulated in all states and the District of Columbia, requiring the fitness of prospective parents to be approved by the court. Five states—Delaware, Connecticut, Massachusetts, Minnesota, and Michigan—allow only agency-approved placements while the others allow independent, non-agency adoptions as well.

Would-be parents began seeking international adoptions after World War II. In 1948, 3,000 Japanese and 840 Chinese children, hundreds from Germany, as well as 1,806 from Greece were adopted in the United States. The Korean War left another large group of children parentless. South Korea's severely depressed economy sustained a continuing adoption program during which more than 100,000 Korean children were placed in families throughout the Western world, many in the United States.

THE ASIAN AND LATIN AMERICAN EXPERIENCE

Studies on the adoption of Asian children by American or European parents show excellent outcomes—particularly surprising since many of the children were more than a year old when adopted and had experienced abandonment, malnutrition, and varied care in orphanages. Children adopted as a result of the Vietnam War have consistently demonstrated the same positive adaptation. Vietnamese children have "a major spirit or trait of hardiness and achievement orientation,"[4] explains adoption expert Christopher Bagley.

Though war fostered many intercountry placements in the mid-twentieth century, it is not the only form of accumulated suffering that affects adoption. The spontaneous flow of children for adoption out of Latin America since the 1970s is a good example of this. The adoption process is different in each country, and inconsistent, depending on the national leadership in power. In *Adoption in Worldwide Perspective,* a publication of world adoption studies, a Latin American respondent said: "Intercountry adoption of Latin American children has caused concern, misunderstanding, and, at times, suspicion of foul dealing . . . due largely to lack of information about a phenomenon that is relatively new in Latin America, together with the sensational coverage that the media accord this issue."[5] Despite problems, sociologist Francisco J. Pilotti concludes that since adoption represents a solution to the plight of many of Latin America's abandoned children it is worth the effort to preserve.

Studies in Sweden, Holland, Britain, Germany, and the United States show outcomes for Latin American children equally as favorable as other transracial and same-race placements within a country. Studies consistently reflect good health, linguistic, and emotional adjustment. There may have been problems when these children arrived, but with timely and appropriate care solutions were typically found. These same studies, however, raise some concerns about racial identification and discrimination.

"I worked through an attorney," Nancy says, "who flew to Honduras and visited orphanages and hospitals. He located my son, Mike, and a little girl. I wanted to raise two together, but it

never worked out and now I know why." Nancy leans over her desk.

"Two would have been my death as a single parent!" She bursts out laughing. Nancy's long sandy curls keep her looking young; she is short and trim. "Because, as you probably know, older adopted children come manipulative, streetwise. I was so caught up in loving this little live wire that I didn't see those problems at first. Once I had established patterns, it was too hard to change. I've lived with behavior I don't think is for his betterment or mine, but we do have a relationship."

"You see, I really wanted a child," Nancy says. "There were no men in my life at the time and I felt part of me was missing. Three years of deep soul searching passed before I contacted the attorney. I learned a little Spanish and flew down carrying Mike's photo, Spanish storybooks, and clothing. I got there Friday night and visited the orphanage the following day. When they brought him out, I lost it—grabbed for my sunglasses, wiping tears away."

"'Do you want this woman to be your mom?' they said. He acted like, 'You're not getting away from me!' It was as if he had grippers on the backs of his hands. He waved good-bye to everyone at the orphanage. We spent the rest of the day together. That night I put him in pajamas, and read him a story in bed. Then he got up, went over to the closet—started taking off his pajamas and putting on his clothes—he thought it was time to go back to the orphanage, that the outing was over!" Nancy tilts forward in her chair. The phone rings; she ignores it.

"I don't know how much Mike's been influenced by his early environment. The first two years of his life were spent with the mother who was malnourished when she gave birth, the second two were in the orphanage. Whenever I tried to find out more about his background they told me I was asking too many questions. But I was required to live in his country for two months and I watched the people there work just as hard as I do to survive. The children in the family I stayed with studied like demons, like college kids. However, I can't seem to motivate Mike—I can't turn him into what I think he should be. Mike has excellent social skills but he flounders in the classroom." Nancy speaks fast, directly.

"I'm a schoolteacher from way back; it breaks my heart. Mike's

hyperactive, easily distracted. He stayed on medication for several years but it caused paranoia and now, at his age, the medication has a street value. He says he wants to be a businessman, an entrepreneur. I don't see a whole lot of follow-through yet—he's a big talker, but he's just fourteen." The phone rings again. Nancy's flower shop is filling with customers.

"I hold my breath every day. I just need to get Mike through these middle school years because at this age he doesn't want to be different from anyone else. He definitely feels discriminated against and wants to have his Spanish name, Manuel, removed. He doesn't have as many Spanish friends as black; colored skin, rather than the nationality, seems to be an equalizer. They're 'bros' when they're darker, except for his best friend now who's white."

"I'm coming to help you—" she calls out to workers in the next room, *"—hang in there."*

"The way Mike looks these days is pretty good. A couple of months ago he wore all black—dressed by his mood—black shirt, black pants, and a black face, really scowling. He has a tender side though, even with no interest in religion for himself, he is encouraging to me. When I traveled one Sunday and stayed home sick the next he said, 'You're grouchy. If you'd go to church maybe you wouldn't be so hard to live with.'" Nancy laughs. *"He nailed me!"*

Intercountry adoption is a demanding option. Single parenting is additionally challenging. Single adults who are willing to take on such dual responsibilities are selfless and strong. Most important, however, is that they be aware of the deficits inherent in their situations and prepare to compensate. LDS Family Services is posited to facilitate "ideal" placements as often as possible. The LDS Church does not encourage single-parent adoptions, as evidenced by its agency policy that places all babies with temple-worthy couples. Notwithstanding, there are older abandoned children and unmarried adults—both single and excluded from the ideal family model through no fault of their own—who are sometimes led to find each other through other means. Their path may require more persistence and creativity.

"Being a single parent is hard and not good for a child," says a single woman (trained as a family and marriage counselor) who adopted. "If asked whether I would encourage someone else who is single to adopt, my answer would be 'Absolutely not!' I have to work harder than ever to get good role models, work harder at discipline. I wouldn't trade my situation because it all came together in such a miraculous way, and thankfully I have a wonderful family support system, but I didn't realize how hard it would be. It is gradually working out fine but is definitely *not* ideal."

Racial prejudice impacts the adjustment of children adopted internationally just as it does their availability. Brazil has no waiting list on adoptions, allows singles and people over forty to adopt, and requires only a week to ten days in the country for completion of legal procedures. Brazil had a slave trade in earlier years and much of its population, including the children available for adoption, is of African descent and therefore darker skinned. But adoption in Chile is more difficult to achieve because even the poor children, more likely to be available, tend to be very light skinned, a preference for the vast majority of adopters, who are white.

Since the 1970s, when the first Latin American children were adopted into this country, most have come from Colombia where the populace is a mix of Spanish and indigenous inhabitants. Since 1995 the number of orphaned children coming out of Guatemala has greatly increased so that it now leads, by a substantial margin, all adoptions from Latin American countries.

In intercountry adoptions it is important to obtain all possible information about the child and her country before adoption, and all helpful assistance from pediatricians, speech therapists, and family counselors after the child arrives. The first children adopted from Latin American countries are now reaching adulthood.

Kara and Marcie are both comely, petite young women who

were born in South America and adopted into a white New Jersey family as small children. Kara was taken from an orphanage when she was less than a year old, Marcie was four. Kara has now graduated from high school. She's enjoying her summer vacation before going off to college. Marcie left home during high school to marry a Cuban. She got pregnant and moved in with his family after their baby was born. But now she's back in school working for her GED and housecleaning to buy extra presents for her child.

Kara interprets her past as better than Marcie's, but their environment in the United States has been very similar. They've both been raised in the same stable and loving Latter-day Saint home. Kara has always been aware that she belonged to her new family; Marcie never got past feelings of rejection. Kara does well in school, catches on quickly, and thinks deeply. Marcie reads on a twelfth grade level but her reasoning ability tests like a fourth grader.

"The difference between Marcie and me," Kara says, "is our background—how much time we were uncared for in the past." Kara and I sit together on a bench near the boardwalk.

"Marcie's parents were probably killed or something. Her grandmother brought her to the orphanage because she couldn't care for her. That has always bothered Marcie, along with all the other negative things in her life. It was harder for her to trust people. Marcie didn't know if she could trust me at first," Kara says. "She's never had another close friend that stayed attached. For years we felt connected because of our race, but our friendship is strong now and separate from that. Marcie has darker skin. She said the kids in school used to be mean—said she was dirty—and Marcie used to dwell on her racial difference. I think about it but not until it takes over. I kind of accept it. I never had that kind of a problem.

"Marcie has sought friends of the same ethnic background. I haven't; they've just come, from Puerto Rico, Mexico—and we do have some things in common. All of us know we could have lived in another country, which is kind of exciting, but it doesn't make us sad that we didn't grow up there. We just fit in with each other because of that similarity. It's a feeling—it's not what anybody

says. But I wouldn't like it if all my friends were foreign." Kara pauses, watching the lawn crew mow the grass around us.

"I want to be an international airline attendant," Kara says. "I want to travel to Europe, the Middle East, to see the earth and all the people that go with it. I want to serve a mission. There are so many things I need to think about. My Mom and I are close, we're always doing things together. We're interested in the same kind of things; she's an English teacher and I write poems about world problems. My Dad is strong and kind. He's given me the feeling of always being protected. And I love my sister. I know she believes in the gospel. I wrote about adoption but it's never been a big issue for me. It's not as big a difference between people as race. And the poem's only fiction—the orphanage probably wasn't that bad." Kara smiles. "I'm happy with my life."

WHY REGULATIONS?

Elizabeth Bartholet is a Harvard professor who adopted two Latin American children. In her book *Family Bonds: Adoption and the Politics of Parenting* she says, "From start to finish, international adoption involves an enormous amount of process with very little substance." From personal experience she concludes, "We need to deregulate adoption. The current framework creates obstacles on both a pragmatic and psychological level: it makes the adoption process costly and unpleasant, and it simultaneously degrades and demeans this form of family. . . . We need new policies that focus on the positive rather than the negative potential."[6]

By contrast, Christopher Bagley contends: "The United States is the major importer of babies for adoption, and through its lack of control over legal and social procedures through which intercountry adoptions are financed and arranged, this country is a major cause of the corrupt system which surrounds some intercountry adoptions."[7] Since intercountry adoption in the United States is often accomplished through independent, non-regulated agencies and third party negotiators—possibly even to make a profit—it is imperative that individual participants guard against every risk of abuse to what some believe is a threatened institution.

Serious allegations have been made of illegal involvement

in the placing of babies for international adoption, including sale of babies by the Mafia, kidnapping of babies from poor and transient women, and purchase of babies from poor sections of large cities with enticingly large amounts of money. Of twelve countries where these allegations have been raised since 1980, four are in Latin America. This emphasizes the need for at least some regulation. Many infractions in the process flourish when international adoption is pursued before the troubled foreign country has time to address its own problems.

Romania is another of the twelve disparaged countries where the United Nations' well-enunciated principles on international adoption were ignored. When the traditional government of Romania toppled in December of 1989 there was extensive TV coverage of the 14,000 "abandoned" children suffering in terribly inadequate care facilities. While the new government was busy handling other areas of reform, couples from Europe and North America rushed in and negotiated to take many of these children back home with them, before it was clear whether their biological parents had agreed. The government subsequently banned adoptions until strict procedures were in place.

The United Nations declared a Convention on the Rights of the Child in 1989 to protect the interests of children who may be considered for intercountry adoption. The Hague Convention for the Protection of Children published initiatives in 1993—the work of representatives from fifty-seven sending and receiving countries—which divided up responsibilities to ensure that the *child* is protected at both ends of an intercountry placement.

THE CHALLENGES OF EASTERN EUROPE

With the dissolution of the U.S.S.R. in 1991, Russia and adjoining states have become open to intercountry adoption with emerging systems of control. Since 1995 the number of intercountry adoptions in the United States has risen by half, with more than a third of the children coming from Eastern Europe. Because these children are Caucasian, they do not face the racial discrimination of other children adopted from abroad. But, according to a four-year study at the International Adoption Clinic at the New England Medical Center in Boston,[8] more than a quarter of the children have had serious medical conditions that went unrecognized prior to adoption, and only half of the children were developmentally normal. The natural resilience of most of these children, in combination with the patience and care of their parents, make prospects good, but problems have been far more pervasive than anticipated. The consensus among professional caregivers is that adopted children from the orphanages of Eastern Europe and the Russian Federation demand more attention than any other intercountry placements.[9]

The small audience spreads out around the library auditorium. Spotlights illuminate the aisle in front of the stage, where a table has been set up with stacks of handouts. Those in attendance choose to sit in the shadows. They are mostly couples, but in the middle, third row back, are five middle-aged, single women.

The meeting is efficient. The lady in charge explains and answers questions on information, which includes an application form and step-by-step written procedures for the Ukrainian or Russian Adoption Program. The fee for the program is $300, plus $140 for the Immigration and Naturalization Advance Processing of Orphan Petition. The list of required paperwork follows, including an additional $325 home study fee.

She moves on to step two. "Now you will be prepared to travel and identify a child from the orphanage. Below are the associated costs." The Foreign Source Fee of $4,500 includes procuring the actual adoption as well as the calculated sum for a driver and translator, an orphanage humanitarian aid fee, and a foreign adoption center fee. Then follows the train fare, housing for ten to fourteen days, and the Russian Embassy fee for the legalization of documents, all listed before the $1,000 airline travel cost per person. Individuals around the room are adding the figures. There is an additional escort/translator expense to get to the Ukraine. Several couples leave.

Then the lady in charge turns on her charm. She is wearing a plaid skirt and red sweater, but her handsome face and flowing

*brunette hair draw attention overall. She relaxes with her subject;
everyone does. This woman is the mother of a large family,
including five children who are internationally adopted. She has
gone with her husband to Russia and the Ukraine. She recounts
their fear going through customs, standing before the city coun-
cils to be evaluated, and entering the orphanages.*

*"All I wanted was a fundamentally healthy child. I have been a
nurse and could look past pus coming out of ears and noses, to
signs of permanent dysfunction. But what captured my heart was
a child who had been placed in a crib far off in the corner. He was
blind. My heart said, 'I want the child no one else will take, who
needs help the most.'*

*"What other kinds of problems do these kids generally have?"
a man asks.*

*"Hepatitis B is almost a given. Malnourishment can—"
Other couples leave.*

*"Don't let the money discourage you," she says. A hardy rem-
nant remain. "A year ago our family sold Christmas trees to pay
for our last trip. Children with handicaps cost substantially less."*

The meeting ends with a lull.

*"One more thing," she adds, "Please respect my office hours. I
take calls from 1:00 to 3:00 P.M. on Tuesdays and Thursdays only.
I don't make any money. The most important thing to me is my
family. If this service ever interferes with them, I will not be able
to continue."*

*People collect around her and a couple leaving for Russia the
next week. An attorney, who offers to handle stateside re-
adoption[10] for $175 plus the filing fee, answers questions as well.*

*For forty-five minutes couples stand and converse, absorbed in
their interest with another corner of the world. They are upper-
middle-class Americans, nice looking people who don't stand out.
Finally, one single woman gets a chance with the lady in charge.
She's wearing a blue nylon parka and white tennis shoes.*

*"I think this is something I can do," she says. She sways back
and forth, puts her hands in her pockets. "I want to care for a
child, especially a handicapped child. I'm glad a single woman
could be considered acceptable."*

ETHICAL DEBATE

Since ancient times adoption has been a crucial means of supplying good options to birthparents but not necessarily in the exclusive way we see it implemented in the United States today.[11] There are culturally traditional types of adoption that Americans must comprehend and respect if they will be able to fairly evaluate the rightness of intercountry placements. For instance, Christopher Bagley wrote about the end of the "Biafra war" in Nigeria, where more than 10,000 children were immediately labeled as orphans by Western relief groups and destined to be put in orphanages or evacuated. One plane was even chartered for the children's rescue. "Yet in truth no child in Nigeria is ever an orphan," Bagley says. "In Africa, children are prized, and the duties of caring and socialization fall not just on the immediate parents, but on the whole community."[12] As a result a number of local social workers were allowed several months of careful searching and were able to place all but forty-two severely handicapped children with local families.

The world now divides into two camps on the issue of intercountry adoption. Some believe that it is humane and charitable to remove seemingly unwanted children from lives of poverty to material comfort and opportunity. Others see it as imperialistic and self-serving—a form of colonialism in which domineering countries seize weaker countries' natural resources. Since the difference in opinion is far broader than the issue of race, some supporters of transracial adoption within a country still remain ambiguous about intercountry placements.

Opponents point to a gigantic cultural value difference between developing and industrialized countries that challenges the intercountry concept. These critics, who believe that children must grow to love and respect their origins, don't think adoptive parents can possibly comprehend or communicate a heritage they don't share. In addition, many anthropologists, philosophers, and historians aren't sure industrialized nations have net gains to offer children above their Third World neighbors. David Maybury-Lewis in *Millennium: Tribal Wisdom and the Modern World,* illustrates this concern from the work of Emile Durkheim, French social theorist and founder of sociology. Durkheim "conducted an exhaustive study of tribal and traditional societies and concluded that they absorbed the individual into the community, providing social support at the cost of constraint. Modern society, on the other hand, liberated the individual but at the cost of doing away with the sense of community."[13]

Also to be considered in addressing intercountry adoptions is the future of the traditional family. Societal emphasis on equality between adults in America's families of today threatens the nationally stated adoption premise—to value the child. The 1990s have yielded the first generation in this nation's history to do worse psychologically, socially, and economically than its parents. Surveys reveal that "fewer than half of all adult Americans today regard the idea of sacrifice for others as a positive moral virtue."[14] Religious and social leaders are hopeful that the deterioration of the two-parent family has leveled off.

Political philosopher William Galston points out that the erosion of the two-parent family is not an irresistible undertow. "It is more like a swift current," he says, "against which it is possible to swim. People learn; societies can change, particularly when it becomes apparent that certain behaviors damage the social ecology, threaten the public order, and impose new burdens on core institutions."[15]

The family is the best environment in which to teach children moral behavior, to distinguish right from wrong. The family is the basic unit of The Church of Jesus Christ of Latter-day Saints. A strong, two-parent family, where the gospel is lived and cherished, is likely to be attached to extended family and become its own community. Children can grow safely within it and still be liberated as individuals to make their own choices. Children adopted into such a family unit have the maximum opportunity to grow. The family is the topic addressed in "A Proclamation to the World," read by President Gordon B. Hinckley on September 23, 1995. "The family is ordained of God," it states. "Marriage between man and woman is essential to His eternal plan. Children are entitled to birth within the bonds of matrimony, and to be reared by a father and a mother who honor marital vows with complete fidelity. Happiness in family life is most likely to be achieved when founded upon the teachings of the Lord Jesus Christ. Successful marriages and families are established and maintained on principles of faith, prayer, repentance, forgiveness, respect, love, compassion, work, and wholesome recreational activities." All parents who follow this admonition can have a positive influence not only in the lives of their children but also in family trends throughout their country and the world.

So it is not growing up in a country with technology and science that gives a child an advantage. It is because that child is free to receive knowledge beyond any age in history—a heritage that she can then more fully transmit to others. That blessing of opportunity, so fully offered through the gospel of Jesus Christ, is what justifies intercountry placements.

A CONTINUING NEED

Birthparents in all ages and all places who are not able to care for their offspring have been faced with remarkably similar choices. They must choose to relinquish their child to a person or institution capable of giving care, to abandon the child, or to eliminate the offspring through infanticide or abortion. It is always tragic when birthparents don't have an option—or don't believe they have one—other than to eliminate or abandon their offspring. It is also indisputably tragic when parents choose to release their parental rights and there is no receiver to accept the offering—no one to assure that their child will have fair opportunity in life.

Certainly, willing parents are on hand. Since the number of babies available for adoption has diminished with contraceptives and abortions during the last twenty-five years, would-be adoptive parents have increased in number. In addition, one-sixth of American couples between the ages of fifteen and forty-five are now estimated to have some type of infertility. The figures are similar in Europe, where a lower birth rate depleted the supply of babies for adoption even earlier.

Clearly, there are some countries in which parents need help for their children and other countries where parents want to help. In spite of the conflicting yet powerfully defensible arguments for or against intercountry adoption, rightful intercountry adoption has its place for the present. The ideal time—when all countries can care for their own—is still far in the future. Extreme critics encourage an ideology that cannot save the huge number of infants and children whose lives are in peril now. Adoption, however, may provide a family—in place of an institution—for those children.

Crucial to perpetuation of intercountry adoption is sensitivity to a country's national pride. When Korea hosted the 1988 Olympic Games, commentators cynically suggested that the country's chief export was babies. The nation was publicly embarrassed, spotlighted for the inability to take care of its own children. As a result South Korea, which then accounted for more than half the adoptions coming into this country, increased the availability of abortions and started cutting back its foreign adoption program.

As a practical matter, there are strong personal incentives that entice many people to choose an intercountry placement. Some adults simply feel thwarted trying to adopt within the United States. Other potential parents favor confidentiality in a country where openness is encouraged. Single adults, who have a difficult time adopting within the United States, may be looking for an infant or young child without serious problems. Others may fear the courts; "There's no chance of a Baby Richard coming out of China," they say, remembering the front page newspaper photos of a young boy being taken from his adoptive parents when reclaimed by a birthparent he had not yet met.

Ken parks a rental car outside. He looks cosmopolitan—wavy dark hair and a trimmed beard. Under his jacket he wears a turtleneck shirt and a medallion.

"When I was hired to work on a development project in Indonesia," he says, "Shelley was pregnant. The doctor here in America thought he had heard two heartbeats. But by the time we were situated and went to the hospital in Bandung there was only one. We considered adopting a second, so we told the doctor, and

he offered to assist. 'I have a baby in mind,' he said. Then sud-
denly he hesitated. 'What religion are you?' he asked; then he
retorted, 'No, I won't help! Mormons are not Christians.' He was
adamant immediately, and nothing I said could convince him oth-
erwise. Then I pursued a search by talking to the consulate and
others in government organizations. Finally someone told us
about a man who was running a place in back of his house for
orphaned babies." Ken crosses one gangly leg over the other,
stretching back his shoulders.

"*We went to the man's house and he quickly gave us the*
impression we could get a baby girl almost immediately, to go
with our infant daughter.

"'*You may have to pay a million rupiah,' he told us, 'for all the*
arrangements.'

He encouraged us to look out back at the kids; he had about a
dozen living in a shed. Some looked pretty good. Then we saw
Sam—big stomach, big head, toothpick legs. He was not accepted
by the others, cried a lot and had no front teeth; at eighteen
months old they were rotted out.

"'*You can have Achmed if you want,' he said. That was Sam's*
name. 'Take him tonight.'

"*We needed time to think about it. The man became upset,*
angry. When we returned a few days later, he assured us the
adoption would be complete in two weeks to a month. We were
worried about Sammy's bones; would he ever get permanent
teeth? An American doctor at the embassy examined him. He
could find no problem other than the need for a good diet, and
Sammy was not allergic to milk as we had been told. We poured it
into him." Ken's medallion sways on a thin leather strap.

"*In Indonesia, adoption comes under the regulation of each*
province," he says. "So we started out in a court forty kilometers
from Bandung. We were required to pay up front for the whole
process. There were problems, not enough money, we paid more.
After a couple of months, they couldn't complete the process
because the government had stopped all foreign adoptions.

"*We tried right from the first to abide by every legal stipula-*
tion but there was no way we could give Sammy back. We
changed our official residence to another province and started

again, with a different agency, for another fee. After two years the court told us 'yes,' but that we must have the mother give Sam up in court. We nearly died!"

Ken has lived in Egypt, Turkey, and New Delhi. He is comfortable negotiating in foreign countries.

"We tried to find her; we went back to the orphanage, the hospital, paying thousands of rupiah each place. The birthmother had paid her delivery bill by letting the hospital keep her baby, a very common practice. All we knew was her first name, Endang, the same as twenty million other women in Indonesia. Finally the agency said, 'We've found the mother.' But our problems didn't end there—we had to go to Singapore to request clearance." Ken grins. He's eager to report on Sam—now a junior in high school.

"Sam sings, plays electric guitar, is an all-star soccer player, 'A' student, particularly gifted in art, drawing, and his vocabulary is incredible."

"Is he isolated racially?" I ask.

"He's in an ethnically diverse school district but he was beaten up the second day after we moved to California. Some older kid said, 'You're Spanish.'

"'No.'

"'You're lying.'

"Sam avoids that kind of confrontation now. He is cautious in new situations, works his way in gradually. Race has made a difference in his life. But Sam," Ken chuckles, "is not shy."

The essence of life transcends cultural groups. Individuals must be sufficiently free from fear and must want to search out a personal destiny, to discover inner strength and purpose beyond themselves. The ultimate value for any orphaned or abandoned child may be a family that can provide such freedom. And parents who take upon them such a responsibility have "a sacred duty," according to the First Presidency and Twelve Apostles, "to provide for their [children's] physical and spiritual needs, to teach them to love and serve one another, to observe the commandments of God and to be law-abiding citizens wherever they live."

Birthparents in foreign lands may also seek freedom of

opportunity for their deprived children by consciously and lovingly transferring their parental rights to adoptive parents who, they believe, will offer them a better life.

A middle-aged, middle-income white couple went to Africa for their two children. Everything had been arranged previously by correspondence. The couple sensed resistance as they entered the small village.

"We will not take the children," they told the birthmother, "if this will cause disturbance."

"Please," she begged. "The village will forget next week, next month. But my children have their lives ahead of them. There is no opportunity or hope of change here."

NOTES

1. Christopher Bagley, *International and Transracial Adoptions* (Aldershot, England: Avebury, 1993), p. 189.

2. Jean-Jacques Rousseau, *Confessions,* 8th ed., trans. Jacques Voisine (Paris, 1964), p. 424. Rousseau did subsequently regret his actions.

3. Charles Loring Brace, as quoted in Elizabeth S. Cole and Kathryn S. Donley, "History, Values, and Placement Policy Issues in Adoption," in *The Psychology of Adoption,* ed. David M. Brodzinsky and Marshall D. Schechter (New York: Oxford University Press, 1990), p. 275.

4. Bagley, *International and Transracial Adoptions,* p. 213.

5. Francisco Pilotti, "Intercountry Adoption: A View from Latin America" in René A. C. Hoksbergen, *Adoption in Worldwide Perspective* (Berwyn, Ill.: Swets North America, 1986), p. 143.

6. Elizabeth Bartholet, *Family Bonds: Adoption and Politics of Parenting* (Boston: Houghton Mifflin Co., 1986), pp. 149, 231.

7. Bagley, *International and Transracial Adoptions,* p. 174.

8. Patricia King and Kendall Hamilton, "Bringing Kids All the Way Home," *Newsweek,* June 16, 1997, pp. 63–65.

9. Margaret Talbot, "Attachment Theory: The Ultimate Experiment," *The New York Times Magazine,* May 24, 1998, pp. 24–54.

10. A second, stateside-adoption procedure is required once a child has arrived in the United States. Children from Russia, for example, must be formally adopted a first time in their own country before they are permitted to leave.

11. Adoption has a rich history, which reflects an ever-present tension between the interests of adults and children. Adoption was already a complex issue in ancient Babylon in 1750 B.C., as documented in the

Code of Hammurabi. Addressed in the legal code was everything from the compatibility of adopter and adoptee to the conditions under which adoptees could search for their birthparents. The law mandated that birthparents had no right to demand back their child after adoption but also stated that transgressions by adoptees against their adoptive parents were grounds for returning the child.

Instances of child displacement during Canaanite history in the ancient Middle East instilled the concept that giving up a child could lead to a greater destiny. Abraham cast off his young son, Ishmael, who went on to become the progenitor of the Arabs. Soon after, Abraham was commanded to sacrifice his other son, Isaac, who through divine intervention was preserved to become the progenitor of the Israelites. Later, Moses' mother contrived a plan so that Pharaoh's daughter would find him and "adopt" him. These stories convey the concept that parental love is important, but not inherently irreconcilable with relinquishing a child.

Christianity popularized adoption. Christians claimed that as a group they had been substituted—not unlike an abandoned child—for the posterity of Abraham and were all adopted into Christianity with a birth through baptism.

"He was born of my kindness," an adoptive father said of his acquired son during the Roman Empire. Ancient adoption was prompted by abandonment, "a voluntary relinquishing of a child by their natal parents," according to James Boswell in his book *The Kindness of Strangers* (New York: Pantheon Books, 1988). Abandonment, translated from the Greek, means an offering or a putting out, implying the placement of the child outside the home, usually in a public place, where she would be noticed. A common name given to abandoned children of antiquity was *Eutyche*, meaning happily found. The relationship appealed to many because it was voluntary and drew its strength from personal ties of love and kindness.

Boswell estimates that during the first three centuries A.D., when the rate of abandonment for urban children was between 20 and 40 percent, a majority of women who had reared more than one child had also abandoned at least one. A broad acceptance of abandonment had emerged because it was so commonly unavoidable for poor parents, who were driven by necessity, to expose or sell their children. Parents traditionally left an abandoned child with a token—a ring, a ribbon, a painting, an article of clothing, or the material in which the baby was wrapped—to alert the finder to the child's status and make it possible for the parents to identify the child if she should meet them again later.

Even now, parents who adopt Chinese children often find mysterious marks on their child's body, possibly a form of token.

In Europe, Boswell says, abandonment was encouraged for parents unable to care for their babies. By the ninth century A.D. marble basins were designated for the safe placement of abandoned children, and a canonical decree imposed severe penalties for infanticide. While social classes remained fluid, the hopefulness associated with adoption made it often "the cure for chance"—what one lacked in birth could be remedied by adoption. Gradually it became popular in Europe to donate children to the church, a practice called *oblation*. Carried to its extreme, children were relinquished not just because their parents were destitute, but to prevent the fragmentation of an estate and maximize the inheritance of older children. As class structure solidified, would-be parents—who pretended children were their biological heirs in order to preserve property—hid the identity of abandoned children.

Christopher Bagley, in *International and Transracial Adoption*, documented an intensive study of foreign adoptions that gives a clearer picture of systemized approaches to adoption throughout the world. In East Africa, for instance, the Lou people traditionally abandoned their "taboo children" (born of too-close relatives, or one child of triplets) close to Nandi settlements because the "Nandi people were known to be especially generous in taking in abandoned children." In India, Bagley says, where Hindus established a caste system, adoption became a traditional practice perpetuated amongst equals. In the highest castes, parents having no male heir arrange and memorialize adoptions with elaborate religious ceremony. Even the lowest caste adopts; but the children of the sub-castes—the poorest of the poor because of a presumptive sinfulness in a prior existence—are not eligible. In Arabia the Prophet Mohammed in the seventh century A.D. forbade adoption after his own adopted son divorced the wife chosen for him by Mohammed himself. A divine injunction written into the Koran has tended to sustain a prohibition on adoption by many Muslims. But current interpretation by American Muslim Imad-ad-Dean Ahmad clarifies that adoption, called *kafala*, translates best as "foster parenting" and is within Islamic law if the children adopted are able to retain knowledge of their "identity by blood" (see Amad, Imad-ad-Dean, "The Islamic View of Adoption," in *Adoption Factbook III,* [Waite Park, Minn.: Park Press Quality Printing, Inc., 1999], pp. 245–46).

12. Bagley, *International and Transracial Adoptions,* p. 163.
13. David Maybury-Lewis, *Millennium: Tribal Wisdom and the Modern World* (New York: Viking, 1992), p. 88.

14. Barbara D. Whitehead, "Dan Quayle Was Right," *Atlantic Monthly,* April 1993, pp. 58, 84.

15. William Galston, as quoted by Barbara D. Whitehead in "Dan Quayle Was Right," p. 84.

Do justice to the afflicted and needy.
Psalm 82:3

11

THE GROCERY CART
SPECIAL NEEDS ADOPTION

Perhaps prospective parents cannot anticipate whether they desire to adopt a child with disabilities until seeing one who is available. The individual soul, imbued with a feeling of its own purpose, can rarely foresee its course. It feels the force of destiny within itself but then must search out its own direction, its own application of inner promptings. Some people are inherently drawn in a direction that helps to compensate for life's inequalities. Accidents disable and orphan many children. There are adults who see one of these children and sense a personal intimation of purpose and destiny to assist. If the connection results in adoption it joins the parents and child into a family that forges its future together. Such unanticipated events are molded into the soul as surely as fulfilled dreams— not as comfortably, but in a way that makes a person more sensitive, meek, and tough.

Children who have disabilities—physically, emotionally, and intellectually—make up only part of the "special needs" category. Since this chapter explores all special needs placements it is important to clarify at the outset that minority children, older children, and children of sibling groups are also designated with "special needs." These older children, without physical disabilities for example, may have particular needs stemming from their previous neglect or abuse. But the varieties of challenges in all children with special needs often overlap. The strength and tenacity of their adoptive parents is similarly crucial, and the rewards are often more subtle. So it is understandable that emerging programs to assist special needs placements have intertwined.

RANGE OF EFFECTIVE PARENTS

Ann Coyne, in a journal dedicated to supporting the "Adoption of Children with Handicaps," summarizes what effective placement workers in the past have viewed as the ideal parent who tends to adopt children with developmental disabilities. They have "maturity, flexibility, lower-middle-class status, high school education, blue collar employment, family-centered lifestyle, religious orientation, previous parenting experience, experience with stress [such as divorce or another handicapped or troubled child], and a desire to adopt a developmentally disabled child." In addition, she says, many adoptive parents are described by their case workers as "different looking and overweight" and sometimes as "needing a child who would never grow up. A number of the adoptive parents were themselves handicapped to some degree. Adoption workers in successful agencies saw these differences as strengths."[1]

Ironically, the seemingly unfortunate life experiences of some people have already aided their preparation for effective parenting of children with special needs. Other people recognize they are inherently suitable to a life work centered in nurturing. The most typical expressions of parents in Britain who had adopted children with mental retardation were: "We just feel we know more what life is all about because of them." "It's given our lives more meaning." "We laugh a lot more. We see much more the funny side than we used to." "We're just happier . . . a lot more aware of each other."[2]

In response to the growing number of children with special needs, single parents were first approved for adoption back in the mid-1960s. The initial placements were of black children adopted by black single mothers, often women of working-class and lower-middle-class backgrounds. When the typical white adoptive family couldn't be found, agencies then started recruiting other singles, predominantly white women of upper-middle-class professional backgrounds. Now, more than thirty years later, a team of social work professionals led by John Triseliotis has reviewed the results of interim studies and says that "single-parent homes may be particularly appropriate for children who need concentrated nurturing and/or a simplicity in relationship patterns."[3] The current estimate is that 25 percent of children with special needs are adopted by single women and a much smaller number by single men. But this kind of adoption is not typical. It is remarkably problematic and utilized only with the very complex child for whom it is extremely difficult to find a home. Furthermore, a single parent in the Church cannot have a child sealed to them. Still, there are some competent, nurturing single adults who go forward to adopt an extra challenging child with faith in the eventual resolution of all things. They find fulfillment in their roles as "nursing fathers and nursing mothers," administering for the Lord to the needs of some of his most vulnerable children (see Isaiah 49:23).

More people today are compassionate toward children with special challenges. The Americans with Disabilities Act has helped sensitize the United States to the unique needs of challenged children and has changed the way most people feel and act toward them. The range of individuals interested in adopting a child with disabilities, for instance, is now far wider than previously imagined. In the late 1980s a national study sponsored by the Child Welfare League of America[4] showed that when prospective families were given free range to select any available child from photographs, including children with developmental disabilities, only half of those who chose a disabled child had previous experience with disabilities and some of those families were middle- or upper-class. Furthermore, parents who decided to adopt a child with disabilities didn't want to wait for more information, even about the child's long-range survival. When professionals tried to delay the placements in order to allow sufficient time for a more complete prognosis of the child's limitations, the willingness of the adoptive families to assume risk stayed high. The motivation of these families to adopt was plainly different from those waiting for normal infants.

Adopting a child with enormous challenges tempers a parent's expectations. The powerful incentives that may accompany adoption—compassion, mission, duty, adventure, sociability—are distilled down to their simplest form; the slightest progress becomes exquisite, tiny pleasures are exulted over, and a bit of beauty is always noticed. Today's profile for adoptive parents of children with special needs is wide open and expanding. But being alive with compassion for a child with disabilities is just the first step to adoption. Preparation and training must follow until a family is able to provide specialized care and sustain high levels of involvement through the years.

Kitty is comfortable in a housedress and slippers. She earned a degree in mental health, worked in obstetrics, never married but fostered forty children, and ran a day-care center until she was diagnosed with cancer and had two ostomies.

"Now I can't work outside the home," she says. "I don't know when something is going to leak." Kitty laughs.

On a bright Sunday she pushes a blond child in a wheelchair along Nolensville Pike. She pauses often for a muscular, black teenage boy in front of them, who pushes an empty grocery cart; he uses it like a walker.

"The dogwood is beautiful this year," she says, "and oh, the azaleas! I want to fix up the yard." She turns onto a side street and walks to her house with a white fence and tiny overgrown garden. Kitty invites me to return for a visit on Monday. "I'll also invite Dot," she says, "since she's the secondary caregiver of the children."

On Monday Dot sits in the living room on the only overstuffed chair, wearing slacks and tennis shoes. Kitty stands over a table gluing magazine pictures onto the backside of a roll of wallpaper. She is making a life-map for her adopted son Timothy to illustrate his growing-up experiences.

"Timothy is our blond boy," Kitty says. "He was six years old

when we got him. Up to that time he hadn't eaten anything that wasn't bottle-fed. His birth mom had cyto-magla virus when she was pregnant, which is usually fatal to the baby. Timothy survived but was totally deaf and mentally retarded at an 18-month-old level. He also has more orthopedic problems than I can describe. When the foster mom brought him to us at the agency she had three full bottles, and started feeding them to him one after another.

"That's enough of that, *I thought. The bottles were only a convenience." Kitty glances up, smiling. "Timothy is stubborn, which is good, because that makes him willful enough to learn. By the next morning we had him eating cereal and applesauce by spoon."*

"If he doesn't eat that way," Dot says, "we put the food away."

"Timothy can let us know when he wants things. He has a few signs like pulling our arm," Kitty explains. "But the surgeries are hard since it's impossible to explain about them when he can't hear or learn sign language. The nurses wheel him away in the hospital and he comes back with some big clump on his arm or leg that's painful. I think he knows now when he goes in what's going to happen, I read his eyes, like he's saying, 'I'll have to put up with it.'" Kitty rolls out more wallpaper and sorts through the remaining pictures. Dot lounges.

"But Timothy never cries," Dot says. "He goes through operations easily. After arm surgery he was running a small fever and they had him stay overnight. By evening he was falling out of bed trying to get away; we took him down to the playroom."

"He uses a walker at school," Kitty says, "but we don't have a whole lot of space here. So Timothy cruises around holding onto things. And is he a climber!"

There is only one path through Kitty's small living room. Two aquariums, hundreds of books, shelves of blocks, toys, and a table covered with craft projects fill the rest of the space. A plant hangs by the ceiling light and spreads around the room on hooks that still hold Christmas ornaments.

"Is he disciplined?" I ask.

"He's had a lot of experience being that age," Kitty says. "Other people's kids are only eighteen months old for one month; he's

been that old for ten years. That's how we short change retarded children," Kitty chuckles. "But even a baby knows how to push your buttons if you let him."

"Once we got used to Timothy," Dot says, "then we started trying to get this other boy from Georgia."

"Yes, Victor," Kitty adds. "He's our black boy. His birthmother is retarded like he is. She signed release papers when he was born but no one ever inquired. He was never abused by caretakers, just isolated in the same foster home for twelve years. When I first saw him I was not impressed. He was sixteen by then and an awful strong kid. He had been placed in a school for disturbed kids and had learned to mimic their behavior. I could see that what Victor needed was good leadership. Now he goes everywhere with us, pushes the grocery cart, plays in the yard. When he first came he could say only two words, 'bus' and 'book.' Now he uses 150 words. He's thrilled about everything. Oh, he's so wonderful!"

"He gets so excited," Dot says, "that sometimes it brings on a seizure. Victor has cerebral palsy and epilepsy. His seizures occur about once a month. They last only forty to sixty seconds but then he sleeps for twenty minutes—so you can't do anything but let him lie there. He had the first one when we took him into a store."

"On the Fourth of July," Kitty says, "he was so excited that he had a seizure walking to the parade. There was too much traffic for him to rest on the sidewalk so he was helped onto the bleachers. You can't feed an epileptic for a while after a seizure, so that morning was kind of hard on Victor."

"On his birthday we bought Victor a new bag," Dot laughs. "We had been shopping all over the mall, and when we finally found it he had a seizure!"

"He was just so happy!" Kitty joins in. "But we still keep doing things. We went to Disney World thinking, why are we doing this? Victor'll have a seizure. But he didn't—until we were headed back home." Kitty stands up, straightens her back and smiles. "I hope we'll have these children the rest of our lives," she says, "but that's not always possible.

"I adopted one other boy who I thought would always live with me. He was a 9-month-old limp rag when I took him into foster care, retarded, with cerebral palsy too. One day I decided I was

*never going to give him up! I talked to his fifteen-year-old mother
while we waited outside the courtroom for the formal adoption
hearing. From what she said it sounded to me like the doctor had
used a vacuum extractor during the birth process, that you put on
the back of the kid's head to pull, and it caused a cerebral hemorrhage.*

*"I started putting balloons in his crib and one day his left foot
twitched, then both feet. He learned to get those balloons floating
with his feet. After I adopted him he developed to the level of a
bright four-year-old, interested in everything, the nicest child. He
worked so hard all through his teen years and then he developed
a degenerative neurological disease and couldn't settle. I had to
walk the streets with him at night. I was working full-time so I
only got a few hours of sleep when he went to school in the morning. I couldn't keep going with that kind of schedule; he's in a care
center now. We're hoping Timothy can learn to walk. We know as
he gets older we won't be able to lift him and he could live a normal life span—Victor too."*

*"Kitty and I have trusts and wills set up," Dot says. "This
house will go to the Association for Retarded Citizens or be
turned into some kind of group home so our boys can live here."*

*"We listen to the talk shows," Kitty says. "They say, 'It's awful
to give up your children'—and we say, 'Children are not always
sent where they're meant to stay.'" Kitty smiles. "Some people
have bodies made to have children but they are not cut out to be
parents. The children born to them are meant for another family
and it's nothing against the mother who had them." Kitty pauses,
looks up.*

*"Sometimes I hear a woman at church say, 'I think there's
another child in heaven who wants to come to our family,' and I
think, there are 37,000 children without homes in this country.
Maybe there's a child already here! Maybe you don't have to give
birth to it. And they'll think, I don't want a child like Victor; I
don't want a child like Timothy. But there are others, a catalog
full. Some are listed as musical, gifted children! Look at this
little girl for instance—I'm in love with her, I want her!" Kitty
hands me a photocopy, duplicated from the adoption exchange
catalog, of a twelve-year-old black girl with spunky pigtails.*

"There are a few requirements, of course. You have to take a course with all the other men and women who want to adopt, where they tell you all the horrible things that could happen. If you can just make it through they say, 'I'll work with you.' The whole preparation process is designed to weed out not those with little money but little commitment. Most of the adoption fees we've had to pay on these children are reimbursed to us by the government."

"And we're going to add another room onto the house," Dot says. "Kitty is going to start working as a medical transcriptionist here at home, then we'll enclose the patio."

"I could never handle these children alone," Kitty adds. "Dot is here to help me much of the time. Her husband helps also; he takes Victor to handicapped youth night at the church, drives us to school activities."

Kitty's project is finished. She eases down onto the sofa arm for a moment. "I think we have fewer problems than adoptive parents of normal kids," she says, smiling. "Their kids can 'act out' as teenagers. We have none of that with our children."

The school bus arrives and Kitty speedily rolls up the wallpaper life-map. Dot jumps out of her chair. Victor charges in the front door, knocking everything he passes. Kitty uses a firm, forceful voice. "Where are you going, Victor? Do you want a drink?" Victor heads toward the back door; he says nothing. "That's fine," she says, "if you want to go out in the yard." His body is taut, all muscles stay flexed as he strides by, his eyes sparkle with excitement.

Timothy is dropped off ten minutes later in a special van. Dot assists him with his walker into the front yard.

The following spring I call Kitty's home. Dot answers. They have not remodeled but they have adopted another child, a young girl named Alicia.

"Alicia is twelve," Dot says. We're not sure yet but she may be mildly retarded, certainly behaviorally disordered. Her earliest memory is of her grandmother trying to drown her. She was abused all her life and didn't know how to trust. When she came to us nine months ago she wet her bed every night, wanted to be fed, and spent every day playing with dolls. Alicia never had a

childhood—all she learned to do was duck and survive. You should have seen the bathroom the first time we tried to wash her hair—she drenched us. If I said, 'I love you,' or 'You look pretty,' she shouted 'No!'

"Now she will say, 'Do you love me? I love you.'

"Every week we go to an Attachment Class for Parents where we learn about 'holding therapy.' When Alicia gets the doldrums, we have to hold her. Then she screams and hollers, but when she settles down to whimpering we can ask her what's the matter and it's never what you think. Sometimes it's weird things like she's afraid of 'big eyes.' Her foster mother was illiterate, into mystical stuff, and talked about 'the evil eye.' If we don't do the holding therapy once in a while, she keeps too much bottled up inside.

"We want to adopt again," Dot says. "We're looking at two other children. Neither one is as capable as Alicia; they are more on the level of Timothy."

"Where will you put them?" I ask.

"Well, we adopted Alicia without remodeling. Maybe this summer we can get a low-interest loan to fix the bathroom, repair the roof, revise the ramp. . . ."

EXPANSION OF ASSISTANCE

When parents of children with mental retardation started to lobby against institutionalization back in the 1950s, reforms resulted that strongly affected the future of adoption, especially the adoption of children with disabilities.[5] The Social Security Act was amended to create a program of aid to the permanently and totally disabled, and the Association for Retarded Citizens became one of the most effective lobbying groups in the United States.

In the 1960s, along with a concern for black children needing adoption, other concerned groups focused on older children and those with disabilities who were considered unadoptable. There were too many children in government care. New York State led out with a partial solution by passing the first subsidized adoption statute. Then the Adoption Resource Exchange of North America started an adoption registry that could link available children with interested families all over the nation. Aggressive recruitment campaigns were launched which publicized adoptable children in the media. The term "special needs" replaced the concept that children were "defective," "unadoptable," or "difficult to place."

During a Senate hearing in 1975 it became clear that judges in this country hesitated to free the portion of special needs children with disabilities for adoption because they did not believe interested families could be found. Social workers also resisted placing these children because they feared that even the willing families could not cope. Other professionals insisted on protecting the children in institutions. Most prospective adopters lacked sufficient money to meet the increased cost of caring for these especially challenging children.

By 1980 subsidized adoption programs for the whole spectrum of special needs adoption placements were implemented in all states. By this time professionals in the health care field had become supportive of families who wanted to raise their child at home, with community supports. However, research continued to acknowledge that the long-term presence of a child with severe disabilities may not work for the good of the whole family.[6] While it may be better to keep a younger disabled child in the home, professionals acknowledge that as the child gets older and more difficult to handle, the support system of family and friends can virtually dissolve, leaving some parents incapable of handling the situation.

Still other studies in the 1980s proved that children with disabilities can be successfully placed for adoption. In a twelve-month period, 1,588 children were placed by 324 agencies in forty-six states, six provinces, and the District of Columbia. The rate of disruption among these children was lower than for the other groups of children with special needs.

Now many adoptive parents of children with special needs request and receive subsidies from state programs matched through the federally funded Adoption Assistance Program. These benefits may include not only the cost of adoption itself and Medicaid coverage, but also a monthly maintenance subsidy in proportion to the extra psychological and physical needs of the child. A post-adoption worker is assigned to each case, providing follow-up aid where needed to prevent the child from ever returning to the system. State offices strive to ensure adequate support services; however, subsidies may not exceed the amount previously paid to support the child in foster care.

TECHNIQUES FOR HANDLING PROBLEMS

Though all special needs adoptions are categorically difficult, there are well informed, gifted adults in this world who specifically choose to adopt the older child who has been neglected or abused. Good fortune in life does not seem to relieve these individuals of their sense of responsibility for others less fortunate; in fact, it seems to call to them. They believe, like the Apostle Paul, "We then that are strong ought to bear the infirmities of the weak, and not to please ourselves" (Romans 15:1). Parents who choose to adopt these children do not seek their own happiness and they don't aspire to make their adopted children "happy." They adopt disordered children to set them straight, to teach them to grow deep and strong and to work through their disrupted past to a constructive present and a productive future. Their calling is so demanding that these parents are constantly learning and growing in order to stay on top of the situation. But it is their vital example that trains their children as much as their learned techniques. How curious that when such parents develop the skills to help one child with special needs—to learn and to love—they tend to adopt others.

"My son Terry came to live with us after being in a psychiatric unit for eight years," Ellen says. She wears gray slacks and a white cable knit sweater. Her long hair is pulled back, loosely braided. "He had been heavily sedated, which I didn't want to continue. I can't believe the list of medications they had him on. What he needed was a fresh start, to get in touch with who he was, what he was."

Ellen's early morning schedule relaxes during spring break. She sits on the sofa in her living room with feet bare. The ceiling is high, and leaded window panes create geometric patterns on the floor. Photos of African fabrics and wood carvings line the walls.

"The second day here Terry grabbed food at the table.

"'What are you acting ridiculous for!' one of my other kids said—they tend to be rather frank. But Terry never grabbed again; it took just one peer experience. There were ups and downs, tremendous crises. When I asked him to do anything he would mouth off, call me some really gross things, and have a fit. So I put him in a 'double bind.' It's fun to use this technique because it's paradoxical, it encourages oppositional behavior. For example," Ellen says, "I said to him, 'Terry, why don't you go and clean your room, but first I want you to stay here and whine and scream and yell at me and tell me why you don't want to do it.'

"No matter what Terry chose to do he couldn't make a bad choice. If he got indignant and said, 'Well, I can go and clean up my room without screaming and yelling,' he got the job done. If he yelled and screamed, he was ventilating with permission."

"Probably in the first month," Ellen says, "I used the double-bind twenty times on Terry, whether it was for hitting his sister or not wanting to empty the garbage. He never did yell and scream with encouragement; the approach always threw him so much off guard. He got so he could control his emotions and obey. Terry also quit saying the 'f' word. We got him a haircut and some funky looking clothes. I sent him to camp—he loved it— plus youth activities exclusively for blacks.

"When Terry entered public school last fall, he had to be put back on a relaxant. It will take years of normal living to make up for the eight years Terry spent in the psych unit, where the whole time very well-meaning people were escalating the problem— making him crazy with the regimentation, handcuffing, medica- tion. He wasn't schizoid or psychopathic at age four when he went in. He had little behavior problems, just a few, but eight years of confinement—"

Terry walks downstairs into the living room where we are talk- ing. He gazes around, still sleepy.

"Say, hello." Ellen says. Terry stops for direct eye contact. He shakes hands, friendly before he's fully awake.

"Are you okay?" she asks. "Get a muffin, whatever else you

*want, and then get on with your chores so we can get going.
School vacations are so jumbled—" Terry walks on into the
kitchen, out of hearing distance.*

"Two months after Terry came to live with us, his physician at
the psychiatric institute discontinued Terry's long-term contract
for therapy. He told me, 'Further treatment is a waste of our
time—I'd be charging the state for nothing.'

"The double bind technique is just one little model I got from
a program called Love and Logic, the therapeutic parenting part." *Love and Logic is a parenting approach developed by Foster Cline,
a psychiatrist, and Jim Fay, an educator. They publish books and
tapes together on how to parent children and teens.*

"Another principle I learned is to treat yourself—the parent—
as the center of the universe," *Ellen says.* "Then your kids eventually understand respect." *Ellen has adopted six children with
special needs transracially, five before her husband left her. She
adopted Terry two years after that.*

"I don't need to tell you what a jolt divorce is. I was immobi-
lized, like I'd been smashed by a truck or had surgery. So much of
my recouping from the pain of losing my husband was taking
care of myself. The result is that my struggles helped my parenting a lot. The way I think now relieves me of guilt and from taking
on my kids' problems. People come here and say, 'I couldn't live in
your house one day, it's too hard.'

"And I say, 'Hey, in comparison to what I went through with
my husband, this is a piece of cake, because it isn't personally
damaging to me. It's hard. I don't like the language. I don't like
some of the things my kids are doing, but I love them.'

"Another technique I've picked up is to give my children genuine but temperate empathy. Luke was the one always abusing
me. The police would call from the detention center at 3:00 in the
morning. He had been out jacking stereos. If I didn't agree to
come pick him up, he'd yell at me. I'd shout back.

"'Why do I have to get up from my bed?' I'd say. 'What makes
you think your problems should ruin my night's sleep?' So I
learned to contract with him.

"'What time do I need to start worrying about you?' I ask
before he leaves in the evening, and I keep flexible. I don't set a*

standard night curfew for him because I don't come in every night at the same time either. According to this philosophy, and I believe it, the best approach is to get these kids to function in an adult world, to learn to think, figure out their lives, and grow up."

"The day after I left Luke in detention," Ellen says, "he was mad at me. 'You're the meanest!' he yelled. 'All the other parents picked their kids up.'

"Instead of saying, 'Well, they're not a single parent, they don't have to work as hard to earn a living'—I just said, 'Probably so.'

"Acknowledgment diffuses anger; I had to practice it." Ellen repeats, "probably so, probably so."

"Now, when the police pick Luke up for truancy I say, 'Is it warm? Can he get a good meal? Great, Luke can stay overnight.'

"'Aren't you going to come and get me?' he asks.

"'Too busy, honey,' and then he spits out some horrible stuff. 'You're right, this is sad,' I tell him. 'What a bummer.'

"Instead of trying to get him up in the morning—going through all those battles—I say other things like, 'You know, Luke, I've never had a child who had to repeat ninth grade before. That would be an interesting experience.' If Luke doesn't make it to school one day, it's okay. It used to be that I couldn't live with that. Now I say, 'Hey, no worry, you can make it up.' My emphasis changed from screaming at him, being tangled in his mistakes, to letting him live with them, just like God lets us live with ours. Maybe if there was a man around here it would be different. That's always the component I'm not sure of. But then, maybe if he weren't adopted, maybe if he weren't black. . . .

"Foster Cline is sort of a guru in the adoption world. Cline started helping people understand unattached children, those who experienced a serious interruption of the bonding cycle because of trauma anytime from conception through the first two years of life. Cline and Fay believe that unattached children have not learned to trust and so have become oppositional. A parent who then enforces success on that kind of child leaves them with only one option—to choose failure. But a trained parent is not intimidated by an oppositional child and can leave him the option of failure, which actually liberates the child to choose success. The techniques don't always work for the most severe psychopathic

and sociopathic kids. For those kids, trained therapeutic foster parents and therapists actually start the kids over—have them drink from bottles and wear diapers to get the rage out of them and then reteach them to trust and to love.

"But the same theory works when my kids become opposi-tional," Ellen says. "It worked with Terry, Luke, and my other chil-dren who don't respond to the 'let's sit down and talk it over' way I was brought up. I've learned to communicate to them that 'I love you, but I won't rescue you.' Ellen's voice is caring and adroit. 'Have a great life,' I tell them, 'and if you need advice, ask me.'

"My experience with troubled kids," Ellen says, "goes way back to when I was running the adoption exchange, trying to place kids from the psych unit. I spent time with them, filmed them for TV clips to attract potential parents. I would say to the profession-als, 'I believe this child is ready to meet a family,' and they would say, 'He's not prepared. We need time.' And I would say, 'Well, he's been in your unit for two-and-a-half years now; how much more time do you need?' They were getting thousands of dollars a month and the adoptive family would get only a few hundred. I thought, wait a minute—you just want to keep your fees.

"'But he has to re-enter the world at some point,' I said, 'so why not let him visit potential adoptive families on weekends.' Then I had a profound personal experience. I adopted Clint, a teenager with Down's syndrome who had been institutionalized for twelve years at a cost of $3,500 a month to the state. They paid me $500 a month. During the four years Clint was in our home, he transformed to the point his therapists didn't recognize him—because he became part of a family, part of the real world where he had to do chores. He saw the good and bad in people as they really are, not just the limited view of a caretaker who changes shifts every eight hours. Clint made the same significant transition that we've seen in Terry."

Ellen walks me to the front door. On the porch Ellen's daughter, Bridgette, is brushing the cat. Bridgette is the only child still at home who has severe mental retardation. "You're doing such a nice job," Ellen tells her. She smiles and gently rubs Bridgette's shoulders. Bridgette stays hunkered down below the mailbox in a new pastel sweat suit, drool oozing from her mouth.

.

Out on the sidewalk Ellen says, "I have to realize that some day Bridgette may also need to go into some kind of government supported care program like Clint. I don't know if I can manage her during puberty—" then she stops talking. Ellen leaves future issues alone and focuses on every technique available to enhance the present situation.

ESSENTIAL PREPARATION

The vision has to be clear and the strategy carefully thought out in order for adoptive parents to successfully implement change in the lives of many children with special needs after placement. Children who have been neglected or abused bring with them an assortment of behavioral problems which adoptive parents need to identify and correct. Otherwise the child will force the adoptive family to accept his dysfunctions—a disservice that reinforces them and may render the adoptive family unable to cope.

"Families are not neutral settings,"[7] says Vera Fahlberg in *A Child's Journey through Placement*. Children who have been in adversarial adult-child relationships most of their lives believe there are only winners and losers in a family. A major goal for adoptive parents is to help the young person recognize that adults and children can benefit each other. Studied patience is needed. It requires discipline for these children to live within reasonable limits of behavior, discipline that will enhance the child's self-esteem as he learns to meet his parent's expectations. "The distinction between discipline and punishment is an important one,"[8] says Fahlberg. Discipline is used when parents focus on helping the child to achieve; punishment when parents are venting their own frustrations. The distinction should be understood not because parents can be expected to be in perfect control all the time but because parents of at-risk children will be stretched to their limits and beyond. Though 70 percent of these children will eventually turn out okay, they will all have problems, and with approximately 30 percent the problems will be severe. A parent's basic assumptions may need to change. The customary teaching patterns—isolate a child when misbehaving, reward a child for good conduct—may be useless. Children who have been severely neglected or abused are used to being isolated and are best disciplined by having to stay close. Children with no self-worth can never be motivated by rewards they believe will never come to them.

Anne Loux, who wrote *The Limits of Hope* after battling through an almost insurmountable task of raising two high-risk children, recommends "that parents prepare themselves carefully for the adoption of an older child—that is, a child aged more than one year—by reading widely on early childhood development, by working directly with troubled children in shelters and homeless centers, in group homes, and mental hospitals, by becoming foster parents, by tutoring children with learning disabilities, and by asking as many questions as possible of social workers, pediatricians, therapists, and adoptive and foster parents, and listening to their responses."[9]

All special needs adoption stories make dramatic telling. They will include moments of exasperation and courage, devastating honesty and fleeting empathy, which may never completely obscure an enduring hope. Few people want to anticipate such pain, but blind hope is not sufficient for the challenge of adopting a child with special needs. The requisite patience must be learned, practiced, and applied consistently. "In your patience possess ye your souls" (Luke 21:19).

NOTES

1. Ann Coyne, "Administrative and Policy Issues," *Journal of Children in Contemporary Society* 21, nos. 3, 4, as quoted in *Formed Families: Adoption of Children with Handicaps,* ed. Laraine Masters Glidden (Binghamton, New York: The Haworth Press, Inc., 1990), p. 97.

2. Laraine Masters Glidden, "The Wanted Ones: Families Adopting Children with Mental Retardations," in *Formed Families*, pp. 177–78.

3. John Triseliotis, Joan Shireman, and Marion Hundleby, *Adoption: Theory, Policy, and Practice* (London: Cassell, 1997), p. 224.

4. Ann Coyne, "Administrative and Policy Issues," pp. 99–100.

5. Elizabeth S. Cole, "A History of Adoption of Children with Handicaps," in Laraine Masters Glidden ed., *Formed Families,* pp. 43–60.

6. Jan Blacher and Barbara E. Bromley, "Correlates of Out of Home Placement of Children with Handicaps," in Larine Masters Glidden ed., *Formed Famlies*, pp. 3–35.

7. Vera Fahlberg, *A Child's Journey through Placement* (Indianapolis: Perspectives Press, 1991), p. 289.

8. Ibid., p. 290.

9. Ann Kimble Loux, *The Limits of Hope* (Charlottesville, Va.: University Press of Virginia, 1997), pp. 260–61.

*We have endured many things, and hope to be able to endure
all things.*
Article of Faith 13

12
CODE GREEN
ADOPTION DISRUPTION AND
CARE OF DIFFICULT CHILDREN

You may not want to read this chapter. It is written for individuals already committed to a difficult adoption situation or those who are considering a tough placement. Few people have within them the call and training for such extraordinary service. The cases that follow are not typical and are not meant to discourage general adoption. Taking in too much information on the risky side of an issue can throw a person off-balance, obscuring the worth of the full proposition.

A "disruption" is an adoption placement that breaks down *before* it has been finalized by a court of law. A "dissolution" is an adoption that breaks down *after* finalization. In the United States, where there is a specified time between a child's placement in a family and her legal adoption (usually six months to a year), the majority of problems are realistically considered before finalization. Intercountry adoptions, however, may not allow for that transition time. "In most countries, including Russia and China, which accounted for 55% of all international adoptions to the U.S. in 1997," says Linda Perilstein, "children generally are not permitted to leave their birth countries until they have been legally adopted."[1] Adoptive parents of these children are immediately legally responsible.

So a disruption of a stateside placement might conceivably be comparable to the dissolution of an adoption involving a child from abroad. Because both situations describe "breakdowns" in adoption placement, I will simply refer to the concept as "disruption." After all, by far the greatest number of adoptions in the United States occur between parents and children who reside in the States.

Disruption has replaced the word *failure* in adoptions, "reflecting a viewpoint that a child's removal from a particular adoption placement signifies an interruption in the path to a goal, rather than a final outcome,"[2] explains Trudy Festinger in her paper on why adoptions may break down.

REASONS FOR BREAKDOWN

In the early days, when agencies claimed to match children with parents, and special-needs placements were rare, disruption occurred less than 2 percent of the time. Infants and children with problems were institutionalized. Festinger's article, "Adoption Disruption: Rates and Correlates" states that disruption rates have risen to around 13 percent, a moderate figure since the total includes children with all kinds of disabilities and older children with severe emotional and learning problems who may disrupt 50 percent of the time.

Adoptions that break down most often are of two types: first, when a child adopted in infancy develops early behavior problems from prenatal and genetic causes; and second, when a child adopted past infancy has experienced abuse, neglect, and a breach of trust. A broad summary of several studies concludes that breakdowns generally occur because of the parents' inability to cope with the child's behavior. These behaviors may include serious eating problems, sexual promiscuity, stealing, suicidal behavior, fire setting, wetting or soiling, vandalism, or physically injuring others. Though social workers refer to the children's behavior as the biggest problem, parents say it is their lack of preparation or foreknowledge of the child's problems.

The following case study is truly heart wrenching. But it

belongs in this chapter, which few people should read. It is both a disclosure and a caution. Good intentions in a complex adoption are not enough. Red flags in placement decisions should be prudently observed. Probing for full background information is not only a right but a responsibility. And some disruptions should occur, for the eventual healing of the child and the preservation of the pre-existing family.

"If you foster a child for a while," Connie says, "people praise. If you adopt and it doesn't work out, they disdain. That's people generally, not professionals."

Connie and her husband adopted three children: two boys at birth in this country, and a girl eighteen months old from abroad. After two-and-a-half years they relinquished the little girl, Anna. The broken adoption still gives them pain.

"When Anna's new adoptive family had a home study evaluation," Connie says, "they told the social worker the reason we had given Anna up was that we didn't love her. Since we already had two other children, the social worker initiated an investigation on us. But when the state representative looked at Anna's file, she offered to assist with the official transfer."

Connie works in the preemie nursery at Parkland Hospital and loves to sing in a choir. Her husband, Geoff, is an electrical engineer with a passion for fly-fishing.

"We felt comfortable when we received a photograph of Anna from the native doctor," Connie says. "The night we arrived to pick her up, they brought Anna to us and she was screaming. I tried to rock her, sing to her, but she had terror in her eyes. We kept thinking, if we can just get her back home everything will be all right."

"'But this is crazy,' I told Geoff. We struggled getting her to sleep. Then she awoke with night terrors—screaming, banging the crib, beating her head against the wall. Her body was stiff, rigid. Stroking, cuddling wouldn't calm her.

"The native doctor wanted to give her massive doses of antibiotics, enough for ten days in two. I took over the medication. But without our knowing, he gave Anna ten milligrams of Valium for the flight home. She passed out twice at the airport and yelled so

much on the plane we were forced to stay overnight in Florida. In the motel room, Anna had fits over the mirrors and clamped her teeth together when we offered her water or food.

"It was such a relief to land back in Houston," Connie says. "We stopped at Arby's on the way home from the airport. Some customer had dropped fries on the floor and Anna climbed under the table to eat. That was the beginning of hoarding. She was always in the refrigerator, and even when she was full she kept food in her mouth, refusing to swallow.

"Our oldest son was seven. He had been part of the decision to adopt Anna. He was gentle and eager to play, but Anna didn't know how. She bit his genitalia. I needed stitches after she bit me. During a complete medical examination, the doctor suggested we do a precautionary chest X ray for TB. Then we saw that every bone in her chest had been broken—each rib, the sternum, clavicle—all at different stages. Unholy fear continued in her face. She was off antibiotics for only three weeks of that first year. I brought the breathing machines home, the IVs too. She snapped at everything we did.

"When Anna cried, she made the typical sounds and screwed up her face, but there were no tears. When she had a temper tantrum, she held her breath until she passed out; seizures followed. But what concerned me most was the day she got mad in the tub, grabbed the massage nozzle and fell back, splitting her head open, and did not cry. In the hospital they said, 'Oh, she's being so good.' They gave her shots, cleaned and stitched her head without her flinching. The truth was, she wasn't there!

"We took her to a neuropsychologist. In addition to obvious physical abuse, we could be looking at schizophrenia and drug use or alcoholism in her birthmother, we were told. A team of seven physicians agreed she needed an antidepressant—she was put on low doses of Tofranol at age two, which minimized the highs and lows in her behavior. She started to sleep better.

"Anna had a favorite doll with long black curls," Connie says. "She tugged on the doll's hair, fascinated by it. I took her to a beauty salon for a permanent. I thought it might please her to look like the doll. She sat perfectly still while I held a Tupperware container of Cheerios for her to snack on. During that afternoon

Anna handed me one Cheerio, the only token of affection she ever gave.

"The psychiatrist suggested day care, 'Enroll her for a couple of hours twice a week. Interaction with other peers might help dilute her demands for exclusive adult attention.' After a few months I was told not to bring her back.

"Anna was constantly in treatment. We worked on eye contact, rage therapy, hope therapy. The next day-care supervisor understood that Anna was involved in all those programs and worked closely with her. After a few months she told us, 'When Anna walks in the room, the other children give up their toys. She'll hurt a child and then start to cry herself. She has killed the birds, the fish, tried to cut a baby with scissors and drop him off the slide.' The clincher was the day Anna broke a child's arm." Connie pauses, rubs the back of her neck.

"It had been two years since we brought Anna into our family, and I was wearing down. My youngest boy didn't dare play at home. An EEG showed Anna was borderline abnormal, with the medication. The doctor resisted doing a CAT scan.

"'It will just discourage you more,' he said.

"A nagging anxiety never allowed me to relax. Anna was prone to running away.

"Geoff and I investigated our options.

"'You could put her in respite foster care,' a doctor suggested, 'but you'd have to pay the bill, and she'd be back in six months. You can enroll her in rage-hold therapy for a flat fee of $3,000, but you may not be able to see results for ten years.' Finally, the neuropsychologist said, 'She was probably abused from day one. There is less than a 5 percent chance of improvement. You may spend years and never see change.'

"We went home to our Anna who by then was four years old and never said more than three words together, never played by herself, and never gave any affection. She remained aggressive or emotionless. Someone else noticed we were struggling, a mother of seven children, including two who had been adopted transracially.

"'We'll take Anna,' she said, 'if you don't want her—' That stung, but Geoff and I were on the verge of living separately: the

two boys with him, Anna with me, and I had never bonded with her.'

"'—Then you need to go with us to the psychologist,' I said to the woman and her husband.

"'No!' Her husband was adamant. 'We don't believe in that kind of thing. We have a child with epilepsy, another with Attention Deficit Disorder. We know about these kids—if you love them, they're fine.'

"The husband finally came to the psychologist's office with his wife, and gritted his teeth through the disclosure session. After they left, the psychologist told Geoff and me, 'Sometimes a child has to go from one home to another, until they can see the norm versus their past. You may always be the bad guys, because you started the rehabilitative process.' Geoff took Anna to her new home; my heart was being ripped out.

"'Please don't take her off the medication cold turkey,' I said. I sent a six-month supply with her. Our nine-year-old was devastated. Geoff explained to him, 'It's like building a puzzle and you can't find the last piece. The part of Anna that had so much anger left her incomplete. No matter how hard we tried to make a piece fit, we couldn't.' Geoff's family criticized. Other adoptive parents condemned.

"Geoff dropped by to see Anna at her new home," Connie says, "after she had been there three months. 'There was no more than a flicker of recognition,' he said, 'that left immediately.' Anna had been given a new puppy. As he left he heard the family cautioning her, 'Anna, don't hold the dog so tight.'

"When six months had passed and the new mother hadn't called me like she promised, I called her. 'Anna's fine,' the mother said. I tried to draw her out.

"'Does Anna sleep at night? Does she laugh, make tears, sing? Does she ever mention us?'

"'Well, Connie, to be truly honest, she has never asked about you, or Geoff, or your children.' I knew she was telling the truth.

"'The funniest thing happened,' the new adoptive mother said, 'when a UPS driver arrived with packages at Christmastime, Anna went out in the truck and left with him.'"

Connie sighs and says, "I feel I failed."

Later I learned that Connie nursed her father with Parkinson's disease until he passed away and she underwent treatment for breast cancer while caring for Anna. Connie is not the type to justify breakdown in adoption, but she had significant reason: preservation of her own life, marriage, and family. And no one can ever judge another's inspiration in the matter because the Lord sometimes allows us to enter into difficult situations and then strengthens us to endure them. Connie and Geoff were blessed to find another family in the Church who could continue the rehabilitation process with Anna.

The large number of foreign orphans arriving with physical and emotional problems (particularly those from Eastern Europe) are causing more clinics to offer pre-adoption counseling.[3] Doctors examine medical records, photographs, and videotapes to help prospective parents evaluate children ahead of time. Making informed decisions about international placements and reputable agencies decreases some of the risk, but if a child arrives with unanticipated problems the focus has to shift from "What if?" to "What now?"

Children available for adoption in the United States may have similarly difficult impairments. Parents who are willing to try a risky adoption and fail may not deserve criticism. Adoptions can break down for legitimate reasons. It's the knowledge we can gain from those complications that becomes productive. The hope is that children will end up where they can be helped the most. Parents at the "end of the line," who are willing and prepared to adopt children with the most consuming problems deserve respect. The comforting actuality is that they do not feel it is a burden, just a challenge. This is reassurance that they are the right ones for the job.

I drop in on Lynette, who works for an adoption agency in Denver. It is early in the morning, and she greets me at the door with a baby. Lynette is the mother of older children (her youngest is fourteen), so I am surprised when she puts this baby in my arms as she finishes the dishes.

"You must hold this precious child while I tell you his story," she says. The baby is adorable—curly black hair and big black

eyes that follow the direction of her voice. As I hold him close I
can see an IV tube still taped to his wrist, inside a furry blue
sleeper.

"Isn't he a treasure?" Lynette asks, waiting while I adjust to
this cuddly infant, who is tentatively reaching out of the blanket
towards me with his tiny arms and perfectly shaped head.

"He's only two weeks old," she says. "The young couple who
had planned to adopt him is from Louisville. But his temperature
escalated and he started into convulsions the first night in their
home. They spent five days at the hospital—around the clock—
learning that he has herpes and that his birthmother was either
on drugs or alcohol or both. If he is sent back to the agency in
Detroit, where he came from, I know what will happen!"

While Lynette is telling me of this tragedy, her voice is jubilant.
She turns around to see my reaction.

"So I went to work and found him another family. They are
perfect. They are middle-aged with three other children who have
significant disabilities. They are already into the medical care reg-
imen. They are thrilled to have this child."

The tiny bundle is leaning on my shoulder but still craning his
head around toward Lynette. She dries her hands and takes him
back.

"Just think of his opportunities now, he'll be sealed in the
temple!"

Lynette's fervor is not only infectious but also befitting.
Holding such a vulnerable baby conveys again the "spirit of adop-
tion," which will carry parents through once they have received
it. "The Spirit itself beareth witness with our spirit, that we are
the children of God" (Romans 8:16; see also vv. 14–8).

ADVANCE EVALUATION

A comprehensive study of adoptions through the child welfare system, entitled *Adoption and Disruption: Rates, Risks, and*
Responses, was conducted by Richard Barth and Marianne
Berry. They cite studies that verify that some disruptions occur
because parents are encouraged to "stretch" or adapt their
expectations concerning a child's handicaps and needs in
order to minimize the wait to adopt. Since child welfare
professionals are constantly pressured to place children with

minimum delays but have a general shortage of available homes, they may be stretching parents beyond their own ability to recognize personal limits. When asked what problems contributed to disruption, adoptive parents reported "that they had sought to adopt younger children without disabilities and had agreed to adopt older children with disabilities."[4] Also, the adoptive parents commented vehemently at times "that they were not provided with adequate information about the child they adopted prior to the placement."[5] Interviews revealed that large percentages of the children had emotional and behavioral problems, learning disabilities, and had been physically or sexually abused, while a third to a half of the time parents were not given that information before placement. Parents were generally told about the child's previous neglect, history of placements, and physical or developmental disabilities.

The more favorable outcomes were reported among parents who were flexible and patient and who attended church regularly. The mothers tended to be older and the children younger. One great surprise in the Barth and Berry study was that higher education of parents correlated with a higher rate of disruption. Those with college degrees disrupted 26 percent, those with high school degrees 11 percent, and parents with less than a high school diploma had no disruptions. Too great a gap between high achieving families and disturbed children, causing more of a reactionary extreme than gradual adjustment toward a middle ground, is one possible explanation. Certainly, education per se is never a substitute for experience in dealing with challenged children. Barth and Berry caution that since these findings contradict previous research, we can only safely argue "against overlooking less educated adoptive applicants for more educated applicants and for not assuming that professionals—yes, even human service providers—are beyond the need for adoption subsidies and complete pre- and post-placement services."[6] Prospective parents need to understand and discuss why disruption can occur, not to curb optimism but to face the reality that adjustment will be lengthy and uneven. Some children may actually need to try several families until they find one that will work. The current trend toward foster care-adoption placements saves many people in that regard. These trial placements are often not officially labeled disruptions.

The truth remains that there is a small percentage of high-risk youth that need an incredible amount of help, and all adults have limits to their strength. Pushing ahead on one mission can render a parent dysfunctional in other aspects of life. Making a decision not to continue with the totally consuming care of one child with serious difficulties may save the breakdown of the rest of the family.

INSTITUTIONAL CARE

Teenagers who were adopted and are severely troubled may require institutionalized treatment just like some of their non-adopted peers. Remember, this is rare; only 3 percent of the whole adolescent population needs extended inpatient care during their teenage years, and only one-half of one percent require repeated or long-term psychiatric hospitalization. Of that small group 15 percent are adopted. Therapists maintain that hospitalized adolescents may respond negatively to society, not because they have been abused or neglected but because they are more comfortable in a state of opposition or rage. Adolescence can be a hazardous stage. Teenagers may be hospitalized not only when their disturbed behavior becomes dangerous but also when remaining with their family exacerbates the difficulties. High costs limit this type of care to children from affluent families, those with excellent insurance coverage, or those in state custody at dangerous risk.

Long-term treatment involves several stages that can be protracted to fit varying needs. First is a containment phase where the patient learns to be regulated in an environment of limit-setting and support. The second phase is designed to achieve personal insight and identity; more freedoms are eventually extended in direct correlation with more acceptance of responsibility. The third is a separation phase where the patient is assisted to move back into the community after a period ranging from a few months to a few years.[7]

"I entered the treatment center for a two-week evaluation,"

Sherrie says. "They diagnosed me as bipolar, put me on lithium, and kept me in programs for the next two years." She turns off the TV—Rescue 911 is over. My mother approved the use of medication for me because our insurance wouldn't cover hospitalization otherwise.

"The medication affected my bladder, my sleeping patterns," Sherrie says. "I have natural artistic gifts—I taught myself to play the piano, paint, sculpt—but the 'meds' changed all that. I could no longer be creative." Sherrie is fifteen now, with dark curly hair pulled tightly back. She wears jeans and an overblouse.

"After three months of hospitalization I was discharged, and that same day I skipped two doses of medication. I felt so ugly looking in the mirror the next morning that I broke it. They put me in another treatment center for six months. After that I went to a girls' group home for ten months; I did well there with no physical restraint and more caring." Sherrie's long legs stretch out in front of her, crossed at the ankles. She stares at the blank TV screen.

"Partway through all this a therapist wanted to increase the medication, but I resisted. He agreed to try it my way—even lowered the medication instead—but I went into depression for a week; I couldn't pull out on my own. So they raised the medication higher than ever and kept me on it for the rest of the time. I haven't told anybody yet, but this summer I took myself off all meds, so I must be doing good." Sherrie lives with her father, who was recently laid off as a driver for a carrier service.

"My dad is on medication now—depression almost got him down—and he doesn't use his mind these days. But I disagree with the kind of treatment they give in psychiatric hospitals," Sherrie says. "I don't believe a person should have to go on medication to be admitted, and I don't believe in physical restraint. I had a friend die during a restraint. He had heart problems. He pleaded, 'Please get off me, I can't breathe.' They said he had to calm down first.

"I was restrained two times. One day I awoke sick, with a headache. So I didn't get breakfast and they said, 'If you stay in bed at all, you stay the day.' When I felt better, I wanted to be with peers so I sat in the hallway. A therapist talked to me, listened to

my point of view, then insisted I go back in my room. I disagreed with him but went back anyway, slamming the door—I didn't mean to—and he issued a code green. Ten people came to my room. I struggled.

"'You need to go into isolation,' they said, keeping me face down on the floor. I was lifted onto the bed with my feet pulled behind me, shackled. I had to be quiet for fifteen minutes in that position before going to isolation for four hours." Sherrie glances around to make sure I'm listening.

"Sometimes I did get out of control. I was easily angered— especially over issues of staff versus peers—stubborn, but kind of like a teeter-totter. I guess there are times when restraint was necessary . . . I saw five men trying to restrain a guy before they finally had to call the police . . . but the time I helped with one it made me feel real uncomfortable." Sherrie pauses, flapping her sandals against each other.

"While I was in treatment I went to a joint therapy session with my mom. She said, 'You remind me of when I was little.' Maybe that was the problem—I was too reminding. My mom had to take care of all of her siblings growing up. I was too hard to raise; she gets along with kids who obey. But my dad has love that won't quit. His nineteen brothers and sisters are just like him, totally supportive."

"You see," Sherrie says, "my parents adopted me because they were asked to by a church agency looking for black parents to adopt black kids. But my mom didn't really want to. She already had four jobs and a big PMS problem—took tranquilizers. Whenever she had a bad day at work I wedged a piece of wood against my bedroom door to keep it closed so she wouldn't grab and hit me. I didn't have my mom's love. I used to cry at home all the time.

"But I never cried in the treatment center," Sherrie continues. "The second time I was ready to go home my parents insisted I get on birth control. Then my mother called me a slut for wearing shorts and tank tops. And nobody in my family did anything with me. They were too busy. My family expected me to change, but they were no different. After a month I ran, lost my virginity,

*drank for the first time. I remember everything I did but I still say,
'That was not me.' I was just scared crazy.*

"Since I've been out of the group home and living with my dad
I feel good about myself. I'm kind of his caretaker now. Sherrie
stares at the wall. Pieces of white construction paper splashed
with her brilliant tempera designs are taped around the room.

"Each person's experiences are different," she says, "because
it's God's way of teaching them. I'm unique. I've been through
what I needed and my thinking patterns are unusual, but that
makes me more creative."

LOW COST THERAPY OPTIONS

There are support groups (the National Adoption
Information Clearinghouse has identified more than 1,000 of
them),[8] child welfare classes, educational books, and training
tapes available through public libraries, LDS Family Services,
and other child welfare and social service agencies that can
advise and replenish parents. Parents whose children are
unmanageable must seek help from all available sources to
avoid an unbearable dead end where they "police" the child,
permit the child to act self destructively, or accept the agony
of a failed placement. Short of the child leaving home, there
are less expensive therapeutic options available to parents with
the time, energy, and desire to continue working through their
child's acute problems. Therapists who run these programs
believe most of the toughest difficulties are plainly correctable
while the family continues living together if everyone is willing to try.

The process is marvelously like repentance and forgiveness,
but all participants must be able to do their part. If a child who
is misbehaving can repent sincerely it will be obvious. She will
confess and forsake the wrong behavior. If the parent and
other siblings are willing to frankly forgive, the family can
mend and move on with their lives together. This process may
need to be repeated time and time again, utilizing repentance
and forgiveness over and over—allowing small changes to
gradually improve family interactions. But changing patterns
of interaction within a family takes strenuous effort. Jane, a

social worker and family therapist, explains one type of assisted option.

"I opened an adoption center in New York City," she says, "and focused on changing the interpretation of negative behavior. Before that I had been trained in the psychoanalytical mode, but then I came onto this brief therapy model which made sense to me." Jane is a short, black-haired woman who wears expensive, practical clothes.

"Instead of blaming problems on adoption, causing the family to stay stuck and feel guilt, we accepted adoption as a fact and looked for other causes or explanations of the problems that could be changed.

"For example," Jane says, "constant temper tantrums by a child are interspersed with some normal behavior. So we would sit back and curiously question the family about the interludes when there weren't difficulties. It's not the clever therapist approach," she laughs. "It's where one is willing to be humble and magnify the family. We help them to be more conscious when things accidentally work well. We try to broaden the family's capacity to emphasize the exceptions to bad behavior.

"It's an ideal model for adoptive families," Jane says. "Most situations aren't hopeless. We didn't get everybody all better, and we didn't do all that well in New York City where I suspect too many adults are still fashionably into psychoanalysis. But 80 percent of the families did say that their problems were solved, including the 25 percent of our cases with the most complex difficulties."

The Brief Therapy Model,⁹ first used at the Center for Adopted Families in New York and currently practiced in a Brief Family Therapy Center in Milwaukee, assumes that people have within them the ability to overcome difficulties. The therapist is there to focus the family on the present and future instead of trying to change the past. All former events are irrelevant to a solution. The cause of the problem does not need to be known because insight and awareness are not necessary for change. Examination of the symptoms may not serve a function either, because the problem has usually become a habit no longer related to the original situation. Finally, the Brief Therapy Model assumes that people can change their behaviors, even if only slightly.

Therapists focus only on what the family requests help with and are cautioned to not "do too much." Small changes in any part of the family system frequently are found to bring about a lasting solution. Just a little adjustment changes the attitude of everyone involved; they instantly feel a sense of progress with minimal effort. The time frame is crucial. Suggestions are given as an experiment with a definite end. "Most people can alter their behavior temporarily," they say, "and in the process discover that the new behavior has benefits."

Dramatic cases are not atypical of families with children referred for "brief therapy" treatment. For example, five-year-old Missy[10] was placed with adoptive parents who did not know she had been the victim of repeated sexual abuse in foster care. As Missy grew to trust them, she told her new parents about her past experiences. The parents contacted the adoption agency but the agency took no action because Missy was adjusting well and there was no way of confirming her story. Two years later Missy and her adoptive brother were discovered having sex. The family was mortified. They were told by their pediatrician and a psychiatrist that Missy was damaged beyond cure. Not only was it Missy's fault, they said, but she was likely to repeat the pattern.

The first brief therapy session started by encouraging the parents to evaluate the problem. They were terrified that "it" might happen again, but they had also thought of an alternative meaning for her behavior. The mother said, "We have to teach Missy to be a sister to her brothers, since she has never had a chance to learn that." The father suggested that Missy needed to learn respect for her body, and what it means to have an appropriate relationship with a boy.

Except for the one grave incident, the therapists affirmed that the family was an exceptional, well-connected group, committed to Missy even when discouraged by counsel from the "experts." They explained that Missy's mistake could have been an attempt to show caring that was inappropriate rather than pathological, and that Missy was far better for having lived with their loving and concerned family during the past two years.

Then they stated the facts. Missy's past was unalterable; her future could be changed. The parents had already dealt with the problem by setting limits and giving support to assure that such an incident would not happen again. The therapist praised Missy for trying to learn how to be a part of the family through actions that her parents felt comfortable about. The son was praised for learning new ways to be a brother and show caring.

"Next Sunday," the therapist said, "we would like the whole family to gather in the backyard. Before this gathering, Dad will dig a small hole with a shovel. Each family member will put their painful memories into that hole and cover them up with a shovelful of dirt. When the hole is covered up, the family will have cake and punch to celebrate its new future together."

In the following years the family reported that Missy engaged in no inappropriate behavior and that she made excellent progress. According to the therapists, "This one session helped the family focus on the solutions they had already developed. It empowered them to have confidence in their ability to be parents to a child with a history like Missy's, and offered them an alternative 'expert' explanation." The specific mistake that caused the major crisis was "buried" and the future filled with hope. This "brief therapy" approach "is effective with those individuals who come to treatment with a clearly defined difficulty and the motivation to resolve it."[11] For people who aren't clear about the nature of their problem or whether it can be resolved, therapists start by helping them to define their goals. The brief therapy approach is helpful only occasionally for those who come reluctantly. However, most families have a combination of participants. The child is rarely eager for help, so the suggestions are focused on the one who is—often the parent. The chance of success is multiplied by the adult's flexibility. Although many adoptive families enter "brief therapy" favoring termination of the adoption, after an average of seven sessions only one family in 300 proceeds in that direction.

THERAPEUTIC TREATMENT PARENTS

Imagining solutions to one's family problems takes time. Difficult children need strong, self-assured parents who can patiently endure fearful crises, work out solutions, and give the child space and opportunity to develop her own self-assurance. Ideally, the most effective treatment therapy is a home environment full of exciting opportunities for growth. Parents can protect themselves from excessive stress by distancing themselves a bit psychologically from a child with difficulties, by constantly nourishing themselves spiritually, by spending time in their own areas of interest, and by allowing professionals to carry some of the load. Parents are effective only if they can retain sufficient composure to treat their child somewhat objectively.

Treatment parents are individuals who have been extensively trained to work with displaced children. These parents work in their own homes; and the displaced child lives there in a structured behavioral program. The child attends public school and interacts in a suburban neighborhood, but the atmosphere in the home is supervised intensively. Treatment parents are carefully trained in "corrective teaching interaction," a consistent series of procedures that reinforce the consequences of both positive and negative behavior with genuine praise and empathy. They also learn to calmly handle explosive situations.

Paul is ten. He has a fresh crew cut. He looks straight into my eyes, smiles, and extends his hand.

"I'm very happy to meet you," he says. "Would you like to look around?" Paul leads me into his room, a remodeled garage freshly painted, with a new carpet, daybed, and computer. He is remarkably polite. His mother, Rebecca, joins us.

"You're doing a great job, Paul. Would you like to give her a tour of the house?" Rebecca is in her late thirties, friendly and assertive, certified as a treatment parent to give therapeutic foster care.

Paul beams, takes a breath, and walks on ahead. Afterwards he excuses himself to work on his agenda—grooming, prayer and Bible study, breakfast, and ten-minute segments of math and reading, with breaks for video games—all before lunch. It is summer in Minneapolis. Swimming, piano lessons, and excursions are afternoon activities.

"I believe in building bridges," *Rebecca says.* "There is a lot of grieving in older children as they adjust to foster care and adoption. Being taken away from their family is similar to death in that once they are separated the child can only remember the good about their parents and long for it. I build bridges to help them remember the bad, so they know, 'Yes, my mother does drink, I was abused.' I keep track of the original family in case I need to reach them, and I assure Paul that I will help him reconnect if he needs it. Everyone who once lived with biological parents deserves a window to that part of their life."

There is a second boy, Dwight, also living in the home. He is ahead of Paul on his routine. But Paul catches up and they eat corn flakes together. Both boys check back with Rebecca when they are ready to go outside for "summer school."

"When Dwight started living here seven months ago," *Rebecca says,* "he bit me so severely I needed a tetanus shot. I thought, I'm the one who fixes your meals, tucks you in at night, and I get this? He needed to hear my anger and feel remorse. It's impossible to feel love for a child through that kind of behavior. We don't say we love each other around here unless it's true. We have to be honest. In the past other people have said they loved Dwight and then abused him.

"So after Dwight does things wrong he has to spend time in his room. But I shorten discipline when he apologizes—then he gets to use the Game Boy while he finishes his time-out. But if I asked Dwight about possible adoption right now, he would be angry at me. I don't want the anger. So I help him with, 'While you're waiting . . . maybe you could learn to play the piano.' Dwight didn't want to take piano lessons at first. Now he spends hours, in addition to practice time, figuring out things on his own. He thinks of himself as waiting until he's reunited with his family, but that will probably never happen.

"The type of abuse and abandonment that displaced children have experienced," Rebecca says, *"triggers dangerous aggression in them. As a result they have a wide range of deficits in their development and have often become very good at avoiding treatment. In the initial stages of adjustment into a new setting any instruction may bring on tears, tantrums or terror. Even after thirty minutes spent calming them down, another instruction often brings on a repeat cycle. A difficult child like Dwight has taught other caretakers to leave him alone."*

"But you've adopted Paul?" I clarify.

"Yes, but he came three years ago. When Paul arrived, at age seven, he could not speak a word. His jaw jutted down, tongue out, and he made just awful grimaces and grunts. He had been raped almost nightly by his mother's drunken boyfriend and had killed a dog. But now he is up to fifth grade in math and reading skills. He is full of heart." Rebecca smiles.

"Some people think that a child who has seen inappropriate behavior, violence, or sex will never be normal. But they can regain their innocence. Now Paul sees a magazine with women's underwear and gives the typical 10-year-old response—'Ugh, I don't want to look at that!'"

Rebecca runs errands while Paul and Dwight do their summer school routine. Midmorning, the boys disagree over use of the video game. Rebecca returns at noon.

"How did things go?" she asks. "What kind of a score do the boys deserve for behavior?" Rebecca glances at the weekly goal charts posted on the refrigerator. There are marks beneath both the positive and negative columns.

My "almost perfect" response is not good enough for Rebecca. She interrogates the boys. Dwight admits to blaming Paul for using the video game too long. Dwight apologizes immediately. "Please let me do time-out before lunch," he pleads. Paul explains that he had forgotten to set the timer, and Rebecca gives him positive points for honesty. Then Paul changes his story—he says the timer didn't work. Rebecca points out his inconsistency but won't take away his positive points.

"I don't want the points!" Paul starts to cry.

"Why?" Rebecca says.

"Because I didn't earn them. They don't belong to me."

Rebecca walks outside with me. "I wouldn't fuss over such little things with normal kids," she says, "but eventually both Paul and Dwight need the freedom to function independently in the community, and that will be restricted if they don't learn appropriate behaviors. Paul has some mental retardation, and Dwight's biggest challenge is accepting responsibility for his own acts and not blaming others. I can promise that resolution of this morning's problem will make the next visit more enjoyable."

The plight of children who have been damaged in this country provokes polar responses: anger at the adults who injured them in the first place and gratitude for treatment parents who help the healing. Children who are abused the worst can be strengthened by the best. Paul and Dwight stand in front of the refrigerator after breakfast each morning—scrubbed, brushed, and radiant— to recite their favorite scripture for Rebecca.

"When my father and my mother forsake me, then the Lord will take me up. . . . Wait on the Lord: be of good courage, and he shall strengthen thine heart: wait, I say, on the Lord" (Psalm 27: 10, 14).

NOTES

1. Linda Perilstein, "International Adoption Disruption," in *Adoption Factbook III,* (Wait Park, Minn.: National Council for Adoption, 1999), p. 545.

2. Trudy Festinger, "Adoption Disruption: Rates and Correlates," in *The Psychology of Adoption,* ed. David M. Brodzinsky and Marshall D. Schechter (New York: Oxford University Press, 1990), p. 201.

3. Patricia King and Kendall Hamilton, "Bringing Kids All the Way Home," *Newsweek,* June 16, 1997, p. 64.

4. Richard P. Barth and Marianne Berry, *Adoption and Disruption: Rates, Risks and Response* (New York: Aldine De Gruyter, 1988), p. 75.

5. Ibid., p. 108.

6. Ibid., p. 101.

7. Wells Goodrich, Carol S. Fullerton, Brian T. Yates, and Linda Beth Berman, "The Residential Treatment of Severely Disturbed Adolescent Adoptees," in *The Psychology of Adoption,* pp. 255–56.

8. For more information about adoption support, see the National Adoption Information Clearinghouse's Web site: www.calib.com/naic or call 888-251-0075.

9. Judith Schaffer and Christina Lindstrom, "Brief Solution-Focused Therapy with Adoptive Families," in *The Psychology of Adoption,* p. 243.

10. Ron Kral, Judith Schaffer, and Steve deShazer, "Adoptive Families: More of the Same and Different," *Journal of Strategic & Systematic Family Therapy* 8 (1989): 36–39. This case study has been summarized. See also Schaffer and Lindstrom, "Brief Solution-Focused Therapy with Adoptive Families," in *The Psychology of Adoption,* pp. 249–50.

11. Schaffer and Lindstrom, "Brief Solution-Focused Therapy with Adoptive Families," in *The Psychology of Adoption,* p. 251.

All children are alike unto me.
Moroni 8:17

13

A HAIRPIN CURVE
ADOPTION OF FOSTER-CARE CHILDREN

"Children are so very important," says President Gordon B. Hinckley. "I never get over the thought that every man, good or bad, was once a little boy, and that every woman was once a little girl. They have moved in the direction in which they were pointed when they were small. Truly, 'As the twig is bent, so the tree is inclined.' The time to mold the pattern of virtuous youth and faithful adults is childhood."[1]

More than a half million "important" children are in foster care in the United States, many because their teenage mothers rejected adoption in favor of trying to parent their children. The tragedy is that these women often grow tired of poverty and parental responsibility. Half of the children now in foster care were born to unwed mothers.[2] These children, added to others from dysfunctional families, may ultimately become available for adoption after multiple foster-care placements. But children do best when they are adopted before age two, and typically children placed in foster care will be more than five years old by the time they are available for adoption. By then they have often developed some distrust of life in general and have become more difficult to direct.

VARIED REACTIONS

Eventual adoption is still an excellent step, even though the child who has been in foster care may have to work through feelings of abandonment and *learn* to trust their adoptive parents' loyalty. They may remain anxious for a while about the permanence of their position, but over time all of these insecurities can dissolve in the constancy and support of a loving family.

John Triseliotis and Malcolm Hill determined—from two British studies comparing children who were adopted with others who grew up in foster care or institutions—that "a separate surname, welfare visits, very sporadic appearances by a natural parent or sibling, the comings and goings of short-stay foster children all contributed to a sense of 'unusualness' which stressed their difference from, rather than oneness with, the [foster] family."[3]

Triseliotis and Hill interviewed fifty-two children who were adopted between ages nine and eighteen years, after having lived with the same foster parents for years, to see if the actual adoption procedure really mattered to them. The adopted children said things like, "adoption meant 'permanence' [their word], 'being there for ever' and 'being part of the family'; also that 'no one can remove you' and 'no more social workers visiting.'" The children also attached great importance to their family membership becoming legal. This was true even for those children who were almost adults. They felt the relief of not having to explain to friends and teachers why they have a different surname.[4]

"We received our foster siblings one by one," Meg explains. Meg and her husband, Dylan, cared for several foster children before adopting six of their own (two sibling groups).

"The social worker felt it was better to work into it gradually; older kids have to want a placement for it to work, so [the children] came to us at two-month intervals. The last one to arrive was ten-year-old Blessing. I picked her up at the airport in time to meet the other kids as they came home from school. The windows were down in the car, and Aaron, her next younger brother

whom she hadn't seen for two months, was walking by the side of the road.

"'Blessing,' Aaron yelled. 'I'm so happy to see you.' Blessing ducked down, flushed. 'Oh,' she said. 'I wish he hadn't called me that name here.'

"The happiest day for all the children was when they got new names. Blessing changed her name to Linzi; she didn't know how to spell yet and sounded it out phonetically. Aaron chose to keep his middle name and Chastity, the baby, we renamed Allison; she didn't get a choice. But the change they liked best—since they all had different fathers—was to have the same last name.

"Everybody should have the experience of taking in an older child, for the child's sake," Meg says, beaming at the ruckus her children are creating after school. "There are so many out there, eager to be taught and loved. Our children would never let us miss a Family Home Evening. They are so hungry for spiritual guidance they always remind us."

Dylan's arrival home from work increases the noise. His tall, lanky frame collapses on the floor in a tussle with the boys. The little girl climbs on top. Dylan works on a power crew for a telephone company outside Sacramento. On the side he repairs tractors. He walks outdoors before dinner.

"We adopted our first two foster children, siblings by birth," Dylan says, "when they were six and eight years old." Dylan leans against one of the tractors and rubs the wheel hub with his oily rag. "They came with ADD and had been sexually and physically abused. The birthfather was of average intellect, alcoholic, and abusive. The birthmother was of lower intellect and neglectful."

"What's not fair," he says, "is that when it's obvious the parents aren't going to change, the system doesn't get the children placed immediately. It was a year after we adopted the first two before they let us know a third sibling was also available. By then the two-year-old had lived in seven foster homes."

Censure of foster care programs is ongoing. It's easy to look for others to blame when badly neglected children wait long periods of time for a stable family. A primary goal of the child-welfare system is family reunification. In two-thirds of child-welfare cases sufficient change in family life is made so that children in foster care can return to their original homes. But the return is not always permanent; nearly one-third go back to foster care either once, multiple times, permanently, or until adoption placement.[5]

Social workers agree that the first removal of a child from an abusive or neglectful situation is the momentous one. Children are deeply conservative creatures and need their environment to stay the same, even requesting the same peanut butter and jelly sandwich for years on end. Children are particularly set in their ways when it comes to family, friends, and schools.

The initial placement of a child into foster care is very disruptive. Grief, separation, and loss are issues foster parents must help foster children handle. In addition, foster parents must adjust their own feelings when the children they have become attached to leave. Regrettably, the foster child's return home may not be in his best interest.

RIGHTS OF ORIGINAL PARENTS

Our society has been very hesitant to terminate parental rights. Returning children to their original family whenever possible has been supported by law in the United States. For example, the Oregon Supreme Court in *State v. McMaster,* 1971 held that, "The best interests of the child are paramount; however, the courts cannot sever parental rights when many thousands of children are being raised under basically the same circumstances . . . transiency and incapacity, poverty and instability. . . . [This situation] is duplicated in hundreds of thousands of American families."[6]

In 1982 the U.S. Supreme Court struck down a New York statute permitting termination of parents' rights by a "fair preponderance" of evidence. The court maintained that the due process clause of the United States Constitution requires that permanent neglect of the child be proved by at least "clear and convincing evidence." For many children needing permanent homes this ruling is unfortunate, but it is the charge of the U.S. Supreme Court to protect constitutional freedom, and its decisions reflect our nation's enduring respect for the right of parents to rear their own children.

However, the Adoption and Safe Families Act, passed by Congress in November of 1997, focuses more than ever before on the health and safety of children. It requires states to place children coming from abusive situations for adoption or with a legal guardian in a timely manner and requires termination of parental rights to be initiated if a child has been in foster care for fifteen of the previous twenty-two months. The act is fortified with financial incentives to states that increase adoptions of foster children. The act also requires states to provide health insurance coverage for children who would not be adopted without it. The results have been significant. Finalized adoptions of children previously in foster care have risen significantly, and 64 percent result in the children being adopted by their foster parents.[7]

FORTIFYING THE PROSPECTS

Two years later Meg is subdued when I return to visit. She washes dishes in front of a window framed by flouncing curtains. The kitchen is cozy. Seven chairs are pushed in under the table. The youngest child, Allison, sits in the eighth chair eating a Popsicle.

"Allison is the one of our six children who I believe will be totally free from the impact of her earlier life," she says. "Yet all the children are making amazing progress.

"Michael, the youngest of the first sibling group, in some ways surpasses all our other children. Though he was marginally handicapped like his siblings at birth, he brought home straight 'A's in four regular classes at his junior high school last semester—no one in this home has ever done that! I thought, They're making allowances at school. *So I asked the teachers.*

"'Not really,' they said. 'We have someone read for him but he does the rest of the work—answers all the questions by himself.' Meg wipes the sideboards, smiles at Allison.

"The social worker told us when we adopted the first two, 'What they will learn to do in a positive environment no one knows—the results are so varied.' I want to find that social worker to tell her that one of those children now gets 'B's and the other one completed resource classes at the local high school and goes on to the community college this fall. They are doing great!"

Meg and Dylan own a modest home. The front room is big enough for a sofa and upright piano, an anonymous gift they received for Christmas. One bathroom adjoins three bedrooms.

"When we started adopting we were on our own financially," Meg says, "and that was fine. We had sufficient income to raise two children. But with their abusive history we soon encountered the need for counseling. We learned we had a right to medical cards. With our adoption of Michael we were given a monthly subsidy," Meg says. "We could never have afforded to take him without it. Money isn't the problem."

Meg leans on the broom handle, "It's one of our children—" *she hesitates again,* "Linzi is trying to distance herself from us. In her view we represent everything that is disconnecting her from the past. And it's not that Linzi likes the drug scene her mother was into, or even that she had a loving, devoted relationship with her. But she stubbornly clings to some dream that never existed, 'I'm not going to let go!'"

"Does her behavior affect the other children?" *I ask.*

"She puts down the oldest two because she's quicker mentally." *Meg sweeps slowly as she talks.* "And her struggle tears at the younger ones who want everyone to be happy, to be together all the time. Twice she has tried to run and then come back on her own. But this is all recent, in the last year, ever since—" *Meg sinks down into a chair* "—ever since last summer when we decided to take the kids to Reno. We promised the second set of siblings—Linzi, Aaron, and Allison—that they could see their friends, former foster family, and the grandmother who has been so kind. The birthmother had just completed a drug rehab program, and before we ever went the foster family asked us if we would like the children to meet with the mother too. We considered carefully and said 'no'—the birthmother is still a prostitute. Well, the foster family took our kids to a bus stop and waited there until that certain lady walked by.

"'Here's our friend!' the foster parents announced to the children. Allison didn't even recognize her. Aaron kind of did, but Linzi was all over her. There were tears, hugs.

"'Oh, my babies,' the lady cried. Obviously we no longer have communication with the foster family," *Meg's eyes droop,* "but

Linzi's done a tailspin since then, caught in a confusion of iden-
tities. So," Meg sets a smile, "we keep going to therapy!

"People in the neighborhood talk like they envy me. 'You're so
lucky,' they say, 'to have missed the diapers and the toilet train-
ing.'

"'I'll trade you straight across,' I say, 'for all the years of ther-
apy.' Yet I don't know what I'd do without it. I learned this week
that Aaron doesn't view me as a happy person. He received an
assignment from his therapist to work on me. Aaron came home
and asked, 'Please say when you're happy, Mom.' Meg puts on a
bright face.

"I guess he only sees the surface things I worry about. So we
just keep trying, like other parents keep trying. I want us to be a
family forever. And I don't believe the risks are greater for us. We
share the same risks with all parents; children can wrench your
heart around but they can also bring you the most joy. The worst
of our problems we discuss with parents who are experiencing
the same thing in kids born to them."

Couples who adopt a foster child can multiply exponentially
their child's opportunities for growth. The children, typically,
are already in the midst of their most productive learning
years. Their personalities are fairly well developed, and any
developmental problems they may have are somewhat visible.

Marianne Takas and Edward Warner in *To Love a Child* point
out that no form of adoption is without risk. Even the "adoption of an infant, often believed to be a guarantee of a 'clean
slate,' may actually entail some risks greater than those in the
adoption of an older child. Some disabilities [such as prenatal
drug and alcohol exposure] may not show up in an infant, but
may prove to be quite severe as the child reaches later developmental stages."[8] So foster children, if one understands and
obtains training to handle their needs, may be a preferable
route to adoption. As least parents can see a bit more clearly
what they are receiving, and the number of available children
is plentiful.

Almost all of the children in foster care who are being
adopted can respond to consistent, caring discipline. "Some

people have the impression that foster care is a 'dumping ground' for children who are out of control," says Patricia Ryan, administrative director of the Institute for the Study of Children and Families at Eastern Michigan University. "This is a complete misunderstanding." Ryan adds that children who are so out of control as to be dangerous to themselves or others need a more structured environment than foster or adoptive families can provide.[9]

Furthermore, children in foster care with significant problems should not be relinquished to adoptive parents without substantial safeguards for their future care. The adoption agreement, which both the adoptive parents and the agency sign, is a legal document itemizing the parents' rights and responsibilities along with the child's rights and the agency's responsibilities. But its most important function may be to assure coverage of the child's special medical and therapeutic needs. The Child Welfare and Adoption Act makes continued medical coverage possible through the state social services department, but it must be specified in the agreement to be guaranteed. Having a lawyer who specializes in child-welfare issues—one who is separate from the agency—review the agreement to ensure that health coverage and any other needed services are provided could prevent a financial catastrophe. Prospective adoptive parents should also be aware that federal law requires health insurance companies to protect children who are adopted in the same way they do birth children.

The transition of foster children into an adoptive home is understandably hard work. The preadoptive placement is an opportunity for parents and child to get acquainted, a standard procedure in most states. During that time the development of trust merely commences, and the separation anxiety a child may feel towards previous caregivers gradually eases. Throughout this early stage young children may ask innumerable questions. They need answers and an understanding of the family "rules"—a sense of structure right from the beginning. But the potential parent's discipline should never overshadow the nurturing of communication. The older a child is the more significant ties he may have with his foster family, his original family, or others from his past. A child's desire for contact should always be respected. Parents, however, must use their own judgment, drawing on the additional skills of an adoption worker or therapist to confirm when perpetuating the variety of previous connections is constructive or destructive to future development. Facilitating the continuity of constructive relationships is extremely important, but assisting the child in disengaging from adverse ones is also consequential and may require great skill and sensitivity.

THE FOST-ADOPT ROUTE

Some social service agencies have found a way to minimize the multiplicity of placements and, consequently, the difficulty of preadoptive transitions for foster children clearly headed toward adoption. Children who are not legally free to be adopted but for whom adoption appears likely are placed with families who already qualify to adopt and have made a commitment to provide foster care in the interim. This more permanent type of foster care is sometimes called legal risk placement or foster care adoption. The advantages are obvious: it assures consistent care for the foster child as long as needed and offers the foster family the right to adopt in the event the birth parents' rights are terminated. Such clear-cut cases naturally receive agency attention. Social services departments are relieved to resolve the child's impermanent situation as soon as possible. Takas and Warner still counsel parents that "foster parenting should not be viewed as a route to adoption," undoubtedly as a protection to parents and children if the expected adoption plan does not work out. At the same time they recognize that for parents who are willing to take in a child for as long as needed—or for parents who are already foster parenting a child who becomes available for adoption—"a fostering-to-adoption route might be just right for your family."[10]

"The future of adoption is in foster care," says Brenda, "which has been going on for thirty years." She watches over youngsters playing in a jungle of T-swings and climbing ropes.

"America," Brenda says, "is finally coming out of the stereo-type that all adopted kids need to be matched, perfect children." Brenda is white and short, in striking contrast to her tall, black husband Javan. They have fostered a girl of mixed race (whom they later adopted) and a baby boy at birth who is black. In between, they adopted two other children through an agency.

"The birthparents of our oldest daughter were living on the street," Brenda says, "for the first year of her life. Our daughter was traumatized at two weeks and at eleven weeks. When we received her two years later she would hoard food, hide it, and eat very quickly. The mother sent a letter once a year, the father came to visit after he got out of prison, and the state left us on our own with no strings attached. We knew we could have her if she ever became available. Both of her parents were into drugs and pros-titution. A year ago, when she was nearly six, the adoption went through." The daughter is a comely, slender blend of African-American and Native-American ancestry.

"The foster-care system," Brenda says, "is not nurturing to fos-ter parents. You feel like you are always walking on eggshells. They will almost discourage you unless you're a nurse or a psy-chologist. My husband, Javan, has been a correctional officer, exposed to life on the street and legal procedures. Fingerprints, TB tests, approved baby-sitters, and a safety code in the house are all part of the foster-care system; Javan is used to all that. We had to put smoke alarms in every place that a child could possibly sleep. Neighbors came by and saw us installing them. 'What a nice thing to do!' they said. For us it was legislated."

Brenda quit her job as a flight coordinator to be with her chil-dren. She started a home preschool. Brenda holds the back door open for a child who needs to use the bathroom.

"Our baby boy was abandoned at the hospital, somewhat at risk. His parents have shown up since but failed to conform to any necessary guidelines. Once we had him in foster care we stayed very much on top of the attorneys and social workers. They were the center of our attention—we were not the center of theirs. But we could choose from the options they gave us. Nothing was final until we said so. We made it clear with Social Services from the beginning that we were committed to the

foster-care system," Brenda says. "And in both states where we applied for foster children we were also totally open with them about our desire to adopt. But Social Service's priorities aren't necessarily ours.

"'Will you take this cute baby?' they ask. Others are willing to grab it right up. Then they learn this cute baby has a dad who's finally been off drugs for a year, and the cute baby goes back to him. It's not just what the agency says to you that counts," she says. "When birthparents are involved it can become very complicated. So when the foster-care agency gets custody of a child where the evidence is concrete—the child's been abandoned and permanent neglect is easy to prove in the courts—they're not just acting expeditiously for humanitarian reasons. It's definitely more of a win-win situation for them and they give the placement priority." Javan waves from inside the kitchen window. A girl with spunky braids is riding piggyback on his shoulders; she waves too. The last of the preschool children leaves, and Brenda escorts her own little boy inside the house.

"More and more people are trying to come into the system," she says. "But the feeling among those who adopt through foster care is totally different than among those in regular agency adoptions. When we worked through an adoption agency the couples were kind of competing. With people anticipating foster care there's a great shared desire. They're far more diverse, but they all have that big heart. Sitting around a table with them you can pick out the ones who will make it in the program. It takes real special people." Javan's deep laugh echoes on the hardwood floors. Brenda smiles.

"And total dedication," she says. "To complete the adoption for Chandler it took a year and five months. It could have happened in six months because he was abandoned at birth, but a new social worker came on board who took over the case. And then there are always eighty-five cases ahead of yours, and the paperwork trail is endless." Brenda straightens her back, smooths her khaki slacks.

"Just last week someone called me from Social Services asking for my copy of a hospital billing on Chandler—he's almost two, the adoption is complete, and they're coming to me! But that's

simple compared to our first one where the parents were in and out of the picture for five years. The system is designed to be very protective of the birthparent." Brenda walks to the front room and looks out the window. Javan is unloading supplies from his white van parked in the driveway. The children are helping.

"And Javan is very protective of our children. When our daughter asks to sleep over at some Susie Q's house, even if I've met the mother, he isn't about to approve unless he's met Susie Q's dad. Javan's never had a strong sense of where he needs to live—his parents raised him in the military, and moves mean nothing—but he has a powerful allegiance to the importance of home life." Brenda opens the front door; Javan and the children fill the threshold, loaded down with gallon jugs.

FOSTER PARENTS' INTERESTS

Foster-care adoption has been shaped by supply and demand. Most observers claim that money has never attracted foster parents, who are paid a daily fee, which in some states is lower than $10 a day per child. The reality is that, whether motivated by economics or not, foster parents traditionally came from lower economic levels. But the typical profile of foster parents is changing for multiple reasons.

Foster parents now have legal rights. For years the courts disparaged the whole idea, but in recent years they have suggested that foster parents have a liberty interest in preserving their relationship with the child. In *Berhow v. Crow,* 1982, the ruling stated, "As the nature of the foster parent/foster child's familial relationship becomes closer and stronger, so as to approach the level of the relationship between natural parents and their offspring, so, too, do the rights of foster parents to preserve that relationship."[11]

Adverse publicity regarding various aspects of the foster-care system has led to a significant change in the application of laws and the attitude of professionals toward foster parents who want to become adoptive parents. Foster parents can now become part of the treatment plans for their foster children. They can also have access to available information about the child; although in the past some caseworkers gave them very little.

Public requests have gone out for more foster parents, as the huge number of children in foster care has been made known. When Utah's overflow of foster children exceeded the capacity of state-run shelters, the First Presidency of The Church of Jesus Christ of Latter-day Saints issued a statement encouraging families to consider (as citizen volunteers and not as part of any Church calling) the plea of Utah's governor "to be a family to a child who isn't safe going home."[12]

The decreased number of babies available for adoption is another substantial reason the foster-care system is now attracting adults of more affluence; 25 percent of foster children end up becoming available for adoption.[13]

STEADFAST PERSISTENCE

Few things surprise children—since everything they experience is new to them—and those who are neglected often develop a passive acceptance of their situation. But children shed passivity when given opportunity and a chance to discover. Then they become suffused with the enthusiasm of growing up. Children's imaginations depend on interaction with their surroundings. If no opportunity comes, children live on with a dull, permanent hopelessness.

For children caught in their parents' despair, going from foster care to adoption is the hairpin curve. It can turn life around, not in the twinkling of an eye, but steadily. Because abuse and neglect stifle ethical growth, the first step may be to help older children develop basic moral character. They may need very fundamental lessons in honesty, dependability, chastity, and kindness to others. Also lacking in their development could be such sensitivities as gratitude, respect, and reverence. Parents may need to be satisfied with bit-by-bit progress. Church activity could be a totally new experience for them and may be offered most effectively by degrees in the way Paul describes as "are become such as have need of milk, and not of strong meat" (Hebrews 5:12).

Adults who adopt foster children also teach them inherently. They demonstrate their own depth of character, not so much by what they do or say as how they do it. Their children are gradually exposed to the myriad of possibilities for a life's work and the qualities of persistence for achieving goals—a mode that can be perpetually invigorating. The effort adoptive parents expend is great but commensurate with the possible rewards. Foster children are powerful transition figures; they have the capacity to change the course of future generations as they themselves change.

Social service agencies should prepare adopting parents for their challenges by openly disclosing what problems they might anticipate with a specific child. Adoptive parents can responsibly insist on access to all background information. Once the adoption decision is made it can be comforting for parents to remember, as they live out day-to-day challenges, that children who have suffered through significant trauma can heal. The timetable may be incomprehensible, but these children are, after all, the Lord's children too. Adoptive parents of children who have tough backgrounds can become the Lord's tools, and the essential aspect of their job is to point the child in the right direction.

Supplied with facts and fortified through training programs and personal faith, potential parents must strive to comprehend the qualities of character necessary within themselves to tackle the unanticipated problems. The following case study illustrates the attributes that assure parents will influence for good the lives of their most nonconforming children.

CJ is twenty-three years old. She's been truck driving for two months, since soon after her baby died. CJ has twenty-four hours off duty while the eighteen-wheeler is in for servicing before going on to Pittsburgh. She chooses a booth for us in the corner of the cafe.

"I was adopted when I was four and my brother was eight," CJ says. "They told me that my mom and dad dropped us off at the welfare office. I don't remember that because I was only a year old when it happened. But I was scared to death when I moved in with my adoptive parents.

"'This is where we live,' they said, 'call us Mom and Dad.' At first neither me or my brother attached to anyone but ourselves. And we gave our new Mom and Dad a hell of a time. My brother

was a terror—he knew more what was going on, but he'd been abused more too." A waitress brings ice water. Hootie and the Blowfish is blaring through the sound system.

"My adoptive parents had this philosophy: the more people who loved us, the better off we'd be. They were taking a chance, bless their hearts, but they took us up to Springfield to visit my foster family, who were really good friends with my birthparents."

The music pulses on. CJ sips her drink.

"So we kept a close friendship with my foster brother and sister, my foster mom—all except for my foster dad, who divorced. They adored me," *she winks,* "—this big, blue-eyed blonde—and gave me extra special treatment." *CJ orders a salad to go with her hamburger, dressing on the side.*

"I'm up to 180 pounds," *she tells me. CJ is six feet tall and statuesque in tight jeans and a T-shirt. Her fingernails are long with dark red polish. Short clipped hair shows off a collection of pierced earrings.*

"I thought my adoptive parents were mean to lay down the law. We had to do all kinds of jobs; they didn't even give us an allowance. If we wanted something we had to earn it, even our clothes. I had to clean the bathroom, rake the leaves. They were well-educated, read to us a lot, and were real active in the Church. My dad taught seminary so we knew we weren't supposed to smoke and drink or have sex before marriage. I was stubborn." *CJ gently glides her ringed finger under one eye, navigating below the mascara.*

"Back then I didn't understand that they were trying to teach me responsibility. When I took money from them I had to earn it back, and my parents always said they still loved me. But my friends got beat on the head for stealing or whatever—they got beat every day. Their parents were alcoholics, didn't know how to show love. Those friends are practically bums on the street now." *CJ blinks, wide-eyed.*

"Me and my mom got close after I married and had a baby who was handicapped. My husband wanted to throw our baby away—like put him in the garbage." *CJ winces.* "I wasn't about to do that!"

"Taking care of my son was a twenty-four-hour-a-day job, and *that finally broke up our marriage. My son had cerebral seizures for a year, then sodium diabetes—got sick easy—was in and out of the hospital most of his life, and Mom would come and sing Primary songs to him, to us. They found five cysts on his brain that obscured the optic nerves. That's why he was blind. It's still hard to be around kids who are normal; my son never walked. The first time he got up on his hands and knees I cried for joy." CJ teeters a fork over her salad.*

"When information came out on fetal alcohol syndrome my Mom sent me a copy of the newspaper clippings. Before that nobody had fully understood the problems me and my brother had been born with. But I was six weeks along before I realized I was pregnant. I stopped drinking then, but my baby was born with problems far worse.

"He was four when he finally died, and I blamed God." CJ closes her eyes, tips her head back, and mouths the words to another of Hootie's songs.

"I'm past that now," she says. "My life experiences have made me who I am, stronger because of them. Everyone goes through trials. I want to get back in school. I finally got my high school diploma through the college. I took one of my dad's courses. I walked into class with a nose ring—it was like, 'the preacher's daughter dares!'" CJ grins then leans forward, speaks faster.

"My goal is to be an RN. I like taking care of other people's kids, and sometime . . . I want a good marriage, a family by one person. So it won't be one of those fast hookups like when people just think they're in love." CJ pushes her plate away, rubs the back of her neck.

"I wish I'd done things differently, wish my parents had understood my problems earlier, wish society hadn't had such a big effect on the way I was raised. But my mom and dad wish they had done things differently too; we kids didn't come with an instruction book. My parents are good people. They always had the courage to admit it when they made mistakes—'We didn't know better,' they said. 'We're learning a lot.'"

CJ tidies up the table, scoots the crumbs onto her napkin, lines up the salt and pepper shakers next to the ashtray.

"And we just keep on learning."

NOTES

1. Gordon B. Hinckley, in Conference Report, October 1970, p. 102.
2. Lincoln Caplin, *An Open Adoption* (New York: Farrar, Staus, and Giraux, 1990), pp. 124–26.
3. John Triseliotis and Malcolm Hill, "Contrasting Adoption, Foster Care, and Residential Rearing," in *The Psychology of Adoption,* ed. David M. Brodzinsky and Marshall D. Schechter (New York: Oxford University Press, 1990), p. 112.
4. Ibid., p. 113.
5. Lois M. Collins, "Foster Care: Children's Lives in a State of Crisis," *Deseret News,* April 24, 1994, pp. B1–2.
6. *State v. McMaster,* 1971, pp. 572–73, as cited in Andre P. Derdeyn, "Foster Parent Adoption: The Legal Framework" in *The Psychology of Adoption,* p. 337.
7. www.acf.dhhs.gov/programs/cb/index.htm
8. Marianne Takas and Edward Warner, *To Love a Child: A Complete Guide to Adoption, Foster Parenting, and Other Ways to Share Your Life with Children* (Reading, Mass.: Addison-Wesley Publishing Co., 1992), p. 14.
9. Patricia Ryan in ibid., pp. 13–14.
10. Ibid., p. 122.
11. *Berhow v. Crow,* 1982, pp. 371–72, as cited in Derdeyn, "Foster Parent Adoption: The Legal Framework," p. 341.
12. Michael Leavitt in Mike Cannon, "Volunteers Are Urgently Needed," *Church News,* December 16, 1995, p. 5.
13. www.acf.dhhs.gov/programs/cb/index.htm

And we know that all things work together for good.
Romans 8:28

14
PEOPLE—
NOT TERRAIN
WHY SEARCH?

Many children who were adopted in confidential place-ments become curious about their origins, even if they don't care to meet their birthparents. A much smaller percentage (current estimates start at 2 percent of the country's adoptees) is driven to find them. Advocates of open records project that 30 to 40 percent of adopted persons will ultimately search for their birthparents during their lifetimes. Obviously the dis-crepancy in opinions and predictions of search patterns is enormous. Nevertheless, the number of adoptees who do pur-sue searches is increasing, in spite of sealed birth records in most states. "For some adopted persons the absence of a sense of human connectedness assumes intolerable propor-tions at a conscious level," say adoption specialists Marshall Schechter and Doris Bertocci. "For them, search becomes a rational response to certain irrational circumstances over which they have heretofore had no control."[1]

THE ASSERTIVE FACTOR

Typical teenagers strive toward independence. Often they begin to resist authority figures—especially their parents.

When resistant teenagers are adopted they may have a more complicated developmental challenge. A struggling teenager who was adopted may assert herself by considering a search for her biological family. The search may have nothing to do with the quality of relationship she has with her adoptive parents or the need for a relationship with birthparents. It is often part of the need to choose for oneself—to be a free agent.

Psychological studies substantiate that in most families a reunion with the birthparents *improves* the relationship of the child with her adoptive parents. "Often a meeting with the birthparents actually brings the adoptee and the adoptive parents closer together," concur David Brodzinsky and Marshall Schechter. "Even after a searcher has found his birthparents, it is still his adoptive parents whom he calls Mom and Dad."[2] The typical person who actually pursues the search is a young adult woman, between twenty-three and twenty-nine years of age.

Samantha, however, illustrates the profile of the passionate teenager who awakened clinicians and society at large to the fact that searchers in a closed system are not "sick youths," unless we make them that way. Searching is not pathological. Young adults who search have normal but intense curiosity and persistence—qualities that are also respectable.

"Samantha was our only child to pursue a search relentlessly—until she had an answer, until she was shredded," Mary says. Samantha was adopted by Mary and Charles Krause when she was five days old, their second of three adopted children.

"In grade school Samantha asked me to call the adoption agency. 'Please find out anything you can.' I asked. I was told that the files were closed. Samantha accepted that. By middle school she was angry, lashing out. In high school she hired a private detective who illegally copied information about her biological mother from an agency file. Samantha went directly to a genealogical library in Voorhees and found everything she wanted to know—names and birth information of grandparents, brothers, and sisters. We learned about her findings after coming back

*from an evening in Philadelphia. Parallel to us on the freeway
was Samantha in her spiffy car. She waved to us, grinning.*

*"When we all arrived home she said, 'I have just met my
mother's brother and his wife.' Samantha held a cloth rabbit
shaped from a washcloth, trimmed in bows, that she fiddled with
in her hands; it turned out to be a token of the new relatives' welcome and love. She was thrilled to pieces that she had found her
family. Samantha's biological mother called our home soon after.
I answered the phone.*

*"'Thank you so much for your daughter,' I said. She talked to
Samantha, sent her a birthday card.*

*"Then the bottom dropped out. The biological mother forbade
anyone in her family from having further contact with Samantha.
Her brother came to our front door. 'Make Samantha leave us
alone. She was a mistake from the beginning, and my sister
wants to rid her mind of it. We are going to abide by her wishes.'*

*"'Please accept their desires,' we told Samantha. 'Do not pur-
sue it anymore.'*

*"Samantha ignored us. Then all her emotions spilled out at her
biological mother instead of me. That was a great turning point,
but I could hardly stand to live with the anger. I felt bad for the
whole situation. She wrote scathing letters to her birthmother.
Her mother responded by threatening her, 'Do not contact my
parents or you will kill them. They have weak hearts.' A letter followed which Samantha shared with us—notice the spelling of her
name:"*

Sinantha, I'm sorry you are having difficulty with accepting
my decisions and wishes. Your happiness is important to me,
however I made a decision twenty years ago that I know was
right. I have never looked back or wished to have done things
differently.

Maybe if I would have known your biological father or had
any relationship with him, I would have felt a bond to you. I
was five months along before I even realized I was pregnant.
My parents did not know of my condition until seven months.
I made the decision for adoption on my own will. I never had
the feeling that the baby inside even belonged to me.

I never knew or wanted to know if the baby was male or

female. I never even asked to hold the baby. I always believed that the Lord placed a special baby inside my body for a family that was unable to have children of their own.

Sinantha, please understand that I have my own reasons for not wanting to share any of this to my friends or family—yes, not even my husband and children. I do not want to relive the past.

Please do not feel that I have rejected you. I cannot reject someone who really never belonged to me. Please close your search and go on with your precious life. You are a very special person. Be happy for all your many blessings; you're intelligent, pretty and have so many wonderful opportunities ahead of you. You must place all your sad thoughts away and use that determination and pride to build a wonderful future.

I will think of you on your birthdays and will pray for your happiness.

Love, your friend

"Samantha let me read one of the letters she wrote back," Mary says. *"I was very embarrassed. I tried to help her understand her birthmother. But Samantha saw the relationship with her another way. She told me, 'I prayed that if I was able to find my mother it would be for a positive purpose, and that if I was not supposed to find her, I wouldn't.'*

"I thought to myself, Samantha was praying?" Mary says as she arches her brows.

"During Samantha's teenage years she had only a few girl friends and they had lots of problems. Meanwhile, everything physical that boys were doing Samantha liked to do. She wore her hair straight, cut short. At school, when she went into the bathroom, the girls would screech and squeal, 'Get out of here! Sammy's a boy!' Her sexual identity was destroyed. Her boyishness, smoking and drinking friends, and eventual ostracism from church activities kept her in constant trouble. But Samantha was born with charity and she stayed true to her friends.

"At age fifteen she lied about her age and got a job washing dishes at Braddock's Tavern, ambitious to own a car. She bought the neighbor's Chevy Vega when she turned sixteen, then a BMW,

an Audi, a CRX—she owned five cars in seven years, negotiating personally with car dealers and mechanics. Samantha would talk with Charles for hours, working out the financial deals. She was pretty good morally; there was only one boy in her life, and he was homosexual. 'Don't need to worry about him, Mother.' That boy walked in our house like he was the owner—of everybody in it! Nothing was sacred or private in her life that he did not invade." Mary slumps down in her chair.

"She forged our name and got $1,000 from our checking account to buy a motorcycle. That was our limit. We dropped everything, took her out of school, and went to the bank. When we finished the paperwork that boy was waiting for her. She left with him and flipped us off. Charles and I stood there in the parking lot and decided to put her in a psychiatric treatment center. We didn't know what else to do!

"Samantha became good friends with counselors running the program. She helped the staff with other kids who were much worse. Her charitable nature had stayed intact; I was not able to see that aspect of her personality during the teenage years, except for this brief glimpse. But she came out of treatment burning mad.

"Her favorite act in those days was to slam—the front door, her bedroom door, her bike against the house, her bike against me, me against the wall. Charles couldn't defend me because he was never here when she was slamming. I thought the gates of hell had opened in front of us. Just before she finished high school Samantha moved out. She barely graduated."

Mary walks into the dim living room. She opens a leather scrapbook. The curtains are open, and she moves close to the window where there's enough sunlight. "This is her graduation picture." Mary grins.

Samantha is stunning, posing like a model in a skimpy, black knit gown. "She didn't even own a dress," Mary says, "until she bought this one. Charles and I were scheduled to go on a business trip that June. We gave Samantha a ticket to France under the guise of a graduation present; we were competing with the gay boyfriend who wanted to take her to Myrtle Beach.

"Samantha came home a month later. 'If I ever marry,' she

said—you know she was never going to marry because of her friends—'I want to marry a boy like Matt Jones.' She had met him at Tour de France. They were both bikers. In a month Matt was on our doorstep. Three weeks later they were engaged. He was a charming boy, shorter than she, very slight and very good. Matt transformed Samantha into the girl she was always meant to be.

"I went to bed sobbing during their engagement," Mary says, "begging to be forgiven for how I had felt about Samantha. She had been in pain—all she could exhibit was hate. Out-of-control teenagers don't know how to change, and their parents cannot help—they are the victims of their children's anger.

"The wedding was called off when she and Matt had their first argument. A detective caught up with Samantha four weeks later. Several months before, her friends had arranged to drive her CRX into the river while she was at a movie, so that Samantha could collect the insurance for a new BMW or whatever car she owned next. The judge let her off with a high fine; she dropped her old friends.

"Samantha worked as a dental assistant during the day and threw freight for Super Fresh at night. Her birthmother called our home the evening of March 17, 1991. I remember the date because it was my grandmother's birthday. That woman was furious.

"'We've been getting obnoxious phone calls,' she said accusingly to me, 'that have to stop.' And I said, 'I'm not sure they are from Samantha, but you can talk to her yourself—when she gets home.'

"'While you are on the line,' I told her, 'I think you should listen to me, please.' I told the birthmother what Samantha had gone through in her life. I told her how much we had struggled. "And in my opinion,' I said, 'you need to own some of it.'

"The woman calmed. 'I have not asked your first name before,' she said. 'May I call you again?'

"Samantha came home at 11:00 A.M. the next morning to get ready for her day job. She looked dreadful.

"'My mother called didn't she?" Samantha grabbed her portable phone and sat down on the floor while I ironed, waiting for me to say something. I told her about my conversation the day

before. Samantha listened intently. I told her that someday she would understand who she really is. The phone rang. She jumped up, ran into her room, and shut the door. A long time later she found me in my bedroom.

"'Mother,' she said. 'I did not get angry.'

"'I didn't hear what you said,' I told her, 'but I could tell.'

"'Why didn't I?'

"'Because you are not like that,' I said."

Mary shifts her gaze from a hummingbird feeder in the yard. She speaks directly, slowly. "That is not really a true statement, after all I've said about Samantha's actions," Mary says, *"unless—you consider her basic charitable nature. After that conversation I still thought,* she is better now than she's ever been, but the other shoe will drop tomorrow, she'll slam the door next week or next month. *I was wrong. Samantha never did again. She went into the bathroom, blew her nose, used the toilet, and it's as if the anger flushed away."*

ELEMENTS OF MATURITY

Samantha described herself to me the night before an anatomy midterm at Penn State. We talked during a study break. "I was very insecure as a child," she said. "I wasn't one to have a lot of friends—kind of a loner. I didn't do very good in school growing up because I didn't have self-confidence. Since I found 'her' [the birthmother] and kind of resolved that, I've been able to learn a lot better. Now that I'm in college, it's amazing." Samantha is now married to a business student. She wears a bulky sweater over tights obscuring the last trimester of her pregnancy.

"People get the wrong idea of adoption reunions from TV shows, and they build false hopes. I still believe that children should have a right to meet their biological parents. I don't regret my search. Honesty is the lesson I've learned from this whole adoption experience—" Samantha slows down, choosing her words. "And I feel bad for my biological mother. She never told anybody else about me all these years, and she's petrified I'm going to show up."

Frustrated parents of a groping teenager may do well to reflect on the positive attributes that were evident during their child's earliest years. Viewing life backwards provides glimpses of fundamental strengths which may be obscured during subsequent phases. Mary continued to recognize Samantha's charitable nature; it was a source of perpetual hope that welled up in her at a peak moment to ease resurgence of Samantha's essential character.

Teenagers like Samantha are not typical; yet they demonstrate that for some the search may seem constructive—their lives are chaotic without it. When the reunion with a birthparent does not confirm dreams of a loving relationship, the compelled grown child still tends to be glad she searched. Betty Jean Lifton, a professional writer whose reunion with her birthmother was not successful, still sees compensatory benefits in the process because "maturity comes when we can accept the complexities and ambiguities of our situation and make them work for us, rather than against us—and go on."[3] Lifton quotes Marshall Schechter's advice, "Adoptees must learn to say: 'Yes, I may have come from that, but this is what I am now.' They have to learn that there's a difference between being related and developing a relationship."[4] Samantha is comfortably mature now with the knowledge of her biological heritage. She recently sent me a newspaper article written from the viewpoint of a sensitive birthmother. She and her husband live in Chester with their four children; the oldest is five. "Samantha's an amazing mother," says her aunt, who just returned from a visit. "Interacting with all those children she is calm and wise and fun. I think she is doing what she was born to do."

The strongest craving of the person who was adopted is simply to see the physical similarities between themselves and their birth families—if only through photographs. Many children, whether they search or not, fantasize positively about their birthparents, believing they are of humble origin and exceptionally caring. Those who pursue a search are eager to confirm their birthparents' inherent goodness and to share what they imagine to be a mutual sense of loss. In a broad sense, many adoption therapists say, *all* people who were adopted engage in a search process. They search for the underlying reasons behind their adoption and seek to integrate these facts into their identity, which is healthy. Generalizing the concept of the search reduces the fear for some individuals involved in a traditional adoption situation, but popularizing the search as "a modern rite of passage," Wayne Carp says, may "undermine the legitimacy of adoptive kinship." Dr. Carp is a historian who used his sabbatical to work at the Children's Home Society of Washington, assigned to the Adoption Resource Center. Carp maintains that when the search process was first made popular in the 1970s by the media, it was *idealized* with "a happy ending that was also therapeutically beneficial" and was fueled by the national fervor to search for one's roots.[5]

CONFLICT OVER RIGHTS

The courts view the search movement skeptically (when associated with the opening of sealed records) because it challenges individual constitutional rights. The battle over rights is raging. The clash was fueled by strict closed-record policies implemented in the 1970s to protect the thousands of unmarried mothers who had demanded secrecy in the 1950s. At the same time, the children who were adopted in the 1950s—now young adults—clamored for rights to their birth family information. Generally, America's legal system during the last twenty years has continued to support birthmothers' rights to privacy *over* adoptees' rights to knowledge, but the fight between individual rights is periodically tested.

Meanwhile, society continues to change as judges, psychologists, and journalists continue to speculate about the consequences of opening sealed records. Most can only guess at how much has changed in the attitudes of birthmothers who were promised confidentiality or how many people who were adopted really want access to records in order to search for their birth families. Paul Sachdev, who conducted a survey questionnaire in Ontario, Canada on 123 individuals,[6] thinks he has the answers. More than four-fifths of those who were adopted were pleased or moderately pleased with meeting their birthparents; three-fourths of the birthmothers were moderately to strongly enthusiastic when contacted by the grown children; and the majority of adoptive parents supported their child's search. But the conclusion obscures the fact that *all* participants were part of the minority who ever chose to search.

Currently, many adoptive and birth families commence the adoption process by sharing enough information to make a search easy if the child, when grown to adulthood, desires it. Other families who are living in a totally open arrangement—between both sets of parents and the child—will never face the search issue.

People who were adopted, however, are not the only ones who traditionally have wanted to search. Data collected by Carp from the Children's Home Society of Washington during the last century revealed that grown children who were adopted have made up slightly less than half of those returning for information, and most of them wanted the nonidentifying type—birth certificates needed for employment, military enlistment, and social security benefits. An additional 18 percent were birthmothers, who generally returned within three years of placing their child. Over 15 percent of the searchers were adoptive parents whose children had behavioral problems; they were looking for medical history and additional facts about the birthparents. The nearly 20 percent remaining were composed of siblings, birthfathers, and other blood relatives of the children who were adopted.[7]

BEING FOUND

Blaine didn't initiate a search. Barbara, his birthmother in Tennessee, did—just before his thirtieth birthday.

"I got a letter," he tells me.

"'I hope that you don't get angry with me,' Barbara had written, 'but I've been waiting so long.'

"I wrote back, 'No, I don't mind you writing. I'm in the same situation you are. I have feelings. I need to hunt this down out here first, and find that you really are who you say.'

"I found the lawyer who assisted my parents with my adoption," Blaine explains. "In front of a judge I asked, 'You just tell me on the record "yes," or "no," if she's the one.' Then I felt like I should bomb her with a bunch of pictures. I figured, if she's been

looking for thirty years, she shouldn't have to endure any longer.'
That's when Barbara, my birthmother, called me on the phone.

"'This is your friend from Tennessee,' she said. 'I didn't contact
you ten years earlier because I didn't want to mess you up. People
told me not to get into your life as a teenager.'

"'I'm glad you didn't,' I told her, 'because you would have!'

"I heard from her a lot at first," Blaine says.

"She talked to my wife and kids. I talked to her husband,
daughters, and then I said, 'What would you like to do now,
Barbara?'

"'I'd like to come and see you on your thirtieth birthday.'

"'You're welcome,' I told her. 'You're entitled to that—you've
persevered, and it's like you were supposed to find me.'

"'I would like to be able to walk off the plane,' she said, 'and
have someone call me, Mom.'

"She was the last one to disembark.

"'Barbara,' I said, putting my arms around her before she had
a chance to think. She started to cry and I cried a little bit, not a
lot. My wife cried, the kids too. We passed the Dallas Temple on
the way home. My five-year-old asked, 'Are you in our church?'

"'No, child!' she snapped. 'I am not!'

"I liked her right off. She's a woman who acts on what she
believes. She's tough, this belle from the South. Her husband is a
wonderful guy—she calls him 'a Yankee from Minnesota.'

"Barbara had goals during her visit beyond the tourist agenda
of Dallas we had arranged.

"We sat up one night," he says, waving at the sofa, "—she was
hitting me with personal questions. At one point I felt like, 'I hope
I don't crack under this pressure, and start doing what she wants
me to do.' Barbara wanted a close family-type relationship. She
still wanted me to call her 'Mom.'

"'The reality is,' I told her, 'I've been here as long as I can
remember. I belong to another family.'" Blaine still lives in the
same neighborhood where he was raised, a short walk from his
adoptive parents.

"She stayed with us for two weeks over Christmas and my
birthday. She brought a big train set with her. 'I've always wanted
to see the baby,' she said, 'the boy I gave birth to, playing with a

train.' So my son Jeremy and I set it up. 'Well,' I said, 'look at Jeremy and you can kind of imagine how I would have been.' She met my parents for the first time at a Christmas party we hold in Furrs Cafeteria each year." Shaking his head, Blaine slows down and looks at the carpet.

"This whole 'finding thing' was really hard for my folks. I didn't want to tell them because they're very sensitive. I talked to my dad at his office first. He's been a military man all his life. I said, 'Hey, I would like your help.' Right then I think he knew.

"'I'd be happy to,' he said, 'but . . .' I could see fear in the questions he asked. And then it came down to telling my mom." Blaine pauses. "She couldn't sit in the same chair while I was talking; she had to get up and walk around and finally leave the room. She was crying.

"'This has been harder on her,' Dad told me.

"'I can understand that,' I said, 'because it's been hard for me too, but I have to do this. It's not like I'm doing anything to get away from you. I've been happy my whole life. If I'd been unhappy, I would have taken care of this as a youth. I feel connection with you guys; I always have. I'm just curious.

"But Barbara, my birthmother, who is made of stone as far as her emotions go, froze the night of the party when they were supposed to meet.

"'I don't know if I can go through with this,' she said. She had trouble getting dressed. Driving there was a big crisis. I think it finally hit her, 'I'm going to meet the people who raised him.' For her it wasn't just meeting more people—she envisioned me with them my whole life. She felt really alone and I just kept reassuring her. 'You're here, you're my guest, you're not out of place, you're fine.' But I couldn't be wishy-washy. I introduced her to 'my parents, Vern and Pat.'

"Religion was a big deal for Barbara. She is Pentecostal. We took turns praying while she was here. One night she asked, 'Would you mind?—in my church we give blessings—would you mind if I put my hand on you and said a prayer?' I thought, she believes this way. It's helping. Let her do it. Then a few days later she fell down while visiting Trail Dust and bruised her tailbone. That night I kept checking on her in the bedroom.

"'I'm not feeling too great,' she said.

"'Would you like me to give you a blessing?' I asked, '—like we do in our church?'

"Now I am very interested in Barbara, more than before when finding her was just exciting. My dream came true; I know my genealogy. I'm part Cherokee—so can I claim any rights?" Blaine laughs.

"After she had gone home," he says, "Barbara got unhappy with me. She was really quiet on the phone. That made it rough because I'm not one to pry things out of people.

"'Barbara,' I said, 'aren't you glad we met? Isn't it better that you found out I was taken into a good home, that I'm having a fine life, that I'm not dead?'

"I know Barbara went on a talk show to tell about our reunion, but she never sent the transcript. She had told me during our first phone conversation, 'If I don't like a situation, I walk away from it.'

"And my wife has had enough of this thing." He softens his voice to a whisper in the front room of their apartment.

"My wife was raised in an old house, with things always breaking. When we were driving around Highland Park together, Barbara said, 'Do you know what kind of house I really like?'

"My wife looked at me in terror. Barbara pointed to the one oldish Victorian-type house in all of Dallas, the house I liked best."

Many states have now legislated the establishment of a mutual-consent voluntary registry to facilitate the reunion of birthparents and adult children who were adopted; some states release mutually requested information without a registry. Other privately run registries are designed to connect interested participants living all around the country or within different countries. One of the earliest to be organized, and the most popular, is the International Soundex Registry in Carson City, Nevada. Adoption agencies are often willing to release information if both parties request it. LDS Family Services will accommodate an adult who was adopted and requests a search by turning over to her all *non-identifying* information in her file (medical and autobiographical information on the birthparents as well as any accumulated correspondence). All these organizations support the concept that a reunion should occur *only* if there is mutual interest. Inherent in a voluntary registration policy is the legal assumption that justice is served when that which is desired by both parties, who have reached the age of maturity, is accomplished.

There exist also, however, hundreds of private search groups for people who want to find their relatives, even if the other party to adoption has not registered its interest. Two states, Alaska and Kansas, now allow direct access to original birth certificates for individuals eighteen or older. Nineteen other states allow certain categories of adopted adults access, usually depending on when they were adopted or whether birthparents have consented. Ten of those states also allow a birthparent veto.[8]

WEIGHING THE CONSEQUENCES

The relatively small percentage of individuals who feel compelled to find their birthparents when combined with the third who claim—according to surveys—that they desire to search could make it increasingly popular. Searching has the intrigue of discovery. And birthparents who search for their offspring may add momentum to the trend. But people, not terrain, are involved. Sensitivity to the rights of others and consideration of possible consequences lessen the chance of injury to participants and their concerned families.

Adults are the most likely to search, often motivated by a life-changing event: marriage, the birth of a child, the death of adoptive parents. They tend to be searching more for medical and genealogical information than for a relationship, but the process itself generates powerful feelings. In *Searching for a Past,* Jayne Schooler describes the emotional stages a searcher typically endures. First, the searcher is likely to feel a sense of neutrality. She may think, "This isn't a big deal." But then comes a second stage full of anger and frustration, usually marked by the question: "What—no information?" In the third stage a searcher may start to become obsessed with the search. In this stage the searcher will begin to feel as if the search "consumes all [her] thoughts and [her] time." During stage four the searcher will feel withdrawn, thinking, "This is overwhelming." And finally, in stage five comes acceptance and the feeling that "whatever happens is okay."[9] The searcher who proceeds to open up a relationship with the birthparent(s) faces another barrage of poignant feelings, for "all reunions," Lifton reminds, "no matter how positive, bring a tidal wave of emotions with them, and Adoptees ride these with varying degrees of skill."[10] And a negative encounter is especially discouraging since the possibility of a fulfilling meeting is finally destroyed.

Research on the subject of searching will always produce conflicting results. Only the individual soul can know what to do. One who has studied the facts may then wisely put them aside and pray. "Let your hearts be full," Amulek wrote, "drawn out in prayer unto him continually for your welfare, and also for the welfare of those who are around you" (Alma 34:27). Because the decision to search may drastically affect others—and also because there are more important missions in life than trifling with unknowns that have the potential to harm—Church leaders discourage individuals and their adoptive parents from seeking to identify the birthparents. They acknowledge that in some confidential or semi-open placements it may be important to obtain genetic or medical information, but any personal contact should be avoided.

Using too much strength in accomplishing a goal as elusive as a search for birthparents may prevent individuals from getting a hold on the real essence of life. The search for understanding of oneself is transcendent. Outward searches—for knowledge of the world, of people, and of places—come and go in worldly time. But individuals laboring with an inward search can begin to comprehend their own timelessness. They build and prepare themselves from within, which may not yield the ready answer but the lasting resolution—an attitude that will always illumine.

NOTES

1. Marshall D. Schechter and Doris Bertocci, "The Meaning of Search," in *The Psychology of Adoption,* ed. David M. Brodzinsky and Marshall D. Schechter (New York: Oxford University Press, 1990), p. 65.

2. David M. Brodzinsky, Marshall D. Schechter, and Robin Marantz Henig, *Being Adopted* (New York: Doubleday, 1992), p. 141.

3. Betty Jean Lifton, *Lost and Found* (New York: Harper and Row, 1988), p. 173.

4. Marshall Schechter, as quoted in ibid., p. 52.

5. Wayne Carp, *Family Matters* (Cambridge, Mass.: Harvard University Press, 1998), pp. 159–60.

6. See Paul Sachdev, "Adoption Reunion and After: A Study of the Search Process and Experience of Adoptees," *Child Welfare* 71 (1), 1992, pp. 53–68.

7. Wayne Carp, *Family Matters,* p. 71.

8. See Patrick McMahon, "Adoptees Demand Right to Past," *USA Today,* June 26, 1999, p. 3A.

9. Jayne Schooler, *Searching for a Past* (Colorado Springs: Piñon Press, 1995), pp. 75–77.

10. Lifton, *Lost and Found,* p. 101.

He loved them unto the end.
John 13:1

15
CHEERS
LONG-TERM STUDY OUTCOMES

---

*"There's always a way to link one notion to another," Eric says.
He stands in the doorway of his San Francisco apartment.*

*"The art I practice does not have wide appeal. In essay form I
make a collage of ideas—ethics, science, literature. I write in
loops, referring back and forward, linking ideas until the com-
pleteness of the relationship is apparent." Eric's eyes are bright
and profound; this morning his shirt and trousers are wrinkled.
He never needs a mental warm-up.*

*"I move through heady, almost delirious mental stuff," he says,
"to find the flesh and blood connections on issues—one wants
what one writes to have relevance to life."*

*"Eric is a genius," Sarah says, "too eager to sleep much." Sarah
is a vocalist, a career that started as a hobby. Her husband is a
medical doctor who collects railroad accoutrements on the side.
They adopted Eric at birth.*

*"At age three," Sarah says, "Eric sat on my bed with the thick
Bible picture book, while I read from the King James Version. He
didn't move for three hours that evening while my husband went
to a meeting. Months later, Eric recited the garden of Eden sce-
nario to my neighbor—Eve's dialogue, Satan's, the whole thing
word for word. I read constantly to him. He would sit very close to*

me on the couch, and I would sing and rock and read my days through. I read him the Tolkein trilogy before he went to kindergarten." The idea of books is heart-pounding to Sarah. She flushes.

"I remember a lady at our kitchen table in those early days— we were living in an apartment on Ashbury Street—I don't know who she was or where she came from, but I can visualize Eric sitting next to her, in his little infant seat. Now I think she was a witch or gypsy lady because when she found out he was adopted she prophesied, 'Watch out—when he is a teenager he will break your heart.' I looked at her with defiance, 'Not my child! We are raising him in love and he will never cause us grief.'"

ROAD TO RESOLUTION

The notion that teenage children who were adopted may break their parents' hearts is outdated, but not unused. Research shows that the long-term outcome is equivalent for adopted and comparable nonadopted children. Usually, children who are raised in stable homes turn out okay. A study by Michael Bohman and Sören Sigvardsson[1] in Sweden compared children who were adopted with children who were taken back by their biological mothers and children who grew up in foster homes (all of similar background). The results showed that the children who were adopted turned out to be better adjusted.

Within the adopted group Bohman and Sigvardsson studied were some children adopted at birth from strong backgrounds and some adopted at birth from disadvantaged backgrounds. Not only did both groups of adopted children fully adjust, but the great majority who were adopted sometime after infancy into well-balanced families fared well too. It is the long-term framework that generally assures the value of adoption; within that framework challenges—that may develop during stages of the growing process—fade.

Eric's story follows, not because Eric is eccentric, but to demonstrate that even his fantastic struggle had a resolution. The message is that the problems good parents may have with a variety of children who were adopted usually resolve themselves. The grown child may never be what the parents dreamed of, but that may not be within the child's control. Some parents have effectively put aside their dreams and worked to help a child accomplish his own dreams instead. With consistent caring and love the children generally become productive—in their own unique way.

Eric's mother, Sarah, is a striking, angular woman. She starts out her story somberly. "Eric's birthmother was from a prominent religious family on Long Island," she says. "A year after giving up Eric she was killed at age seventeen in an automobile accident. Eric was also seventeen when we told him about her death. I wasn't consciously thinking that we would tell him then—from the beginning he knew everything else about his adoption. We were just having a conversation one evening in the living room. That was during his senior year in high school. Eric was the editor of the high school newspaper and recipient of two scholarships to the University of California. Afterwards, Eric got up from the couch and walked down the hallway sort of stunned, and then came back and said, 'She was my age, now.' He came back again and wanted to love me, the tenderist he ever had.

"But on January 25th of that same school year Eric went berserk. He came home stoned; he cried and slept the whole week—physical things he had never done around us before. On Valentine's Day we found drugs in his pocket. That night he said, 'I don't want to be saved, let me fall.'

"I went to his priest's quorum advisor and took him by the lapels, 'Do something!' We will rescue him now, *I thought.* Certainly, immediately this can stop.

"Then we took him to a prominent psychiatrist. After spending an hour with Eric alone the psychiatrist told us, 'It would be wise to warn Eric that he has to leave home if he becomes abusive.'

"In March of Eric's first year at UCSF he turned on us with such hatred that my husband, John, said, 'Would you like to leave now, or in the morning?' My heart stopped, and Eric went white as a sheet. He grabbed his coat and bath towel—" Sarah pauses to smile, shaking her head, *"—and drove off into the night. He went to Chicago the following summer and returned looking like*

death warmed over. You see," she says, "his rebellion compelled him to do things distressing to his nature. He lost his scholarships—never filled out the forms necessary to perpetuate them. After Eric left home, I went to visit every place he lived— on the street, in apartment houses that would make you cringe. I went to see him after my rehearsals at night, when I could find him, and somehow I was protected.

"Eric spent months sitting in Denny's Restaurant, drinking coffee, and writing essays. He earned money by renting his body to the University for drug studies; they furnished a phone, food, and bed. The only regular job he had was at night, in a home for autistic adults. He came to his sister's wedding dinner in balloon pants, blouse, vest, effusive jewelry, and gloves. The maître d' said to me, 'Have you seen that strange man? Does he belong to a cult or some kind of religion?'" Sarah looks down at her hands. She extends her long fingers and clasps them together.

"I could say, calmly, 'He's my son.' But Eric is a different person now," Sarah says, "—no flamboyant clothes or braided tail down his back. He is warm and kind and learning patience from his girlfriend."

The next fall I meet Eric for the first time. He agrees to talk with me in a crepe and coffee shop at 10:30 A.M. French music is playing. "I believe you would enjoy their hot raspberry scones," he says. "What would you like to drink?"

Eric leads the way to a table near the window. He breaks a piece off his scone. Delicate silver rings and a simple chain enhance his plain clothes. He explains that he is open to any questions I might want to ask—use of a tape recorder is fine.

"When I found out my birthmother had been killed in a car accident," he says, "things were already iffy with my parents. I was told of her death in the midst of a light conversation, to forestall the possibility of it coming out in a burst of anger. That information created a sense of loss in me, not because I couldn't do something I wanted but because the option was no longer there. I had always assumed that the woman who gave me birth was someone I could have been friends with; I read her early pregnancy as a form of rebellion." Eric looks up for a reaction.

"Adoption was never something I thought much about—it was

like the color of my eyes," he says. "I feel that I've been sort of thrown into this world, and that makes me pretty much no different than anybody else. I've always been grateful my parents told me I was adopted. They also told me I was a rebellious spirit. That mythological explanation simply says, 'We don't like what you are doing.'" Eric brightens, confident of his position.

"I turned my back on the religious account of my origin, during my last year in high school. I was not going to swallow the religious explanations my parents gave me and shove my questions aside. It wasn't just a matter of intellectual integrity but also of authority, and of my wanting. I've reflected on how deeply frustrating, disappointing, and frightening it must have been for my parents. I could not have been the child they thought they were getting." Eric has finished every crumb of his scone. He is pleased to accept the rest of mine.

"Once the tide of hell had washed away," he says, "and we were on high ground for a time, I told them, 'You were not the failure as parents that you said you must be.' I don't know how well that sank in. I don't think it's the sort of thing they were able to take my word for—it will involve reevaluation of the tradition that told them what being a good parent was." He waits, smiles at the silence and bounds on.

"I didn't feel guilty for my actions as soon as, by some schedules, I ought. It took a long time for me to get past indignation towards my parents. By the time I did I had a sense that I could not have done anything else, and that I was sort of tragically implicated. Like when Agamemnon had to kill Iphigenia, he really had no choice. If he didn't sacrifice his daughter the whole fleet would die, and so he did what he had to do, but afterwards the Grecian chorus reproached him for not feeling badly about it. Just because you have to do something doesn't get you off the hook—I feel that guilt."

Eric sets his cup down above his napkin. "No relationship is fulfilled completely honorably," he says. "But I am content with the relationship I have with my parents. I respect them. I love them. I feel we did all right by one another." Eric holds onto the mug, shifting it back and forth in his hand.

"When I ask myself what repercussions adoption may have

had on me, I wonder if I'm inventing something. Although we humans aren't necessarily free, I believe we're still personally responsible for what we choose to do. I'm suspicious of things we tell ourselves to place the locus of action elsewhere.

"All the inheritance I feel is from my adoptive parents. It was a particularly good match between my mother and me. I will go to my father for advice, but I was not the outdoorsman he had hoped for. And I bequeathed an ambiguous legacy to my sister—she saw me getting away with things she couldn't pull off. I had psychological cunning and a keen eye for my parents' weaknesses. But I'm twenty-seven now, safely away from there."

THE ADVANTAGE OF PERSPECTIVE

Eric has exceptional talents which seem to drive him relentlessly toward some intangible destiny, some pursuit of the soul. Such people are fascinating to observe because their soul-searching is visible and undistracted. Extraordinary people are helpful in understanding more conventional individuals; most people have within them a sense of personal destiny which persists until it finds expression. An intense person like Eric exhibits as a young adult what another may manifest more gradually and acceptably throughout a lifetime.

Bohman and Sigvardsson did their long-range study on more than forty individuals whose adoptions were finalized, for the most part, by age seven. They were then tested at ages eleven, fifteen, eighteen, and twenty-three. The results demonstrate the advantage that adoptive parents have when they have a long-term perspective. "If, for instance, the investigation had been restricted to the first, cross-sectional follow-up at age 11," they say, "then conclusions concerning adoption would have been quite different from those we have now reached."

At age eleven they found that the children born of socially disadvantaged biological parents had a less favorable prognosis than children in general. But by ages fifteen, eighteen, and twenty-three the negative trends of those children who were biologically disadvantaged had dissolved. "In regard to the very high frequency of . . . criminality and alcohol abuse among the biological parents," Bohman and Sigvardsson report, "the conclusion is warranted that adoption largely reduced the risk of social incompetence and maladjustment." Bohman and Sigvardsson believe the improvement of the children they studied was a result of the stable situation provided in adoptive homes where the parents were "psychologically well prepared for the task of rearing a nonbiological child."[2]

If Eric had been part of a long-range adoption survey, he would have buttressed optimistic findings until age seventeen but then thrown them off for a few years, only because he was still in the process of finding his path in life. Adoptive parents endure better if they can understand the length of time a child takes to fully adjust to the idea of being adopted. Ask any parent about one of their challenging children at age seven, and then at fifteen and twenty-three years of age, and they will give divergent responses even though the composite result may be positive. And the more difficult the process—if it doesn't destroy parent or child—the more satisfaction in the result. The child that onlookers may never cheer is often the one for whom parents deserve a little credit.

Everyone agrees that the younger the child is when placed in an adoptive home, the better. Early adoption placement is a form of problem prevention for children from disadvantaged families. Attachment to an older child with challenges can be harder, but it is just as significant. The amount of ultimate risk involved may often depend on the adoptive parents, not whether they are good people, but whether they are well adapted to the lifelong task.

SQUARING WITH THE OLDER CHILD

It is the first day of a training workshop for foster care providers. The trainer asks questions.

"Neil," she asks, "would you allow youth to read the Rolling Stone?*"*

Neil weighs at least 300 pounds. He and his wife, Seini, will take over the management of a group home for teenage boys beginning next week. He leans back on his chair and clutches his hands behind his head. The buttons on his shirt pull precariously.

"No, it's full of bad values." Neil and his wife have a new baby boy who also comes to training; when the baby fusses they take

*turns holding him. During the morning break the trainer goes
over to Neil's table.*

*"Three years is a heavy commitment," she smiles. "What got
you into this program?"*

*"We get board and room, benefits," Neil laughs. "It's a good
thing for us right now. When we're finished with our contract, we
pretty much have a ticket for this kind of work anywhere." Neil
opens a can of soda.*

*"Ya know, I was a foster kid before I was adopted. I had a
pretty rough youth. I think I can help others." Neil bites into a
donut.*

*"When I was thirteen, I went to jail for a year. I'd done some
messing around. I didn't do all the stealing, but I hung around
with other kids who did. Finally, when I went to court—I can still
remember my dad sitting there with tears in his eyes—they sen-
tenced me, and he wouldn't do anything about it.*

*"He'd sat me down when I was eleven and twelve and told me,
'This is how it was. You came to us with hair down your back and
feces stuck up your clothes. You hadn't been cared for, boy, and
those things are still part of you even though you can't remember. But you have choices to make. You can decide what your life's
going to be like. You don't have to keep acting out.'*

*"During the year I was locked up my father came to visit me
every day. I knew how much he loved me. I knew what the other
guys in jail were like—what they were headed for. I changed."*

Neil reaches for another donut, and Seini grabs his hand.

*Neil smiles. "I still have some things to change, but I'm work-
ing at it."*

Older children who are adopted can fulfill realistic expectations when given sufficient consistency and love. Martin
Textor, in a review of international adoption in West Germany,
concluded that even foreign adoptions of older, shell-shocked
children are generally successful. He cited an intensive study
of Vietnamese and Korean children that demonstrated that
"the effects of early deprivation can be totally alleviated."[3]
These adoptive parents were trained to help their children pass
through three phases. The parents stimulated needs in the

child, especially if the child was apathetic. Then the parents satisfied the child's needs for quite a long time—matching extreme deprivation with extreme satisfaction—and finally phased out absolute satisfaction until the child learned to postpone some needs and develop normally. Children adopted nationally and internationally from violent pasts may have to endure, along with their adoptive parents, many difficult phases during the adjustment process. The amazing fact is that these efforts, as a general rule, are sooner or later effective in directing the child toward a constructive life.

FACING THE UNKNOWN

The greatest experiment in raising traumatized orphans is currently in progress in the United States. More than 25,000 children have been adopted from Eastern Europe (especially Russia and Romania) since the collapse of Communism in 1989—by far the largest group of deprived children available for long-term study. Victor Groza, an adoption specialist at Case Western Reserve University, conducted a study on 229 of these American families that was reported in the *New York Times*. "A lot of them have made great strides," says Groza. "But I think if you adopt such a child you at least have to be prepared for someone with special needs that may last a lifetime."[4] About 20 percent of the children in Groza's study continue to have alarming emotional problems and marked developmental lags up to four years after their adoption. Another 60 percent Groza calls "wounded wonders," those who are behind in social and developmental growth but who are making great progress in their adoptive homes. The remainder are "resilient rascals," those who show no obvious ill effects of their institutionalization at all.[5]

"The final results may be good," Karen says, "but it's harder than we thought. And we did a lot of research to prepare." Karen has an inherited disability. She and her husband, Joshua, chose to adopt all their children.

"Our first three kids were almost grown, and we had always wanted a foreign child. We received a magazine through an agency in the Northwest, carrying pictures of available children

with their biographical sketches. We picked out a boy named Ramon from the Philippines and sent for more background.

"When the information arrived, the picture of an older Filipino boy was also attached. That was Marco; he looked like the ideal teenager. Joshua and I had already discussed adopting two from the same country—we didn't want one to feel isolated." Karen slows her story, looks away. It's been a hard year for her. She went through chemotherapy treatments but her thick, wavy hair has grown back.

"We were barely able to get the older boy," she says. "Marco was sixteen, which is the cut-off age for foreign adoptions—he actually turned seventeen before we picked him up."

"Well," she pauses, "those two boys came into our home and literally took over." She sighs, gestures, falters, trying to explain what it felt like to have the thirteen- and seventeen-year-old Filipino boys in her kitchen emptying the refrigerator, in Joshua's library playing with the computer.

"We had expectations that were unrealistic," Joshua fills in, "and they did too. They thought we would be rich. When we asked Marco to help with the housework, he thought we were treating him like a servant. The younger boy, Ramon, had been abused— of course we didn't know anything about that. He didn't want us to touch him.

"The boys were not appreciative of anything. We delayed the adoptions two years, until we were sure it would work."

Karen appears calm; she never stands out in her solid, deep toned clothes. Joshua also blends into the world—lanky and book-ish in appearance with schoolboy enthusiasm.

"Ramon, the younger," Joshua says, "has been the most diffi-cult but he has also said the tender things that touch our hearts. He works long hours to make payments on a sports car. We are closer to him now than to Marco who works part-time at a drug store while he attends a junior college."

"Since Marco was an older teenager," Karen says, smiling, "we recognized he wouldn't be with us long. But now," Karen begins to laugh, "we worry that he will! Marco is far from being fully independent."

Long-term conclusions of research are incomplete without the

*details. A psychology study would rate the adoption adjustment
of both Marco and Ramon as good. The boys say they are glad to
be adopted. I ask Karen, "Would you and Joshua do it again?" She
sighs. "Not the hard experiences," she answers. "But how do you
separate them out?"*

*"There is no way you can be fully prepared," Joshua says. "But
of course it's been positive."*

*People living a miracle may not recognize it. But Karen and
Joshua have applied the greatest rule of life to adoption: those
who lose themselves in a great cause find themselves (Matthew
10:39). Karen and Joshua were uniquely capable of teaching their
sons the gospel. When the boys first arrived from the Philippines
they went with them to the Catholic church, because it was familiar. But Karen and Joshua also lived gospel principles in their
family—praying, reading scriptures, continuing to attend their
own church meetings and bringing the message and Spirit of
those meetings back home to share. Within months the boys
wanted to go with them to church. Both boys have since served
missions—the younger before the older. They went to areas where
they were particularly effective because of their backgrounds;
people were attracted to them and subsequently listened to the
gospel message. The adoption of Marco and Ramon has blessed
hundreds of lives already, and they will be the ones to lead
another generation.*

ETERNAL OUTLOOK

"We are not chance creations in a universe of disorder,"
affirms President Gordon B. Hinckley. "We lived before we
were born. We were God's sons and daughters who shouted
for joy. (See Job 38:7.) We knew our Father; He planned our
future. We graduated from that life and matriculated in this.
The statement is simple; the implications are profound."[6]

Adoption is part of the Lord's orderly plan. The Lord lives
beyond the chaos of the world. His love and understanding are
perfect. He gave the principle of faith in conjunction with the
principle of repentance: the one exists to strengthen the other.
Through him human error can be turned to growth, injustice
to understanding, and sorrow to abiding joy. "How great, how
glorious, how complete," Eliza R. Snow wrote, "redemption's

grand design, where justice, love, and mercy meet in harmony divine!"[7]

The good news of the gospel comes together in the concept of adoption. The Lord knows us each personally, and he kindly prepares us for our life missions. While on earth, each soul needs the opportunity to find its divine identity, to develop talents, to build hope and faith. Through inspiration, individuals jointly participate in adoption, becoming crucially *equal* before God in achieving his significant purposes. Every child who is adopted, every adult—birthparents and adoptive parents—can then go forward with daily motivation, assured that they are being guided in other aspects of their life's work.

Adoption can be an exquisite expression of the mortal soul at its best—the desire on the part of each person involved to give opportunity to every child of God. All parents in adoption are important, and all children can be blessed. And within the difficulty of each person's contributing role lies the power to vitalize that same individual's immortal soul. The Lord never leaves us alone; experience bears witness that *he* is the God of adoption.

NOTES

1. Michael Bohman and Sören Sigvardsson, "Outcome in Adoption: Lessons from Longitudinal Studies," in *The Psychology of Adoption*, ed. David M. Brodzinsky and Marshall D. Schechter (New York: Oxford University Press, 1990), pp. 95–106.

2. Ibid., pp. 104–6.

3. Martin Textor, "International Adoption in West Germany," in *Intercountry Adoption*, ed. Howard Alstein and Rita J. Simon (New York: Praeger, 1991), p. 116.

4. Victor Groza, in Margaret Talbot, "Attachment Theory: The Ultimate Experiment," *The New York Times Magazine*, May 24, 1998, p. 30.

5. Ibid. p. 38.

6. Gordon B. Hinckley, *Teachings of Gordon B. Hinckley* (Salt Lake City: Deseret Book Company, 1997), p. 174.

7. Eliza R. Snow, "How Great the Wisdom and the Love," *Hymns*, no. 195, 1995.

INDEX